# NORTHBOUND + DOWN

## ALASKA TO MEXICO BY BICYCLE

### OTTO ECROYD

GREAT  ORTHERN

Great Northern Books
PO Box 1380, Bradford,
West Yorkshire, BD5 5FB

www.greatnorthernbooks.co.uk

ISBN: 978-1-912101-35-1


Design by David Burrill
Maps by Claudia Walton


CIP Data
A catalogue for this book is available
from the British Library

*For my parents, who never called bullshit.*


*Not even on this.*

## Foreword

Ten years ago, a friend convinced me to sail from Norway to France. We had just finished our undergrad degrees. The plan was to move to his parents' house in rural Norway, fix up the family sailboat, and spend summer in the sun cruising down to the Mediterranean. I had no experience sailing anywhere more challenging than sheltered New Zealand bays, but this sounded like a great idea. The sailboat, a 1970s trimaran, was advertised as having a minor hole in one of the hulls. This had been incurred on a sailing trip two years previously where my friend had crashed into a dock. He had covered the hull in rubber cement and kept sailing. This might have tipped me off that there would be some detours on our journey south.

We first went to look at the boat in March, when the weather in Norway warmed up enough to consider doing work outdoors. The rubber cement still covered the hole in the port hull. We pulled the rubber off. The wood underneath was soft, rotten. We continued to pull. The hull peeled back. We spent the next three months knee-deep in fibreglass and glue, inhaling fumes and rebuilding the hull. By the time she was ready to put on water, the glue was so much a part of her we christened her 'Epoxy'.

Epoxy made it around the coast of Norway. Over long summer days we cruised through fjords, in between coastal islands, around from Oslo up to Stavanger on the west coast. The first test was the crossing to Scotland. We waited days for ideal weather; a strong following wind and sea. As my friend said on Scottish TV news afterwards: "Everything was going well, a well reefed sail, perfect conditions." Halfway to Scotland we surfed down a seven-metre swell. At the base, the nose ploughed into the water. The mast rocked forwards, then back. A front stay snapped. The metal ropes lashed across the deck. A second stay snapped. The floating mast rocked all directions, unsecured. Gusts of wind and the rocking boat competed to see who could pop the mast off its mount first. Halfway to Scotland is not a great place to be with a broken mast. We spent the next few hours trying to improvise something to secure the mast so it would take sail, and calculating whether we had enough fuel to motor to land.

Our calculations worked better than our improvisation. We were going to run out of fuel. We called a passing ship for help. They radioed to shore. Within an hour, an oil service vessel diverted from whatever, doubtless expensive, thing it is an oil service vessel does to pull us two idiots to safety. If you haven't met an oil service vessel before, I wouldn't recommend the North Sea with seven-metre swells and twenty-five-knot winds as the best place to first do so. They are seventy metres long, with multiple stabilising engines. I'm not sure how tall the hull is. When you are trying to catch a thrown tow line from a screaming Russian sailor, looking up from the bottom of a swell trough into the churning engines throwing off torrents of whitewater, it looks like a castle wall.

During the tow to the Shetlands, rocking from the swell snapped the mast off its mount. Hanging off the side from the remaining stays, it smashed into the hull we had spent the last three months building. I leapt from the stern with bolt cutters and cut it away. Somehow we also lost the outboard motor. Don't ask. Then, during the night, the tow line broke. We repeated the afternoon's exercise in whitewater rafting. Spotlights glinted off the waves and the metre-long blades of the stabilising propellers above. After deciding not to drown us for being such a pain, but not able to get close enough in the dark to a motor-less, mast-less raft to attach a line, the oil service vessel called the Scottish Coast Guard. When we arrived in Lerwick harbour, the whole town was out to meet us. We spent the next ten days being bought beers by the locals. They spent the time they'd bought with the beer telling us what they thought of us. No prizes for guessing.

Ten years later, my Norwegian friend and I were reminiscing over the trip. Years had come and gone, and this was still our coolest story. We had moved countries, got degrees, found and lost girlfriends, got jobs, drank beers, gone on holidays, turned jobs into careers, turned girlfriends into wives (in his case, at least). In short, we had done normal stuff. Neither of us were unhappy, but neither of us had done anything that would be worth talking about in another ten years. I am a normal guy. I'm not a professional adventurer. I'm not any kind of athlete. I'm not someone who was at rock bottom, rolling the dice on a last shot at redemption. I just decided that I needed another story that would be worth telling. *Northbound and Down* is that story.

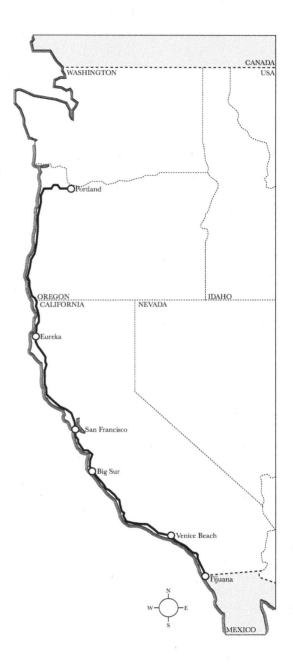

## On planning

I decided to go bike touring because I was bored at work, too old to take drugs in every hostel in Latin America and too poor for a sailboat. When I decided to cycle 20,000km I hadn't ridden further than across town. I dated a girl in the summer of 2017 who had done some bike touring. It sounded like the kind of thing I could get behind. Escape the hostel highway, meet local people, eat unlimited pasta (she toured in Italy). Where do I sign? I decided to find out more about bike touring. Typically, I didn't do this by doing anything useful. I didn't talk to anyone else who had toured before; I did no route planning; I learnt nothing about bike maintenance. I read books. I no longer have the girlfriend, but I now have a large collection of bike touring literature.

The girl had recommended the story of Dervla Murphy. Dervla rode from Ireland to India alone in the 1960s. She carried a gun. She shot at wolves and at men. She befriended Pakistani army generals. She forded a river with a cow. Dervla introduced me to the essence of cycle touring: getting off the beaten path and opening myself up to the possibilities of being on the road alone. Inspired, I worked my way through the rest of the Amazon top ten list. Next was *The Cyclist Who Went Out in the Cold*, by Tim Moore. Tim rode from Finland to Turkey on what he described (at length) in his book as an "East German shopping bike". He started this trip in winter. Finnish winter. Tim was a masochist, and introduced me to the self-imposed challenge of cycle touring. Why do something easy if you can do something stupid? Another British author followed a similar vein. Mike Carter almost rode around the coastline of Britain. He did this with no plan, no training and for no purpose other than to do it. He gave up riding the full coastline when he realised it would require more detours than he had the patience for. He complained about people cycling to raise money for charity. Why not just do it? Mike introduced me to the genre of 'some whinging dickhead goes cycling'. Finally, I read Alastair Humphreys. Alastair rode around the world over four years using £7,000 of scrounged student loans. He changed his route from across Central Asia to down through Africa after the US invaded Afghanistan. He went the wrong way up South America. He crossed Siberia in winter. Alastair's books were inspirational. They conveyed the profound nature of his experience. Reading them opened my eyes to the possibility of having such an experience myself. I decided to follow in his footsteps and cycle from Argentina to Alaska. I bought a bike.

I bought the wrong type of bike. I didn't realise this was possible. That could have been because I didn't at any point Google: "What bike do I need to ride from Argentina to Alaska?" If you're considering doing this, I'd recommend Googling it first. When I went to purchase my first bike in ten years, I was too embarrassed to tell the guys in the bike store exactly what I was doing. I was afraid of having to discuss my lack of experience. I think I told them: "I want to go on a long bike ride." This didn't set us up for success. The only thing I really knew was that I needed space for four bags, two on a front pannier rack, and two on the back. I failed to mention this. The salesman recommended I buy a cyclocross bike: "Jack of all trades, master of all." I thought that was a great line, and that the bike was a great colour. I bought all the accessories. I felt like I was halfway to Alaska. The final thing I needed was a front rack. On closer inspection of the front forks, it wasn't obvious where this would go. "Where would I put a front rack on this bike?" I asked. "A front rack? On this bike?" the salesman replied. The mechanic behind him had just finished mounting the last of my accessories: "I wouldn't put any more weight on this bike if I were you," he said. What? I'd come too far to admit my mistake. I'd lived in England too long to brave the awkwardness. I rode out of the store on my new bike. I bought three front racks off the internet before I found one that would fit.

Months later, I realised that the trip from Argentina to Alaska usually takes the better part of two years. For the first 5,000km the prevailing wind is against you, and the first set of mountains you need to cross are the Andes (quite high). Who has two years? I scaled back my ambitions. Alaska was already in my original plan, so I settled on that. If you think that sounds like a poor decision making process, I'd agree. I chose the default. Except, a better default would have been to just cycle out my front door in England and see where the road took me. Europe, Asia, Africa, all big places, all accessible without £1,000 flights. Hindsight is twenty-twenty. After committing to Alaska, I purchased maps. The maps sat beside my bed for a month until I set aside four hours on a Saturday to really get into some route planning. I spread them out on my kitchen table. After five minutes I realised there was only one possible road out of Alaska, and two roads south through Canada. The first turn-off was 1,500km from Anchorage. I decided that decision was best made on game day. Route planning done, I packed the maps away.

The rest of my planning involved buying things on the internet. Most of them I carried a long way and never used. *The Book of Bivvy* by Ron Turnbull inspired a bivvy bag. I had visions of camping under the stars on the tundra. The Alaskan mosquitos had other plans. That bag made it 2,000km. I'm not sure I even rode through any tundra. I bought not one, but three guides to Alaskan plants, animals and birds. I was only in Alaska for two weeks. I never identified any birds except endless crows and the occasional bald eagle. The guides joined the bivvy bag. I bought a solar panel. This would have been useful in the Sahara. In America, they have power outlets in coffee shops. I bought food. Why buy food when you arrive in Anchorage when you can buy it on the internet in the UK and fly it over the Atlantic? I started the trip with two kilos of dried lentils. This demonstrated a fundamental misunderstanding of lentils. I was still making dal in Alberta. Mercifully, an ill judged internet purchase of front pannier bags two sizes smaller than intended limited the available space. This put an end to my 'planning by purchasing'.

## On training

The first weekend after buying my bike I went for a ride around Richmond Park. This worked. I found the park, I rode around it twice and I rode back home. I'd ridden 30km. And, what was more, I'd enjoyed it. I felt very good about this until I realised that the 1,500km to the first turn-off at Watson Lake at 30km a day would take two months. I'd need to ride a little further than that.

I made a plan to ride down to Brighton. I asked a few friends to join me. They told me they would meet me at the pub afterwards. This was wise, because the ride was a disaster. What should have been a 100km, six-hour jaunt turned into a 120km, nine-hour saga. I was under the impression that, as a relatively common bike ride, the London to Brighton route would be clearly signposted. What I didn't consider was that from London to Brighton is essentially all city. Roads spread like veins, branching out from the beating heart of London all the way to the coastal skin of England. Many of the roads aren't just veins; they are high pressure, eight-lane arteries. I didn't set myself up for success by listening to an audiobook. I quickly lost the route. No matter, I thought, 'all roads lead to Rome,' I'd join up with the main drag if I just pointed south. In hindsight this was a weak assumption. Brighton is not Rome.

My troubles started two hours in. A rubbery flapping noise penetrated my headphones. I ignored it. It ignored me and continued. I looked down to find a flat back tyre. I pulled off the road. No journey is complete without a challenge. I had a spare tube, a patch kit, tyre levers and a pump. What a great opportunity to test my gear! I pulled the bike onto the sidewalk and took off the wheel. I couldn't get the tyre levers in. It dawned on me that the last time I'd changed a tyre was the last time I owned a bike, in undergrad, ten years before. I tried to remember the process. All I could remember was that the tyre levers went in under the tyre and the tyre came off. This was how it worked, right? Well, it wasn't working now. I prodded at the wheel with the levers. Maybe I had the angle wrong. I wasn't even sure which end of my tyre levers to use. In true millennial fashion, I watched an instructional YouTube video. I tried to hide this from passing cars. It's embarrassing to look like you're learning on the job from the internet. The guy in the video had no trouble getting the tyre off. This wasn't even the hard bit. Actually, there was no hard bit. He made it look easy, start to finish. I wondered where the nearest bus stop was. Then I wondered what the bus system was like in Alaska.

After fifteen minutes of this, a man came out of his shop: "Do you need a hand mate? Come in here." I thanked him and told him this was my first cycle trip, by way of an excuse for blocking his shop entrance. "Oh really?" he replied. "I thought you looked like an expert." English humour, I guess. We stepped into Greg's TV shop with the bike and wheel. He got the tyre off in a second. It looked like a magic trick. I couldn't tell what he did that I didn't. I'm sure having the tyre levers the right way around helped. He pulled the tube out, along with an inch-long screw: "I think this might be your problem." I was glad I at least had a replacement inner tube, so didn't look like a total jackass. I handed it over. I'd abdicated control of the process. The valve wouldn't go through the wheel. I now discovered there are two types of valves, and I'd bought the wrong one. The internet is a dangerous place. We set about trying to patch the tube. Neither of us had done this before, and neither knew which side of the patch was supposed to go on the tyre. We had a cup of tea. After ten minutes spent glueing my fingers together, I inflated the tube. It deflated. We admitted defeat. Greg told me there was a bike shop a two-mile walk down the road. I steeled myself for a hike. Just then, the owner of the shop next door pulled up in his Porsche SUV. Greg asked him if he would have his man in a van drive me down to the bike shop. I thanked all profusely and threw my bike in the van. I learned that patching a tyre is a pain in the ass, inner tubes have more than one valve, and that not all Porsche drivers are dickheads.

After these valuable lessons, I was ready for a smooth ride down to Brighton. This was not to be. I gave up on my audiobook and submitted to the ignominy of navigating with Google Maps in my ear. I was instructed to take National Cycle

Route 20. The 20th cycle route in the UK sounded like it would be an established route, a route with signs, a route that it would be possible to follow with the aid of a mobile phone with more processing power than the first moon lander. This was not the case. I went on a tour of Gatwick Airport, circumnavigating it twice. I ended up on a golf course where I rode over a fairway and was justifiably sworn at. I rode through a paddock. It was wet. My wheel got stuck in the mud and I toppled over, in slow motion, into a puddle. Shortly afterwards I passed a couple walking their dog through the mud. They smiled, "Lovely day for it!" Sure. I circled around a motorway slip road like a sailboat around a whirlpool, getting increasingly stressed as the voice in my ear insisted I join the eight-lane motorway below. I was about three quarters of the way to Brighton, deep in suburban hell. I saw no alternative. I caved to the voice. I joined the motorway. I was honked at. My phone ran out of battery. This was briefly worrying. Then I realised I was no more lost than before, now I was just lost with no robotic voice parroting, "Left on National Cycle Route 20, right on National Cycle Route 20." I'm unwilling to admit that National Cycle Route 20 exists. Nevertheless, I was lost and had to ask directions. I approached an old man walking his dog: "I'm trying to go to Brighton." He gave me a solemn look. "Oh, you are well off track. Yes indeed, nowhere near it. Very off track indeed," he said. OK, great, any advice on how to fix that? He pointed me down a road. I asked new directions at every corner. A cyclist in Lycra pointed me down a concrete path at the end of a cul-de-sac: "On from here it's a lovely ride into Brighton!" With red spandex to match his red racing bike, he looked like he knew what he was talking about. One corner after the cul-de-sac, the concrete path joined a motorway slip road. That British humour again. Or maybe this really was as good as it got. The path did lead to Brighton and I made it intact. I bought myself all the curry I could find and hopped on the first train back to London. I spread out over two seats, distributed crumbs and improved everyone's Saturday afternoon trip to the city.

Buoyed by this success, I coerced my friends to do two small bike tours around the UK. The first of these was from Newcastle to Edinburgh. At 300km this counted as real distance. I'm not sure it counted as real training though, at least in the traditional sense of the word. At the first hotel out of Newcastle we ate the restaurant out of oysters and drank them out of champagne. Looking back, it's probably more likely that they just refused to serve us more champagne at some point. In any case, we claimed victory. My memory of the rest of that weekend is hazy.

The second trip was 250km around the Pembrokeshire coast in Wales. This part of the country is known as the 'Welsh Riviera'. It was much harder to find champagne there than in the traditional Riviera. There were also a lot of hills. They weren't large hills, but they were steep hills. Some of them started out with a twenty percent grade. After climbing and descending the first hundred, we had developed quite a desire to keep the momentum from the downhills into the climbs. I overdid this, lost my nerve, braked in a corner and slid onto my side. I ripped one of the sleeves off my T-shirt, and all the skin off one arm. I spent the rest of the weekend wishing I had brought a second T-shirt. One with both sleeves, that wasn't covered in blood. I resolved to carry disinfectant and to not fuck around on descents in Alaska. In hindsight, this was a valuable lesson, cheaply bought. Loath to purchase even more stuff, I cut the other sleeve off my ripped T-shirt. This became a big part of my touring look, for better or worse.

Time running out, and friends now wise to my promises of short rides and long meals, I decided I'd do the rest of my training in Alaska. Why waste time? I was riding 10,000km. My body was sure to figure it out eventually.

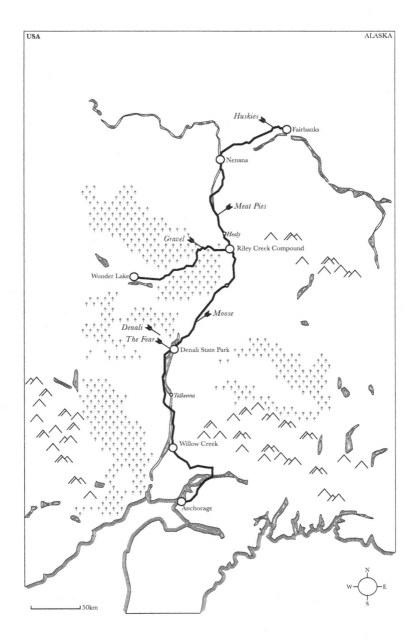

# Day 1 – London, UK to Anchorage, AK

I struggled with my bags through Victoria station. I'd packed as much as possible into my bike box to save on extra bag fees. I half dragged, half carried my life for the next three months across the station floor. I started to sweat. It was rush hour on a June morning. I was getting in people's way. The London commuter is not known for their patience. I had the urge to tell people that I wasn't a tourist. I was one of them. I was wearing my helmet, dragging a second-hand cardboard bike box, and by now sweating profusely. Ranting at strangers was not going to improve my image. I wondered how people normally transported bikes across continents. Maybe I should have wondered that earlier. I was late for the train and the carriages were full by the time I arrived. I led with the box and carved myself a space. I didn't make any friends on the train.

I made it onto the plane to Seattle. I had a window seat next to two legit looking guys. They looked like they had spent a lot of time outdoors, with shoulders that didn't quite fit into the economy class seats. As I sat down, we exchanged standard plane chat: "How's it going, where are you from, where are you going?" The conversation petered out. I felt the awkwardness of having said hello, having nothing further to say, but now not being able to pretend they didn't exist for the rest of the flight. Then I reflected that this was the start of my 'great adventure'. A big part of this was supposed to be talking to people. How was I going to meet people on the road if I couldn't chat to the people stuck next to me on a plane? The guy in the middle seat swivelled his machine gun turret torso and extended a hand that looked like it could eat my hand. His name was John.

John and his buddy Mark were river guides. They were returning to Idaho after teaching a swift water rescue course in Norway. Knowing nothing about rivers and less about Idaho, I struggled for something relevant to say. I told them that I went white water rafting in Iceland a few years before with a guy from Idaho. They asked his name. I couldn't remember, but remembered it was spelled with a missing consonant. "Matt with one T, John with no H, Bob with no B, something like that," I said. "Anyway he had some filthy river stories, great chat." "Was it Zak, Zak with a K instead of a CH?" John and Mark started laughing. It turned out that the brother of my river guide in Iceland three years ago was picking them up from the airport in Seattle. "I've known Zak since he was in diapers," John said. "What was his best story?" I protested that the story was in no way plane appropriate. People were still having breakfast. John insisted, "Come on man, we have nine hours, what else are we going to talk about?" I told Zak's story.

Zak was the head river guide leading a group of three boats rafting in northern Iceland. My friends and I were the only vaguely athletic looking people in the group. Zak took one look at us: "You three, with me," he said. We quietly asked if he didn't want to split us up. "Nah fuck that, privileges of being the boss," he replied. I could tell we would get along. After squeezing into our dry suits, we started to badger Zak for stories: "What's the craziest shit you've ever seen on the river?" He laughed, "Well one time when I was a junior river guide, we were on a five-day trip down the middle fork of the Salmon. We had the usual suspects: the people who don't want to get wet, the ones who have never slept in a tent, the complainers, but also a newlywed couple that couldn't keep their hands off each other, and a big Texan oil man. The Texan was straight out of a cartoon: ten-gallon hat, thick accent, smoked a cigar and drank a whiskey every night in camp. On the third day, we got to one of the best campsites of the trip, on a river bend. The head guide went to the newlywed couple and told them, 'Now, tonight you have the campsite we call 'the honeymoon suite'. It's up the hill around the river bend. You have a great view of the sunrise over the river, and you can get a bit of privacy from the main camp.' They giggled. After dinner the group sat beside the fire, chatting about the day. The couple was snuggled up to each other and the Texan smoked his cigar and drank his whiskey. The couple was first to head to bed. After they left, the group exchanged a glance and a smile. Ten minutes later the group started to hear faint noises of sex from around the river bend. Another glance, another smile. The noises got louder. The glances got more awkward. The noise grew, and the wife started to shout: 'Fuck me in the ass, fuck me in the ass,' over and over. Now the group by the fire was avoiding eye contact. As the shouts built to screams, the Texan had had enough. He leant back in his chair, took a puff of his cigar and shouted in his Texas twang: 'Son, just fuck her in the ass already!' From around the river bend, silence."

This was not a great story to tell on a plane. I tried to be quiet but got carried away. I got a laugh three rows up. John and Mark appreciated it. We spent the flight talking trips, and mapping my route out on the in-seat TV. I had not planned to go through Idaho. This was viewed with scorn. "The whole state of Idaho should be a National Park," John said. By the time we touched down in Seattle, I had added a three-week Idaho tour to my route. It was unclear how I was going to go the 800km inland to get there, but I had all of Alaska and the Yukon to figure it out.

The trip from Seattle to Anchorage was the typical jumble of impressions of twelve-hour flights and ten-hour time zone shifts. After my route mapping session with Mark and John, I was feeling underprepared. There were no road maps in duty free, so I bought all the US and Canada *Lonely Planets* on my Kindle. I didn't read them, but I felt better for having purchased something. As we flew into Anchorage, I looked out the window to see snow on the hills. Other people on the plane were already wearing their down jackets. I remembered that I had originally wanted to start the trip in May. That would have been a poor choice. There was still snow on the hills. Anchorage airport was filled with wildlife pictures and advertisements for nature tours. There was a taxidermy moose in the middle of one of the concourses. Seeing all the animals reminded me how nervous I was about camping. How easy would it be for me to find campsites? How easy would it be for the bears to find me in those campsites? I remembered that I had only ever pitched my tent once, in London, in my living room. I had never slept in it. Tomorrow problems. My bike box arrived intact. I bundled it into a taxi and went to the hostel.

## Day 2 – Anchorage

I had a full day in Anchorage to get ready. The first order of business was to put my bike back together. After an hour dropping screws, I reflected on the value of keeping different sets of parts together and of not trying to do bike maintenance in long grass. Next time. Another bike tourist was staying in the hostel. He joined me on the lawn to play with his bike. Mike was from Taiwan and was doing a two-month tour through Canada. This was also his first major bike tour. He politely pretended not to watch me put my handlebars on the wrong way and drop my bike in the grass. He was nice enough not to offer to give me a hand. We chatted about our routes and where we planned to make our first stops. Mike planned to leave that afternoon. He couldn't remember the name of where he was going or how far it was. This made me feel a little better about my lack of route planning.

I almost got my bike back together on my own. For the life of me I couldn't figure out how to get the back pannier rack on. Where the screws went was clear, but the rack was surely too big to get the screws to line up with their sockets. It might not be a great start to the trip to not be able to put my bike together myself, but I reflected it would be a worse start to break the rack. I gave up and rolled down to a bike shop, rack in hand. I asked the mechanic if he could check my assembly work. He asked if $25 was a fair price. I laughed, "Man, you can charge me whatever you want, as long as you can tell me that the bike isn't going to fall apart 100 miles out of town because I've put a screw in the wrong hole." He was amused: "You can change a tyre, right?" Thanks, buddy.

I went to a camping shop to buy bear spray. Bear spray is pepper spray with a ten-metre range, diluted to avoid lasting damage to the bears. When someone first suggested I carry it, I thought it was a joke. The more I thought about meeting a bear on the Alaska highway, with twenty minutes between passing trucks and 100km to the next town, the smarter it seemed. The shop assistant led me over to a stand. He looked like he had just arrived from hibernating in the mountains, with shoulder length grey hair and a thick beard. The bottles of bear spray were cheerily decorated with pictures of snarling bears showing off two-inch teeth. As the shop assistant handed me a can of bear spray, I asked him how much of a threat bears really were. He shook his grizzled head, "Oh yes, bears are hungry this time of year, very hungry." He wouldn't let go of the can. I tried to pull it out of his hand more firmly. "Very hungry, those bears," he stared at me, "but what you really have to worry about is the moose, oh yes, the moose are very dangerous. Especially at this time of year. Lots of people get hurt by moose." He paused. I gave another tug at the bear spray and it slipped from his grasp. He started, broken from his reverie, "And the wolves, man, careful of the wolves." That made me feel better. Maybe the wolves would scare the bears off.

Bear spray acquired, I searched for something else to do in Anchorage. Anchorage has almost half of Alaska's population. It's for people who like the idea of the frontier, but also like paved roads. It is still the frontier. People still occasionally surprise bears in their backyard and get stomped to death by moose. There was no wildlife on the road at the minute, and the Iditarod wasn't until next March. I collected my bike and rode back to the hostel.

Back at the hostel, I packed my panniers. I realised I'd brought food for three people. Two kilos of dates, two kilos of dried lentils, two kilos of oatmeal, eight packets of freeze-dried fruit, half a kilo of honey, half a kilo of spice mix, and half a kilo of milk powder. It all looked delicious. I knew it was ridiculous. I couldn't bring myself to throw unused food away. I hoped Canadian customs would be okay with me importing lentils.

## Day 3 – Anchorage to Willow Creek

Over breakfast, I met an Alaskan named Mary. Mary was moving up to Utqiaġvik, in the Arctic Circle to run a school. Utqiaġvik is the northernmost city in the US. It is only accessible by air, or by boat when the sea isn't frozen. Mary said it didn't get above freezing until May, and there were no paved roads. Real frontier Alaska. Mary was excited about my trip, and we traced out my route on a map on the wall of the hostel: north-east from Anchorage to Tok, then south-east through the Yukon. As I talked through the route, Mary turned and fixed me with a stare: "If you haven't seen Denali, you haven't been to Alaska." I didn't know how to respond to that. "OK," I said. I had been feeling guilty that I was billing my trip as Alaska to Mexico, yet I was only going to be in Alaska for a couple days, with no real destinations to mark the trip. The National Park with the highest peak in North America seemed like a good compromise between the Arctic Circle and nothing. The benefit of having no plan is it's easy to change. I told Mary I was sold.

After adding 500km to my trip over breakfast, I set out into a sub-arctic summer drizzle. Mike the Taiwanese guy sat on the couch and played with his camera. He'd postponed his departure because of the weather. As I rolled my bike out of the yard he came out to wish me luck. I wondered whether my guilty feeling of pride would be rewarded by wet camping in the evening. Mike was the extent of my send-off crew. The mundane reality of rolling through Anchorage suburbs felt out of step with the thousands of miles of riding I had ahead of me. At least I didn't get lost.

I cruised along a quiet bike path reflecting on the fact that my journey had begun, feeling the weight of possibility ahead. Then I joined an eight-lane highway. I had realised that I was going to have to ride on the highway to get out of town, but I was not prepared for the size of the road. American roads are big, and American cars are bigger. Pickup trucks with double tyres on the back axle grazed the rumble strip. Long-distance trucks towing two containers pushed waves of turbulence along the road. I hugged the right-hand edge of the shoulder, self-reflection banished.

The rain stopped, and I settled into a rhythm. The motorway shed lanes, fading into the peripheral towns of Anchorage. I passed two fellow bike tourers. Jakob and Antoni were a Polish father and son travelling north to Fairbanks and then down to Calgary. They had arrived in Anchorage the same time as me but had ridden straight out of the city to avoid paying for a hostel in town. They had camped beside the road. They were real cycle tourists. They were riding mountain bikes that looked like they had been pulled off a Soviet scrap train. Waterproof duffel bags were strapped down with fraying bungee cords. Jakob and Antoni were planning to go up to Fairbanks and down to Calgary in twenty-three days, ten days faster than I was planning to cover the same distance. We chatted about bears. This was going to be a common topic of conversation. Neither of them had bear spray. I struggled to convey, "Bears are hungry this time of year." They were unfazed. I lacked grizzled legitimacy.

I chickened out at my first opportunity to free camp. I came across an RV park beside a river, swallowed my pride and went to pay my money. Finding campsites was one of the things that I felt most nervous about on the trip. I told myself I hadn't spent a night in my tent yet, or cooked on my stove. One step at a time. It felt like a weak excuse. I settled down amongst the RVs to cook my lentils. I undercooked them. They were horrible. Oh well, 1.95kg left to get that right.

## Day 4 – Willow Creek to Denali State Park

I woke to the sound of Alaska's state bird. Thirty mosquitos whined patiently on the mesh roof panel of my tent, watching their breakfast. I lay cocooned in my sleeping bag and thermal underwear and counted them, for the record. The state bird joke was a standard one: "It's not the bears you have to be worried about, it's the mosquitos, har har." In the airport I'd seen postcards illustrated with mosquitos carrying off unsuspected children, campers and a moose. My tent mates certainly looked bigger than the mosquitos I was familiar with. Bear sized. I packed my gear and exploded from the tent, trying to distract them with speed. This failed. I rolled out of Willow Creek with bitten ankles, wishing I'd brought bug spray.

100km outside of Anchorage now and the population had thinned out. Pine trees lined the sides of the highway. I looked for bears in the forest. There must be wildlife hiding amongst the shadows. Alaska was wild. From a distance, I saw many bears. Upon closer inspection, they turned out to be trash cans, tree stumps, or just darker than your average shadows. I started to wonder how close I was willing to get to a bear to guarantee seeing one. The worst result of a trip to Alaska would be getting eaten by a bear, but surely the second worse result would be not seeing one at all. How much of a mauling would be worth a sighting? How much bear is too much bear?

The bear hunt kept me amused for most of the day. Along miles of highway, the scenery became wilder as I approached Denali State Park, the little brother of the National Park. I stopped at viewing platforms along the road, looked out over an unbroken sea of pine trees towards cloud-covered mountain peaks and tried to figure out which was Denali. Dayglo tourist information signs advertised "There's No Denying Denali". The mountain was first climbed by professional mountaineers in 1913. Three years earlier though, a group of four local miners got to within sixty metres of the summit in blue jeans, carrying a bag of donuts, a thermos of hot chocolate and a four-metre pine flagpole. Alaskans are tough. I selected a likely peak, claimed victory with a photo and pushed on.

I stopped to camp at a deserted campground in the State Park. There were large signs telling me to beware of bears and hang my food from a tree. I regretted my lack of rope. The prospect of meeting a bear now seemed less exciting and more utterly terrifying. I cooked dinner in the car park and stashed my pannier bag of food in the underbrush well away from the campsite. I retreated to the tent, hand on my bear spray, shadows pouncing.

## Day 5 – Denali State Park to Riley Creek, Denali National Park

I woke up and discovered I hadn't been eaten. The bears had also missed my lentils. The deserted campground felt less ominous in the morning. I set off towards Denali National Park in the sun and in a positive mood.

The ride to the National Park was my first introduction to the emptiness of Alaska. The first human habitation north of the State Park, a town called Cantwell, was 80km from my campsite. I did not plan well for this. There was a well at the campsite, but it pumped water orange with rust. I passed no streams. My mood deteriorated as I climbed repetitive hills and ran out of water.

For the second time that morning, I survived. Cantwell reminded me of a typical New Zealand rural town: a shop, a church and a bar. This impression was reinforced by a sign advertising "Meat Pies" mounted on a truck trailer in a gravel lot. A black prefab cabin at the back of the lot didn't inspire hope, but I wasn't in the position to be picky. JP's coffee house turned out to be a heaven-sent patisserie. JP was from Louisiana and baked Cajun crescents of joy. I had a chicken gumbo pie, then a muffin, then a coffee, and then another pie. The staff laughed at me, gear spread out across a table with pie crust covering my Lycra: "Enjoying yourself? Going for round three?" The locals chatted over their daily pie fix and complained about the heat. It was twenty degrees.

I dragged myself away from the pies and cycled on to Denali, my outlook on life substantially improved. At the edge of the park, I saw my first moose. I stopped to watch as this miracle of evolution galumphed along the forest verge. Gangly legs lifted hooves high for each short step forward. From twenty metres away, it was hard to imagine it as dangerous. I set up camp at the park entrance, surrounded by RVs, and listened to red squirrels object to the intrusion into their domain. Between the emptiness of the ride and the wildlife, I felt like I had arrived in Alaska.

## Day 6 – Denali National Park: Riley Creek to Wonder Lake

I got up at 5am to catch a bus to where I would ride the 100km to Wonder Lake in the middle of the Park. I rolled out of the campground into a silent dawn shrouded in mist. As I turned into one of the campground loops, I was confronted by a mother moose with a calf less than a foot tall. The calf wobbled along beside the mother's legs as she grazed. It was a peaceful scene. I stayed well clear. I was in no mood to test whether mother moose were peaceful creatures. I turned around and took another exit to the bus station.

I loaded my bike onto the bus and we set off along the Park road. After an hour of admiring gravel hills I would not have to climb, the bus driver let me out. I hadn't ridden a kilometre when the bus came back to get me. "Fresh bear kill up ahead," the driver said. Oh, good. They drove me through a stretch of road marked with signs saying, "Bear Danger: No Pedestrian or Bicycle Traffic," and dropped me off next to the last sign. I considered asking to be driven a little further. The signs didn't look like they would stop a bear.

I rode on. By the second gravel hill, I was regretting bringing all my gear into the park. Why was I carrying two kilos of lentils for one night of camping? I considered this question at length as I ground out the hills. The view, however, was excellent. The road ran above a glacial plain surrounded by snow-capped mountains. A braided snowmelt drainage twisted the length of the valley. I stared across the valley. There was a moose running full tilt towards the road ahead. The hillside below the road was steep, not quite a cliff, but close. I watched the moose as it galloped at the hill, expecting it to stop. It didn't even slow. It hit the hillside at full tilt and started to climb. Improbable legs bounded over boulders. I came up beside a Park Ranger's truck as the moose gained the level ground of the road thirty metres ahead of us. I greeted the Ranger, "How about that moose, man?" "Moose?" he replied, looking at me with surprise. "Haven't you seen the bears?" Two cinnamon coloured grizzlies climbed the hill on the opposite side of the road. The hill on this side was even steeper. The bears' claws dug into the rock as they scaled the face. The moose was chasing them.

The Ranger told me that the bears had killed the moose's calf earlier in the day. Mama moose was not peaceful. I'm not sure what she would have done if she had caught the bears. The bears were not keen to find out. The hill the bears climbed was too steep for the moose. The bears stopped fifty metres above the road, and peered down as the moose scrambled thirty metres below. After twenty minutes, the moose admitted defeat and wandered off. The bears descended to the road. As the bears approached, the Ranger leaned out of his car, "You. Down the hill. Now." I beat a retreat to the bottom and waited for a passing bus to give me a lift through. I told the story to the bus driver and half the bus, standing in the aisle in my Lycra, recreating the moose's pursuit with waving hands. When we passed the Ranger, the bus driver had a laugh. "We picked up this boy down the hill there. Said he saw a bear. I think it got him a little excited," she said. Whatever lady, I'd seen my first bear, and I didn't even have to get mauled.

As I continued towards Wonder Lake, the adrenaline wore off. It occurred to me that there really were bears here, and they really were hungry. I'd been told that the best way to avoid bears was to make "human noises" so that the bears knew you were coming and could get out of the way. I sang. I talked to the bears. I talked to myself. I put on accents. I ran out of ideas. I started singing, "Human noises, human noises," on repeat. I felt ridiculous, but I saw no more bears, so it must have been effective.

While in full bear song, I came across another touring cyclist taking a break and enjoying the view. Alan was sixty, English, and a proper cycle tourist. Alan had been cycling for eleven months through Death Valley, the Baja Divide and now Denali: "And I haven't even started my trip yet," he said. He was headed up to the Arctic Circle to turn around and go to Patagonia. He hadn't seen a bear though. I shared my adventure from earlier and we agreed that it was just the right amount of bear. "There are some things you want to do," Alan said, "then there are things you don't want to do, and then there are things you want to have done. Getting close enough to smell a grizzly sits firmly in the last category. Great to talk about in the pub afterwards."

By the time I got to Wonder Lake, I was exhausted. My knees hurt. The weather was chaotic. Grey clouds would gather, the wind would pick up and the sky would go dark. I would stop and put on my wet weather gear. The clouds would clear, the sun would start to shine and the inside of my jacket would turn into a sauna. I would stop again to shed layers, always too late, always just in time for the next shower. I gave up changing and committed to getting soaked. I made it. At the campground, I was greeted by a Ranger with an Australian accent so broad I expected his pet crocodile to waddle out of the cabin behind him. I wondered how he ended up at the end of the road in Denali.

I braced myself for another battle with lentils and chatted to the other campers. They were all suitably impressed with my bear story. Chica was from Tokyo but lived in Whitehorse, the capital of the Yukon, where she worked as a trail guide. She had lived there for six years and was applying for permanent residency. Did she want to stay in Whitehorse forever? "Oh, no, I just want to be able to buy a gun ... for the bears," she said. Chica was not a fan of bears. We discussed my route through the Yukon. There were two possible highways. I could continue on the Alaska-Canada Highway (ALCAN) to Calgary, or turn off on the Stewart-Cassiar to Vancouver. Chica encouraged me not to go down the Stewart-Cassiar, "Stewart-Cassiar ... many bears. Many, many bears." She told me my new bear spray was useless: "If the wind is wrong, the spray doesn't work. If it's raining, the spray doesn't work. If the bear is in your tent, the spray doesn't work." Chica had given this a lot of thought. I asked her if the ALCAN was any better. "Oh, no, ALCAN also so many bears."

While we considered this, the clouds cleared from over the lake and the mountains came into view. It was true, there was no denying Denali. Standing 3,000m taller than the surrounding foothills, the peak looked closer than the base, like it was bending around the earth towards us. I'd left my phone in my tent. I knew I should get it and record my one landmark in Alaska. I couldn't be bothered. I was done. I retreated to my tent to dream of bears.

## Day 7 – Wonder Lake, Denali National Park to Nenana

We woke to a fog-covered Wonder Lake. Unprepared to schlep my lentils back over the gravel hills, I boarded the bus back to the Park entrance. I was joined by Chica and three army boys up from Anchorage for the weekend. Chica planned to go backcountry hiking. In the second valley we surprised two bears out collecting breakfast. They appeared from the mist, metres from the road, camouflaged in the brown glacial scrub. In the next valley, Chica stopped the bus and got out to wander off into the fog. She wasn't as concerned about bears as I'd thought. The army boys watched her go, impressed. I chatted to them for the rest of the ride back. One was from Fairbanks, the largest city in the Alaskan Interior, and my next stop. I asked them what there was to do in the city. The Anchorage guys laughed, "Absolutely nothing, nothing at all." The Fairbanks local considered this. "That's not true," he said, "there is great Thai food."

It was raining when we arrived back at the Park entrance. I sat under cover outside the ticket office and tried to motivate movement with coffee and donuts. There were three other touring cyclists doing the same. Nate, Allyssa and Will were heading into Denali and had just met. Procrastinating brings people together. Allyssa introduced herself: "Is it your first tour?" she asked. "How could you tell?" I replied. "Your panniers, they are just so clean!" Allyssa laughed. I was just starting to feel proud that my panniers had accumulated some road grit. She might as well have called them cute.

The small talk of Alaskan cyclists was becoming familiar: the hills, the rain and the bears. Will had hiked the Appalachian Trail and the Pacific Crest Trail "Four hundred nights in bear country," he said. He used his food as a pillow. I questioned his sanity. "Think about it," he replied. "Out here, bears aren't used to your smell, or thinking of you as a food source. If a bear ever does happen to wander into your camp, they'll smell you at the same time they smell your food. Your nasty cyclist stench will scare them off." I wasn't convinced, but it did make me feel better that someone was confident enough to sleep with their sausages. You only need to be the second slowest person running away from a lion.

We debated bear strategies. Allyssa had a bell on her handlebars to warn bears of her approach. A middle-aged lady overheard this: "Hey, hey, what's the difference between grizzly bear poop and black bear poop?" She paused for effect. "Grizzly bear poop has bells in it." She cackled and walked away without waiting for a response. There is an Alaskan State Championship in scaring the tourists with bear stories. My third coffee tipped my motivation over the edge and I got up to go. Allyssa parted with a motivational speech. "You'll feel better once you start moving," she said. "Why do we do this? Because we just really, really like riding bikes!" This was true. I'd found over the first week of riding that once the leg muscles started to work, my mind and body settled into a flow and the mile markers ticked by. Today though, it was raining, and my ass and my knees were having a screaming competition.

After the first 20km my burst of caffeine motivation faded, dissolved by the persistent drizzle. I passed a guy walking on the side of the road. This was an unusual sight in Alaska. There aren't that many people, and those that are there certainly aren't walking. I slowed to say hi and he called out, "Where'd you come from?" "Anchorage," I replied. He gave a big grin, "Right on man, right on." He was wearing Tevas. It's an ambitious move to own sandals in Alaska, let alone wear them. His positivity was infectious. My mood improved. Also, the rain stopped.

I stopped for the night at an RV park in Nenana (like the Rihanna song). I still hadn't worked up the courage to find campsites by the side of the road.

## Day 8 – Nenana to Fairbanks

Day eight was work. Headwinds and hills to Fairbanks. Every time I stood up on the pedals, the front of my knee felt like it was going to pop off into the road. Every time I sat on the saddle my ass felt like my bike shorts were lined with sandpaper.

I amused myself by RV watching. Freed from the restraint of the city and judgement of society, the RVs were getting larger and more ridiculous. One passed towing what looked like a toy car. It was a Jeep. The RVs looked more like rock star tour buses than low rent holiday homes for retirees. One gem was branded "Outlaw" and covered with flame decals. It was being driven by an elderly couple, heads peaking over the dashboard.

The only shop I passed in the 100km between Nenana and Fairbanks was called Skinny Dick's Halfway Inn. I stopped for coffee. The logo on the billboard outside was two polar bears fucking. The door to the bar was covered with a sign saying: "This Place is Protected by God and Guns, if you Trespass You'll Get Both." My curly moustache seemed like it would be unwelcome and I was unprepared to get God. My hopes for a cappuccino faded.

'No trespassing' signs were a theme. Some properties had opted for the standard "Posted: No Trespassing". Others had gone for a more bespoke approach. I saw one hand-painted sign four feet tall saying: "No Trespassing! Violators Will Be Dealt With By The Law Or Otherwise". I considered the implications of "Or Otherwise" as I battled the arctic wind into Fairbanks, my hands curling into claws around the handlebars. Town achieved, I made straight for the nearest coffee shop. I was greeted by a barista wearing a shirt with "human" printed over a rainbow flag. Cappuccinos and moustaches were encouraged.

After checking into a hostel I went for Thai. My army buddy was right, it was excellent.

## Day 9 – Fairbanks

I could barely walk down the stairs in the hostel in the morning. My knees felt like the Spanish Inquisition had gotten hold of them. I decided to take a rest day. I hobbled down to a local diner for breakfast. The customers reflected my impressions of Alaska so far. Parked outside were two American-sized pickup trucks, complete with Trump bumper stickers. In between them was a Prius. It was also covered in stickers: 'Alaska Girls Kick Ass', 'Proud Feminist', and 'My Other Car is a Broom'. I people-watched and searched for something in Fairbanks more interesting than pad thai.

I joined a group of cruise ship tourists to go meet local legend Mary Shields at her cabin/kennel nestled in the woods outside of town. Mary was the first woman to complete the Iditarod sled dog race, in 1974. She had come to Alaska as a post-graduate student, was lent a sled dog by a friend and fell in love. Mary joined the Iditarod, a 1,500km race, because she wanted to go on a camping trip on trails she didn't have to break herself. At the halfway point, she was running 25th. As she came into the camp, there was a cheer. She was curious. People don't cheer for 25th. She found out that the men following the race had bets on when she would drop out, and the cheering was from the women that had bet on her and were coming into the money. She thought she better not treat it as a camping trip anymore and picked up the pace.

We went outside to pet her dogs. They were awesome. Mary told us to howl. We howled. The dogs replied. Mary told us that on camping trips she would howl to say goodnight. The dogs would reply. Then, from the distance, another howl would echo around the valley. A wolf. The attraction of an Alaskan winter started to make more sense. After the cruise ship tourists left, we chatted while I waited for a taxi. Mary was seventy-three and recently had the bottom half of her leg amputated after a broken ankle. I asked how it was going to affect her life with the dogs.

She looked me straight in the eye, "I'll be back on the sled by the end of the year. Easily." When the taxi came, Mary loaded me up with baked goods and wished me luck on my trip: "Just keep going." In the taxi, I reflected that I had essentially paid $100 to pet dogs and get a pep talk. Not quite in line with the bike touring spendthrift ethos, but worth every penny.

## Day 10 – Fairbanks

After a full day of rest spent massaging my knees and eating anti-inflammatories like they were psychedelic, I still winced as I walked down the stairs in the morning. I decided to take another rest day. I now had persistent doubts as to whether I would be able to make it to Canada, let alone Mexico. Was this the kind of pain that would get better or the kind that would get worse? If it didn't get better, the rest of the trip wasn't going to be much fun. I remembered something that Alan, the English cyclist in Denali, had said to me. I'd admitted to him that I took the bus in for the first 30km. He scoffed, "So did I mate. I'm not in it for the pain." Neither was I, in theory. I wondered if I could live down giving up after a week.

I spent the morning in the hostel drinking coffee, eating cereal and going stir crazy. After sled dogs and Thai food, I'd exhausted the worthwhile attractions in Fairbanks. I sat on every couch in the house. I read John Muir's *Travels in Alaska* about his trips in the Alaskan Panhandle. Big mountains, bigger glaciers. I considered whether taking a boat down the coast and cycling around the islands would still count as a cycling trip. I alternately determined to continue and decided to give up until the early afternoon.

Sick of being inside, I rode over to a nearby bike shop to see whether my knee pain was caused by seat position or something else fixable. A wave of positivity flowed through me as I got out into the fresh air. When I arrived at the shop, the mechanic listened to my story, took one look at my setup and said, "Looks fine to me buddy, it's just growing pains." It didn't really matter. Being on the bike had made the decision for me. I told the mechanic about freezing on the hills down into Fairbanks. He laughed. He was from here, he was familiar with cycling in the cold. Apparently, I got lucky: it snowed that day on the Denali Highway. It was June.

To celebrate my decision, I dropped the bike back at the

hostel and went for ice cream. I was reminded of how ridiculous you look as a full grown man eating ice cream in public in the middle of the day. Parents assembled at the ice cream shop regarded me with suspicion. Ice cream accumulated on my moustache. It didn't help my image.

Back at the hostel, I met an oil rig worker named Rory. He offered me a beer. Rory was on holiday and trying to pack in as many activities as possible. He looked exactly like you would expect someone on holiday from an arctic oil rig to look. Hands like bricks, no neck, and a huge smile of freedom. He offered me a new beer twice before I'd finished my first. Rory was going bear hunting the next day, then renting a car and driving down to Haines to go salmon fishing. I asked about bear hunting. "You know the best bait for bears?" he asked. "The best bear bait, by far, is donuts." Why donuts? "It's the fried fat and the sugar. They can't resist." He grinned. I wasn't sure if this was another 'scare the tourists' story. Still, no more donuts in the tent.

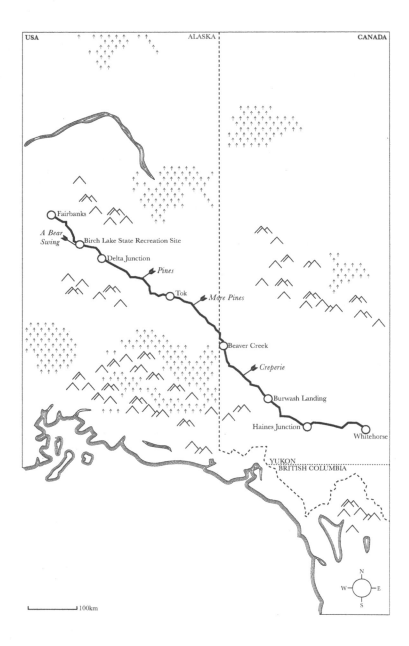

USA     ALASKA     CANADA

Fairbanks

*A Bear Swing*

Birch Lake State Recreation Site

Delta Junction

*Pines*

Tok

*More Pines*

Beaver Creek

*Creperie*

Burwash Landing

Haines Junction

Whitehorse

YUKON
BRITISH COLUMBIA

100km

N
W   E
S

# Day 11 – Fairbanks to Birch Lake State Park

After two days, I rushed to get back on the bike. The cycling was easier than expected. I found that if I moved up through the gears one by one, my kneecaps remained attached to my legs. Ninety flat kilometres later at 3pm I stopped to camp by a lake in a State Park. It started to rain. Two boys played on a jet-ski in the lake. Their dad shouted to them: "It's only when you get so cold that you stop shivering that you have a problem." I wasn't there yet, but after waiting for my lentils to boil in the rain, I was close. I regretted my lack of donuts.

The road from Fairbanks to Whitehorse was 950km through bear country. I decided to learn how to tie a bear swing. I was defeated. No tree branch could handle my absurd supply of food. I'd been told (by the internet) to find a solitary tree. That way a bear couldn't climb up a nearby tree to get at the bag. This proved easier on YouTube than on the lake shore. In the end, I found a tree. It wasn't perfect, but it was far enough away from my tent that the bear wouldn't have to wake me up to get his meal. The next challenge was throwing a rope over the branch. I was glad I was far enough away from the jet-skis not to be laughed at. Rope in place, I pulled at my food bag. It wouldn't budge. I pushed the bag with one hand, jumping and pulling the rope with the other and my teeth. Five minutes of this graceful dance, and the bag was a foot over my head. If a bear had been watching, I might have been saved by curiosity. Or by pity. Frustrated, I put all my weight on the rope. The branch snapped. Fuck it. I resolved to leave my food on the bike. If a bear wanted my lentils, they were welcome to them.

## Day 12 – Birch Lake to Delta Junction

The landscape was monotonously beautiful. Pine trees surrounded the road, green and dark. Up hills through pines, down hills through pines. Thick pine forests, thin pine forests, pine forests in swamps. There might have been other trees, but I couldn't tell the difference. They were big, green, and went on for miles. As the pines beat me into submission, I passed a middle-aged couple. Charlie and Janet were also sick of pine trees. They also hated the weather. Two days earlier, they were snowed in on the Denali Highway. This coloured their experience. Nothing comforts like other people's misery. I rode off feeling much more cheerful.

My only other company on the road during the day were moose. Most grazed by the side of the highway, out of the way of traffic. One thought that beneath him, and stood across the road. Enough people had told me that the furry forest horses were more dangerous than bears. I stopped twenty metres back to shout at him. I shouted, he stared. I hadn't seen a car for thirty minutes. I edged closer. The road was quiet, empty as far as I could see in both directions. I rode to the edge and slowly passed behind him. He picked up one leg as if to move, thought better of it, and continued to survey his kingdom.

A lone butcher shop broke the pines, the only shop I'd seen all day. Although moose were great company, I stopped for some human contact. I introduced myself to the owner feeling like a Jehovah's Witness. She asked what I was looking for. I didn't look like a good prospect to purchase a moose leg. At a loss for valid conversation, I told her I was from New Zealand and was cycling down to Canada. "We had a butcher here from New Zealand last year. He was … rowdy," she said. Not for the first time I wondered how someone ended up in a place like this. I bought some moose sausage and got back on the road.

There were no State Parks between Birch Lake and the Canadian border. I had no option other than to find an off-piste campsite for the first time. I stopped at a turnout to cook dinner before starting my search, steeling my resolve with lentils and the last of the moose. I wasn't about to start camping with sausages. After thinking about bears almost non-stop since I arrived in Alaska and talking to anyone with an opinion about how best to avoid getting eaten, I'd come away with three simple rules. Don't cook where you camp. Don't sleep with your food. Don't be unlucky. After dinner I rode on, searching the sides of the road for a campsite. Once I started to look, with no other option available, everything started to look like a campsite. This made sense: absolutely no one lived here. I found a small clearing hidden from view of the road by a scrubby patch of pine, pitched my tent and crawled in to massage my knees.

# Day 13 – Delta Junction to Tok Junction

I spent the ride from Delta to Tok Junction weather watching. The weather in Alaska was famously variable. A favourite saying of locals was, "Oh, you don't like the weather? Don't worry! Just wait ten minutes..." Pause for effect, "It'll get worse!" I'd given up paying attention to the forecast. Often, there would be patches of cloud, sunshine, and heavy rain moving across the same horizon. The road would either weave through the minefield of squalls or pick them off one by one. I rode towards a range of hills blanketed by a storm. The road snaked along a valley towards the hills and the rain. Cycling is not driving. I had hours to imagine, in great detail, the torrents of water flooding down the hills and down my neck. The road cut left. A solitary raindrop fell on my glasses and I rode away from the storm to Tok. High drama on the open road.

Tok Junction was a motley collection of run-down gift shops, with a supermarket and a gas station strung out along the highway. The town was founded as a road construction camp in 1942 and hadn't gone far since. I headed to the gas station for coffee and donuts, careful not to get any crumbs on my clothes. A guy shouted at me from his car window, asking me about my trip. He was halfway across the car park. Too close to drive, too far to walk. I walked over. Lewis told me he used to have a store where he'd let cyclists camp. "I'd feed them steak and potatoes," he said. "You know man, get them carbed up real good." He tried to convince other shops along the highway to do the same. Now I was interested. Steak sounded better than lentils. Did it work? "No man, no one agreed, cyclists aren't great business." True enough. My dream of steak was short-lived.

As I headed over to the supermarket for supplies, a woman intercepted me on her bike. "Where are you touring from?" she asked. I think the half-empty six-pack of donuts I was holding gave me away. Clarisse was from Montreal but worked in Whitehorse as a biologist. She was two weeks into a two-year cycle tour from the Arctic Circle to Argentina. It had snowed on her for the first three days in the north. Her knees had given out. Clarisse pulled the plug and got a lift south to Fairbanks with a trucker. She was reassessing why she had decided to tour. "Last year I cycled across South Africa. Eight weeks of summer, barbecues and wine," she laughed. "What the hell am I doing in the Arctic Circle?" We had a donut and swapped motivational speeches. I guaranteed Clarisse that her knee pain would improve, and she assured me that the pine trees thinned out further south.

## Day 14 – Tok Junction, AK to Beaver Creek, YT

On the way to the Canadian border, I stopped in at Tetlin Wildlife Refuge. After 80km of cycling without seeing a person, I would have stopped to talk to a bear. Outside the Ranger station, I met two motorbike tourists. Dave and Rob were from Calgary. They had come from the border that morning and were planning to get to the Arctic Circle by night. The previous day they had ridden 1,700km in nineteen hours. I told them they were insane. "Well, we aren't the ones cycling it." Dave had a point. We ran through the standard bear chat and complaints about the pine trees. I told them my plan was to head south through Vancouver. This was not well received. "Why would you go to Vancouver?" Dave asked. "The Icefields Parkway between Banff and Jasper, that's where you need to be. Glaciers, mountains, the most beautiful views of your life." Dave was getting excited. "In fact, fuck all this, fuck all these pine trees." He waved his hand to indicate the last two and the next four weeks of my life: "The Icefields Parkway is the best road in North America." As I cycled off, new route possibilities brewing, Dave screamed at a picnicking family, "There goes a crazy man!" They turned in panic. This buoyed my spirits through the pines.

There was a 30km 'no man's land' zone between the US and Canadian customs checkpoints. It was the most desolate section of the route so far. As I rode through scrub pine I was reminded of something my uncle said after reading Alastair Humphreys' books: "He didn't have much to say about Canada and the US. It was a pretty long period of silence. Why are you going? I'm not sure there is that much up there." Not a lot there, and a lot more of that to go. The emptiness was either impressive or boring, depending on how much coffee I'd had. My reflection on the mind-numbing nature of pine forests was broken by a bald eagle. It was the first one I'd seen. As I approached, it launched into the air, gliding down the road ahead of me. A moment of stillness, then two great flaps of its wings and it was off. This seemed like a fitting farewell to Alaska.

I picked a horrible campsite. As I listened to the sounds of mosquitos assaulting my tent netting, I realised that I had decided to continue to Whitehorse. My knees had improved. They still hurt, but after four days of cycling slowly they were going in the right direction. From Whitehorse, the only option would be to ride the remaining 1,400km of either the Alaska or the Cassiar highway. I tried to put the distance out of my mind.

## Day 15 – Beaver Creek to well before Burwash Landing

I did battle with a headwind. In the morning, there were 450km to Whitehorse. After twelve hours in the saddle, there were 340km left. I spent most of those hours cursing the cycling gods.

50km in though, a break in the otherwise grey sky. 400km from Whitehorse, 600km from Fairbanks, 5,000km from Paris: a crêperie. A bright red billboard was decorated with Canadian and French flags. It was the first shop since Fairbanks that wasn't a gas station, a souvenir shop, or abandoned. I chatted to the owner. Pascal had moved from Paris, to Montreal, to Whitehorse before coming to a rest in this remote stretch of rural Yukon. I wondered how many banks he had robbed. I asked him what life was like here. Pascal laughed, "Quiet in summer, silent in winter."

Enjoying my third crepe, I met two truckers fuelling up for the drive to Whitehorse. I wanted to make a good impression. Trucks were my most constant companion, and risk of death, on the ALCAN. I told them how grateful I was for the space the eighteen-wheelers gave me when passing. Better than London black cabs. They told me they had already passed me twice. They thought I was insane. Wouldn't this be easier in a car? Where did I sleep? What did I do about the bears? My new friends were amazed I hadn't seen any bears along the highway. They had seen two "big old cinnamons" this morning.

Fortified by crepes, I renewed my assault on the headwind. I reflected on my lack of bears. Maybe I was going slow enough that they heard me coming and moved out of the way? Maybe it was just randomness. I wondered what I would do if I saw one. Would it be best to try to ride past? To stop and wait for it to move on? What if it didn't, would I wait for a car to escort me past? While I was considering the possibility of a half-hour watching a bear while waiting for a car, an RV going the opposite way pulled over to my side of the road. They had seen a grizzly bear, three kilometres down the road. They delivered this message in worried tones and drove off. Thanks team, what am I supposed to do now? I rang my bell. I sang. I made human noises. After ten kilometres, no bear. Human noises win again.

In the afternoon, a car screeched to a stop ahead of me. A big man jumped out and ran towards me. Reaching for my bear spray, I recognised Rory. Rory had completed his donut-fuelled bear hunt and was on his way to Haines. He regaled me with tales of the hunt: "They were everywhere, man. So many bears, we had to shoot our way into the blind." He mimed shooting a rifle and advancing through the trees, commando style: "We bagged a beautiful big boar." He showed me a photo. In full camouflage and face paint, Rory stood above a bear with paws and claws spread across a log. He held what looked like a Gatling gun above his head. If I was getting anywhere near those claws, I would have wanted a tank. Each claw was ten centimetres of grey steal. Perfect neck-cutting length. The bear had ten. Rory and his friends made bear jerky. My news was less exciting. I bitched about the wind. Rory offered me a lift. I declined, but was tempted.

My resolve was rewarded with the best campsite of the trip so far. Nestled by a creek, an alcove of pines sheltered me from the gale. The mosquitos also liked the shelter. There was no escaping them. Selected by Darwin to suck blood through moose hide and bear fur, Lycra bike shorts offered no protection. I put on my wet weather gear and put up my tent.

## Day 16 – Burwash Landing to Haines Junction

I woke to a headwind even worse than the day before. If I stopped pedalling, I stopped moving. It was like cycling in syrup. I passed an elderly RV couple at a rest stop, staggering in the gale. The husband stopped and clapped as I passed. Well, I thought, it could be worse; it could be raining. The wind was a warm southerly and I had been able to put away my gloves for the first time in the trip. If I was going north, it would have been beautiful.

My applause high was blown soon after. An RV stopped to tell me there was a bear on the road, "A big papa griz." I rode on. Another car stopped. A young guy leant out the window and screamed, "There's the biggest grizzly I've ever seen up ahead." He paused, looking me up and down as if wondering how long it would take the bear to eat me. "You good?" he asked. Well, mate, you've just said the words "the biggest grizzly ever seen" to a guy on a bike. What do you think? A third car stopped, a big pickup truck. A middle-aged lady got out and offered me a lift. She had the tray down and was helping me load gear before I'd said a word. Cleo was from Oregon but told me she "half lived in Alaska." Her dog, Charlie, tried to get into the front to say hello. We rounded a corner and passed the bear. He was a metre off the road, gigantic, eating dandelions. Cleo handed me her phone to take a photo. Charlie took advantage of the distraction to leap over the seat and start barking out the window. The bear didn't look up from his dandelions. Cleo laughed, "Bear don't care." We drove and chatted for a while. I told Cleo about my trip. One of Cleo's sons had just finished biking around Oregon, so she was on board with the concept. She invited me to stay with them in Oregon and drew me a map to her town, "We travellers have to stick together."

The headwind chipped away at my sanity. The line, "Just keep swimming, just keep swimming," from *Finding Nemo* ran on loop through my head in a sing-song cartoon fish voice. I stopped at a gas station for coffee. A man in a checked shirt and grey beard said hello, "This wind is tough in the truck, it must be hell on the bike." It felt good to have someone else recognise it. I asked him if this was normal and if it would continue. He gave me a sympathetic look, "All day, all year, all the way to Whitehorse."

The road joined Kluane Lake, pine-bordered and covered in whitecaps. At the foot of the lake was a low grey cloud. As I approached, the cloud turned out to be dust. A causeway crossed the southern tip of the lake. Beyond it, a plain stretched towards the foot of the mountains bordering Kluane National Park. The park is 22,000 unbroken square kilometres of snow, glaciers, and the highest mountains in Canada. My headwind was born in these mountains and rushed down across the plain, untamed. The dust storm covering the causeway looked like something out of *Mad Max*. I stopped into a pullout to procrastinate and met an Indian couple. Dev and Meera had retired, sold their house in Chicago and decided to drive to Alaska. They had been on the road for four months. After the usual road greetings, they asked to film me explaining my trip. Dev filmed, and Meera asked me how I found campsites, how I dealt with bears, and what I had discovered about myself. Meera was excited that I was cooking lentils. She gave me a lecture on the benefits of a vegetarian diet. This particularly focused on the digestive effects. Dev looked embarrassed. Meera laughed, offered me some potato curry and told me to get married. I smiled all the way through the dust storm.

## Day 17 – Haines Junction to Whitehorse

I woke to no sound. I rushed out of my tent. The wind had stopped. The sky was blue, the sun was shining, and the tops of the trees were still. I rolled down into Haines Junction for breakfast. It was 175km to Whitehorse, but with no wind, a bed in a hostel at the end of the road, and three day-old pastries for $5 in my backpack, I decided to give it a shot.

10km out of Haines Junction, a car stopped and warned me about a bear, "A big one, right on the road, just on top of a hill." Before I could ask what side of the road, how far, or what hill, they drove off. Sick of singing, I tried a new bear deterrent: waving. I waved to every car, RV, truck and motorbike coming my direction. My theory was that if the person saw me there were three possibilities. First, there was no bear. Second, there was a bear, but the people waving back at me had decided it was far enough from the road not to bother a cyclist. Third, the people waving back were horrible sadists. Waving at everyone was a great way to pass the time. This was Canada, not England: everyone waved back. The waves gave me fresh confidence I wouldn't be eaten before my first shower in a week.

Three hours from safety, I got my first flat tyre. It was a slow leak and I went through the classic phase of denial. Tyre flapping on the road, I realised there was no escape. I laid the bike on the side of the road. It was at this point I remembered that I had meant to test my spare inner tubes before I left England. I hadn't. This seemed reasonable in London. It seemed less intelligent with a litre of water left, 75km left to Whitehorse, and bears behind every bush. There were moments of panic: the tyre levers didn't fit, the tube was too small, the pump didn't work. I completed the simplest of bike repair exercises covered in sweat, chain grease and mosquitos, victorious.

I continued my waving game all the way into Whitehorse. Out of the wilderness, the danger of bears declined. In town there was a new beast on the road. Whitehorse was filled with Harley-riding, neck-tattooed, leather-vest-wearing men glaring at each other. Who owns a Harley in the Yukon? It snows ten months a year. The more hardcore the biker, the more flamboyant my wave. Sometimes I caught them off guard and they waved back. They were still, after all, Canadian. I arrived at the hostel at 8pm. Exhausted, I sat in my bike shorts and ate an entire large Domino's pizza in the middle of a living room full of motorcycle tourists, canoeists and hikers. By the seventh slice, people were starting to stare. "Buddy, where the hell are you putting that?" I'd made an impression.

## Day 18 – Whitehorse

Over breakfast, I met Jay. Jay was a nurse from Ottawa living in Yellowknife, capital of the neighbouring Northwest Territory. She told me she'd moved to the north because she liked the idea of the midnight sun. Jay was on her way up to Tuktoyaktuk on the north coast for a solstice festival. I asked her if it was a good festival. She said she didn't really know anything about it, but she was pretty sure there would be midnight sun. No further questions.

After two weeks on the bike, I decided it was time for a check up and headed down to the local bike shop. Aidan, the mechanic, had done the tour down from Vancouver to Baja. It was worrying that he'd skipped the Whitehorse to Vancouver segment. Aidan checked my chain and laughed. "Here is a new chain." He showed me the chain tool with a half-centimetre gap. "Here is where we would recommend you replace the chain," and the gap doubled. "And here is as big a gap as the tool can measure," and Aidan rattled the tool around in my chain. "This chain is two hundred percent done. Maybe three hundred percent. It's pretty much a rubber band now. Exactly how much weight are you carrying?" God damn lentils.

I met Florian and Matt drinking rum outside the hostel in the long summer sunset. They were paying for their room and board with labour. Florian was a German carpenter and had just built a deck in the backyard. He told me about his time in New Zealand. "I built every house, drove every road and drank every beer," he said. His plan for Canada was the same. Matt was from the UK, a landscaper and a trail guide. He had come to Whitehorse to "get experience in real mountains, big rivers and lots of snow. Lots and lots of snow." Matt was paying his rent by re-turfing the hostel lawn. I told them about my trip; that I'd already ridden the length of the UK and I wasn't even halfway to halfway. We laughed about biting off more than you can chew. Matt had done his first hike here alone and off trail.

He had bushwhacked three miles into a valley before seeing his first bear. It sniffed in his direction, gave him a disdainful look and trundled off into the bush. "What the hell was I thinking?" he laughed. "This is nuts." It was a Friday night in Whitehorse, and my thirtieth birthday. I enlisted Jay, Florian and Matt and an Australian miner named Elle to go out and get wrecked. It was fun.

# Day 19 – Whitehorse

Today, I was hungover. I wandered around Whitehorse to see whatever else there was to see. Whitehorse went from First Nations land, to trading post, to town with the Klondike Gold Rush in the early 1900s. People rushed in with the gold, the gold rushed out, and most people followed. Donald Trump's grandfather, Freddy Trump, (allegedly) ran brothels back in the day before he lost his Bavarian citizenship for (allegedly) dodging military service. The town had peaked. I followed RV tourists through a museum and returned to the hostel to maximise my time on the couch before getting back on the road.

The hostel was now packed with canoeists about to embark on the Yukon River Quest, a 715km race from Whitehorse to Dawson City. I had a coffee with a Polish guy called Jan, about to embark on his Quest. I asked him what canoeing 715km was like. "Paddle, paddle, paddle," he mimed, paddling in his chair. "Paddle, paddle, paddle. Check speed," Jan looked at his watch, paddling with the free hand. We had both had too much coffee. "Paddle, paddle, paddle. Energy gel," Jan mimed, squeezing a gel into his mouth one-handed, other hand holding the imaginary paddle. "Paddle, paddle, paddle. Pee in a bottle," a final mime. Canoe racing sounded fun.

The Canadian motorcycle tourists' chat that the Icefields Parkway from Jasper to Banff was "the best road in North America" was pulling me east of Vancouver. I reviewed my maps with the collective wisdom of the hostel peanut gallery. We realised that the route through Idaho mapped out for me by John on the plane started just south of Banff. The decision was made. So much for Vancouver.

In the evening I cooked my last non-lentil dinner with Sarah, the hostel manager, Matt and Florian. Sarah was a big fan of road trips. Every year she and her husband strapped an RV conversion onto the back of their pickup truck and drove the 4,000km down to California to go to Hearst Castle. Hearst

Castle was the summer house of William Randolph Hearst, the early 20th-century publisher and movie producer. There were dress up tours. Sarah had been on all of them. I told her I would check it out. She made me a birthday cake.

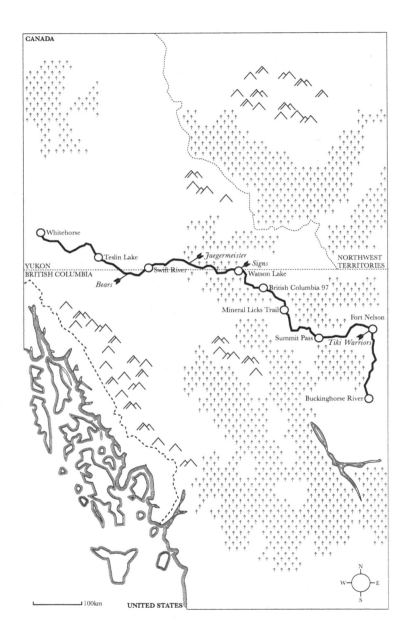

CANADA

YUKON
BRITISH COLUMBIA

NORTHWEST
TERRITORIES

Whitehorse

Teslin Lake

Swift River

*Jaegermeister*

*Signs*

Watson Lake

*Bears*

British Columbia 97

Mineral Licks Trail

Fort Nelson

Summit Pass

*Tiki Warriors*

Buckinghorse River

100km    UNITED STATES

N
W — E
S

# Day 20 – Whitehorse to Teslin Lake

I struggled to pull myself away from the hostel. Florian and Matt were going to a medieval sword fighting contest. What did a medieval sword fighting contest in the Yukon look like? I saw a poster. It looked low budget. But, there was a beer tent. I resisted. Sarah insisted I pick a song for the hostel playlist. It was full of Backstreet Boys. It got more *Scandinavian Leather*.

The 1,400km on the ALCAN from Whitehorse to Dawson Creek was described as impressive overall, but with nowhere overly impressive. I planned to stop in two towns on the way: Watson Lake and Fort St John. The 950km from Fairbanks to Whitehorse camping by the side of the road was right at the boundary of my hygiene limit. Whitehorse was the bustling metropolis of the Yukon, with more than one street. I felt that deeper into the wilderness hope for activities to fill a day might be misplaced. The whole being greater than the sum of the parts is nice, but it usually means the parts are shit.

The scenery improved as I rode away from Whitehorse. The pines gave way to the occasional birch tree. Not often, but sometimes. I rode over the Teslin River where it flowed into a lake. The smooth surface of the lake reflected cotton ball clouds and the last sliver of the setting moon. It was a great day for cycling.

There weren't many people out enjoying it. The only person I talked to all day was Paul. Paul was in his sixties and was covered head to toe in yellow high-vis gear. Paul was in the process of cycling every major road in Canada both directions. He showed me a map with each road outlined in green highlighter, which meant he had done one direction, and pink if he had done the other. I asked him about his motivation. "As I tell people all the time, whenever they ask, it looks like this in this direction," he waved his arm in the direction I'd come from, "and like that in that direction." Paul turned and waved the other direction. The road extended two kilometres to each horizon, flat, black and bordered with pines. Paul was taking a thorough approach to his task. "Two wheels on the ground, that's my rule," he said. "If they won't let me ride through road works, I wait until 6pm and ride through after they are finished. If the road is too broken to ride, I'll walk the bike." Paul encouraged me to start my own business. He had run an occupational health and safety consultancy for thirty years. That explained the high-vis gear. Paul noted down my nationality with a check mark in a notebook, "You're the fourth New Zealander I've met!" and we parted ways.

## Day 21 – Teslin Lake to Swift River

I was greeted in the morning by a 20km stretch of road works. Every car, RV and truck that passed kicked up a cloud of gravel dust. By the end, my bike, clothes and lungs were coated.

After this charming start to the day, I stopped for coffee in Teslin. The rest stop was a tour bus tourist zoo. A fat, white, elderly zoo. I reflected that we were covering the same ground, but our experiences could not have been more different. Covered in roadwork dust with no prospect of a shower for a week, I wondered who had the better end of the deal. I half showered in the cafe bathroom, dirtbag style. The tourists didn't comment, but they knew.

Climbing a hill out of Teslin, I spotted a brown boulder. Fishing for distraction, Stephen King's best thriller voice intoned: "And then the rock moved." Then the rock did move. I was too close to stop and hope the bear wouldn't see me. I decided to ride past. He was eating flowers by the side of the road. As I struggled past him, I realised I didn't have much potential to accelerate. Then again, maybe you never know how fast you can climb until you have a bear chasing you. Some days you find motivation, other days motivation finds you. I had been practising my bear spray unholstering technique. I wondered if I would have the coordination to do it with a bear lumbering at me. I'm not sure panic improves coordination. The bear continued to eat flowers. As Cleo said: "Bear don't care."

After the bear excitement faded, I felt the loneliness of the road. Cars passed every thirty minutes. After Teslin, I didn't see a building for the rest of the day. My hopes were raised by a sign for "Walker Lodge: Wilderness Bakery". I approached, planning my order. The text underneath the sign read, "Turn-off in 56 miles." The taste of cinnamon buns faded.

A van covered in satellite dishes approached. The driver got his full body out of the window to scream encouragement, long hair streaming behind him. I was still laughing when a second car approached, horn blasting. I looked for a bear. The driver pumped his fist out the window: "Go on, boy!" They were coming towards me. They knew the 1,000km+ of road I had ahead. I appreciated the morale boost. I resolved to scream more at cyclists.

The ALCAN dipped into British Columbia for a 15km stretch before returning to the Yukon. A faded welcome sign announced: "Super, Natural British Columbia". Dark clouds swirled across the sky like angry ghosts. I debated where to camp for the night. I delayed too long. Thunder clapped, hail drummed. I struggled to pitch my tent with chilled fingers, then collected marbles of ice as they began to melt and pool beside my sleeping bag.

# Day 22 – Swift River to Cassiar Campground

The hail stopped, but the rain persisted. In full rain gear, I packed away a wet tent. I contemplated the attractive prospect of sleeping in it again that evening. So enthused, I set out into the northern Cassiar Mountains.

I stopped off in a turnout at the top of a hill to make some porridge. This proved chilly. My theory was that breakfasting on the top would give me the downhill to digest the porridge before tackling another climb. This was outweighed by the twenty minutes standing on a ridge in the wind. I attracted sympathetic looks from people inside RVs. They looked warm.

I passed an RV park and rushed in to warm up. Inside a rickety door was a grandmother's house. Floral wallpaper, and framed postcards with slogans like "Children Complete the Circle of Life", and "Beautiful, Gentle, Understanding, Forgiving: a Mother's Love". It looked like the opening set of a horror movie. But, there was a tray of cinnamon rolls and free refill coffee.

Inside, I recognised Nate, one of the cyclists I met at the entrance of Denali National Park. While I went north to Fairbanks, Nate had taken the longer route up to Dawson City. He had now come back to rejoin the ALCAN and head south. We decided to cycle together. After cycling by myself for three weeks I had settled into a comfortable rhythm. This was insufficient to keep up. Nate encouraged me, "You've got almost twice as much stuff, just wait until you get rid of the lentils." He was twenty-six and this was his second long cycle tour. The first was six months after graduating university. Nate hiked and biked to the highest points in thirty states. After that, he went to work and set himself the goal of saving $100k as fast as possible to get back to touring. Three years later, Nate was cycling from Alaska to Patagonia. Nate chatted, and I puffed up the hills in the persistent rain. I asked what he would do when he got to Argentina. "Maybe I'll just keep going," Nate replied.

As I was starting to dream up excuses to stop cycling and crawl into my wet tent, we passed a State Park campground. Nate suggested we stop and see if we could make a fire. In the middle of a clearing of pines was a picnic shelter, complete with a barrel stove. Next to it, a pile of firewood. Thank you, Canada. We built a fire and unpacked our tents to dry, hanging them as close to the stove as we dared. Nate and I sat back to appreciate our good fortune. Then, two motorbike tourists arrived. Klaus and Hank unpacked their bikes and we invited them to join us by the fire. I marvelled at the quantity of kit that emerged from their metal motorbike panniers. "Ja, you young guys, you can handle eating oats all day, every day," Klaus laughed. "We need a bit more of home out here." Hank produced a bottle of Jägermeister. The day ended well.

## Day 23 – Cassiar Campground to Watson Lake

We sat watching the rain fall. The shelter and the fire made leaving difficult. I offered oats for breakfast. Klaus and Hank thought that was hilarious and cooked us all eggs and proper coffee.

My inflatable sleeping mat had developed a leak in the night. When it first deflated, I re-inflated it and went back to sleep. Denial proved ineffective. An hour later, I was again awake on the wooden floor. After breakfast, I repaired the leak with a bicycle patch. This worked for all of a minute. Hank told me he had had the same mattress, the same problem and tried to do the same thing. It didn't work. "You know what worked?" he asked. "Buying a new mattress." Oh good, only 900km until the next camping store.

Nate and I pushed on to Watson Lake. The weather was grey, approaching black. Nate was philosophical about it: "You can't appreciate the sun without the rain," he said. After the last two nights, I decided I could appreciate a dry tent many times for it being wet once. We discussed adventure. "On the spectrum from watching TV at home, to Shackleton crossing the Weddell Sea, we are closer to RV people than sailors," I said. Nate agreed, "This isn't real adventure. There are roads. There is cell phone reception. You have to go pretty far off the beaten track these days to find something truly adventurous." We tried to come up with real cycling adventures. The west coast of Africa. Siberia in winter. The Darién Gap. We dreamed of near death experiences. We passed a grizzly. Neither of us noticed until we were beside him. He was fifteen metres back from the road, foraging in the grass. He didn't even raise his head. Bear don't care. We giggled and sped up. Still no Weddell Sea, but rich enough for my blood.

Outside the Watson Lake visitor centre was one of the ALCAN points of interest. The signpost forest. Seventy-thousand licence plates, street signs, park signs, and anything else people could steal and nail to a post. Nate and I marvelled for most of a minute, took the obligatory tourist photo, and retired to the visitor centre for coffee and warmth. Impressive overall, but not overly impressive. Inside, we both took one look at the weather map and booked a motel. More adventure could wait for dry clothes.

A visitor centre host tried to get Nate to watch an informational video about the ALCAN with a crowd of RV people. He demurred, "I've seen enough of this road, I'll form my own opinions." To justify our lingering, I chatted to Linda, another host, about what was in store for us down the road. Nate planned to turn off at Watson Lake to take the Stewart-Cassiar down to Vancouver, while I would follow the ALCAN to Jasper. Nate had more bison, I had more mountains. We both had bears. Linda was casual about the bears. Her eighty-year-old mother would pick berries in the same patch as a grizzly: "Oh he's doing his thing and I'll do mine," she'd say. "He knows I'm here, and there are plenty of berries for the both of us." I wasn't there yet. According to Linda, managing bears was all about your energy: "No fear, no aggression ... oh, and no food odours."

To celebrate our soon-to-be-dry kit, Nate and I bought microwave pizzas, blueberry pies and litres of ice cream. We checked in to Air Force Lodge, a Second World War barracks that had been converted to a motel. It was full of motorcycle and car tourists too old to camp, but with too much pride to buy an RV. The Lodge was run by a huge blond German. Hans looked like he had been plucked from a Bavarian beer tent and dropped in the Yukon. We sat around chatting as we microwaved our pizza and pie. Hans had come to the Yukon twenty-five years ago when he was thirty. He told us long stories about the sense of community he found on the frontier, the nature, and the Corvette he bought when he first arrived. That was before he realised he couldn't drive it for three quarters of the year. I asked him how he decided on the Yukon. Hans was evasive. "For the first five years I lived out by the lake, no neighbours for twenty miles. No noise, no hassle, no laws." And no German police.

## Day 24 – Watson Lake to Whirlpool River

Nate and I parted ways in the morning. It was great having company for two days, but I was looking forward to cycling slowly. Nate set out at 8am for a 200km day. All power to him.

I procrastinated, ate more pie, and bought the last available sleeping mat for 500km in any direction. It was $27 and looked like a pool toy. It was a pool toy. There were six separate tubes, each with its own valve. My old camping mat inflated in eight breaths, the pool toy took fifty. By the time I finished testing it, I had to sit down. Its one advantage was that it worked.

Ten kilometres out of town I saw a black bear. He was right by the road. I saw him from a long way off. I was wondering how to handle it, when an RV stopped by the side of the road. He had seen me, and was running bear interference. I cycled around him, waved my thanks and resolved to stop making fun of RVs to everyone I met. I really was in bear country now.

Twenty minutes later, I sped down a hill. The rain had stopped, the sun had come out, and I was enjoying the speed. A baby bear ran into the middle of the road. I swerved and just missed him. He spooked and ran back into the pines. He looked like a big black Labrador puppy. All I could think was, "He was cute." Mamma bear would have been less cute. I didn't see her. As I continued to ride down the hill, the shock of the encounter wore off. I realised I'd done everything wrong. I made no noise, I didn't reach for my bear spray, I looked at the cub rather than for the mum. I was lucky I was going downhill, that I didn't hit him, and that mama bear decided to stay in the forest. It took a long time for my heart to stop beating.

I passed another two bears beside the road. The third bear I slowed and hesitated for, the fourth bear I rode straight past. Neither looked up from their dandelions. I started to appreciate "Bear don't care."

I caught up with a Dutch couple 60km out of Watson Lake. Kim and Jan were cycling to Patagonia, their bikes were decorated with Tibetan prayer flags, National Park stickers and an Alaskan licence plate. They were chilling, cycling slowly, chatting away, and carrying twice my gear on each of their fully laden touring bikes. We started to ride together.

There was a new beast in town: bison. I'd been told they were more dangerous than bears. Being trampled is likely no more enjoyable than being eaten, but is somehow less intimidating. The yellow wildlife warning signs along the road looked like the designer had been having a laugh. The black bison icon took up the entire sign, the yellow background relegated to a wafer-thin afterthought at the edge.

That afternoon we found one. The sign wasn't kidding. The bison was massive. It was also in the middle of the road. We slowed and crossed to the other side. A head the size of a moderately priced family car swivelled with us as we passed.

Jan, Kim and I camped above a bend in Liard River. Jan and I had a disagreement over bear tactics. By now I was committed to my approach of not cooking where I camped, but forgoing a bear swing. In his subtle Dutch way, Jan told me what he thought of this: "Ja, that's bullshit! You've been doing this wrong for a month." We agreed to disagree. Jan struggled with his bear swing, and I made sure their tent was between me and the cooking spot.

Tactics settled, we retired to the riverbank. Falling pines had stacked up at the bend and formed a whirlpool eddy. Freshly eroded tree trunks bounced down rapids upstream, crashing into the dam and flowing past. We built a campfire and contemplated the river in the evening light.

## Day 25 – Whirlpool River to Mineral Lick

In the morning, the Dutch and I cooked a great breakfast. At least, Jan and Kim cooked a great breakfast and gave me some. Their extra gear appeared to be mostly food. They had a relaxed approach to touring, aiming for 50km a day. After hanging out with Nate and being inspired by his, go light, go fast, go far philosophy, they introduced a bit of balance. As Jan and Kim forced their endless supply of cookies and coffee on me, I regretted my cold-soak oats and resolved to buy more shareable luxuries.

After our hour-long breakfast, we strolled off to Liard River hot springs. The sun was shining and the wind was behind us. Summer had arrived. The Dutch had no interest in pushing themselves up hills, dropping down into their lowest gears and chatting all the way up. When we arrived at the hot springs, it was twenty-five degrees. Sweating in a stream didn't hold much appeal. However, the hot springs were the only 'attraction' in the 1,000km between Watson Lake and the end of the ALCAN, so we decided to brave the heat.

The Dutch set up camp at the local RV park. The manager came over to chat. "Careful of the bison," he told us. "Don't mind them and they won't mind you. Just don't look them in the eye, go too close to them or make any sudden movements. Actually, just really try to avoid them." We walked over the road to the springs. There was a bison on the road. It wasn't moving, just staring down the highway, its huge head pointed at the tarmac. We skirted around it, trying to be invisible. We asked the Ranger at the springs about it. "Oh, Bob's harmless," she said. Bob's horns didn't look harmless.

After sweating in the hot springs for an hour, we felt like we had justified the entry fee. Jan, Kim and I returned to the RV park and had bison burgers for lunch. Bob was no longer on the road. The ladies that ran the restaurant loved the idea that we were cycling through the Yukon and gave us their two cents on bear management: "Bears can't run so good downhill, yeah? Make sure if you're running away from a bear you're running downhill." Could we outrun them? They laughed, "Oh no, they'll still catch you, you'll just run longer ... you never know, maybe a car will come."

I parted ways with Jan and Kim after lunch to move a little faster towards Banff and Jasper. As we stewed in the spring, we had joked about how the ALCAN was impressive overall, but with nowhere overly impressive. I realised that Jasper, 1,300km away, was the next place that was worth going to. I rolled down a hill out of town. At the bottom of the hill an old suspension bridge crossed the Liard River. Over the river, the road snaked through rolling hills towards a clear horizon. The post-lunch coffee kicked in. I reflected that it didn't matter if this part of the country was worth going to, it was worth going through.

Ten kilometres out of town, I passed a herd of bison. Calves tottered behind their mothers. They didn't quite have the puppy-esque charm of baby bears, but at least I wasn't worried mum would eat me. I slowed to admire them. The bulls turned toward me in a line, backs to the herd. They looked ready to charge. I tried to look unthreatening and crossed to the far side of the road. The bulls tracked me, shuffling round. They spooked. The herd set off down the side of the road. They were thirty metres ahead and going the other direction. It seemed safe, but it was still a lot of bison, moving fast. En masse, they turned and charged over the road. I tried to get my camera out. I took a short video of my front wheel. The bison crunched through the underbrush, flattening trees. I reflected that bears don't have a reputation for molesting sleeping campers. These big dumb bastards would run straight over my tent.

Later in the day, I passed another black bear. After three days of non-stop bison and grizzlies, a medium-sized black bear seemed almost passé. A driver stopped to warn me. I blithely replied, "Oh, a black bear. Yeah, as long as he's not looking for trouble, I'll be fine." The driver looked impressed.

I camped in the car park of a viewpoint. The attraction was a cliff where animals come to eat dirt, for the minerals. I did the short hike to the cliff. There were no animals. The campsite was appealing though. Too hilly for a bison charge.

## Day 26 – Mineral Lick to Summit Pass

I woke up late and surrounded by tourists. RV people are early risers. That'll be the last time I sleep in a car park. Hopefully.

The road passed through the most spectacular scenery since Denali. I rode by Muncho Lake. Muncho meant big in the local language. It was indeed a big lake, bordered by pine-covered hills and a brilliant turquoise. Ahead of me, the road headed into proper mountains. I could tell these were proper mountains because they had snow on top. I was entering the Northern Rockies. Before the climbing started, I stopped into an RV park for caffeine. I asked the receptionist about the hills. She told me that she'd seen lots of cyclists get off and walk. I told her I wouldn't have that issue. She laughed.

600m up, 700m down and 30km later, I realised that this was the first of two mountain passes for the day. The next one might be the walker. Bordering this valley though were folded mountains. The plates either side of the Great Continental Divide had collided and crumpled together coloured bands of rock. Exposed hillsides looked like melted Neapolitan ice cream. I rode through the valley, neck snapping about as I tried to take in every detail.

As I left the valley and approached the second mountain pass, I was given another chance to exercise my amateur bike mechanic skills. Emphasis on amateur. I got the chain wrapped around the axle. I'm not sure how this happened, but it wasn't great. After ten minutes, my bags were strewn across the shoulder. After twenty, the back wheel was off. After thirty, I was covered in chain grease up to the elbow and having visions of hitching back to the last RV park. A candy red Dodge Ram 3500 with two bikes on the back passed and I flagged it down. The 3500 is a pickup truck so big it scares RVs. It screeched to a halt, U-turned across the ditch beside the road like it wasn't there, and stopped behind me. The cab lowered with a hissing sound. A step unfolded from the undercarriage and a seventy-year-old man almost five-feet tall emerged. Bill and Mary were Texan and on their way to Alaska. Bill took one look at the state of me and drawled, "Son, just calm down, we are going to figure this out." He held down the rear derailleur and I untangled the chain. It didn't take long enough for me not to be embarrassed. Mary handed me Clorox wipes until my hand was clean enough to shake. They wished me well and I rolled off to attack the second pass.

I didn't walk, but it was difficult to interrogate the motive behind the selection of every photo opportunity. I found a campsite in the nick of time to beat the rain. Nothing makes you appreciate a dry tent more than the knowledge it could have been a wet tent.

## Day 27 – Summit Pass, YT to Fort Nelson, BC

I rolled down from Summit Pass into the last service stop before Fort Nelson. The roadside sign advertised "The best cinnamon rolls this side of the Galactic Cluster!" The owner enjoyed my confident assertion that the hills were over. "Oh no boy, you've got some work ahead," he said. "Have a cinnamon roll." They were ridiculous. Two inches high, chunks of cinnamon sugar hidden in the folds, dripping with butter. I had read that keeping up the calories on a cycle tour was essential, but difficult. Not in North America.

Through 50km of hills, the scenery deteriorated and the clouds accumulated. The sky looked like the folded mountains. My only company through the climbs were big-horned mountain sheep. They skittered up vertical hillsides as I approached. From the final pass onto the Fort Nelson plains, the elevation dropped from 1100m to 400m. That passed rather quickly.

The visitor centres in the towns along the ALCAN produce guides for the coming 500km of the route. I picked up the last one when I arrived in Fort Nelson. The authors had struggled to fill one side of A4. One entry listed a power station. Fort Nelson was the last "town" before the 450km section to Fort St John and Dawson Creek at the end of the ALCAN. The *Lonely Planet* described Fort St John as "a stop best not made." Fort Nelson wasn't any better. The town was a run-down strip mall built on two parallel service roads along the highway. Between the service road and the highway ran a fetid drain. On the other hand, there was a pizza restaurant.

I checked into the Fort Nelson Hotel. It had of course seen better days. Two floors, fifty rooms and tiki bar themed. I wondered who they were expecting. A mezzanine decorated with snarling wooden masks overlooked an indoor pool. The pool was empty. Two fierce, two-metre-tall tropical idols guarded the deserted bar. Piña colada service had long since ceased.

I chatted to the Filipino receptionist, "Call me Shine"

Sunshine. Shine had two jobs and was studying to be a dental assistant. I asked what it was like moving from the Philippines to Northern BC. "Cold," she replied. "I won't be here much longer." Shine was the only thing on the way up in Fort Nelson. She tried to convince me to stay for the Canada Day parade the next day. I asked her if it would be any good. She laughed.

I did my laundry in the shower, went for pizza and went to bed.

# Day 28 – Fort Nelson to Buckinghorse River

It took a long time to get moving. The tiki hotel was creepy, but more comfortable than the arctic summer outside. It was not a great day for a patriotic parade. Even good parades are shit. The Fort Nelson Canada Day parade was not a good parade. Pickup trucks with Canadian flags draped from front windows starred.

My cynicism was rewarded with rain. I grappled with two age-old dilemmas of the cycle tourist: how strong does the rain have to get before you stop to put on wet weather gear, and how far outside of a town do you have to be to piss on the road?

After the excitement of the last week, I had a wildlife-free day. There were still road signs warning of bears and bison, but the endless pines were now endless fields. Farmers tend to discourage bears. It seemed the safari section of the tour was over.

The road to Dawson Creek was long, straight and grey. This must be what it is like to cycle through Indiana. Or to grow up there. But, the shoulder was wide, the rumble strip deep and a tailwind howled through the pines. I put in a 190km day. The highlight was lunch. I ate leftover pizza from Fort Nelson at the top of a hill. The wind kept the bugs off my prize. I looked like more of an idiot than usual. Lycra bike shorts and singlet-clad, standing over the bike, shovelling pizza into my mouth from a miniature takeaway pizza box. RV people stared. I regret nothing.

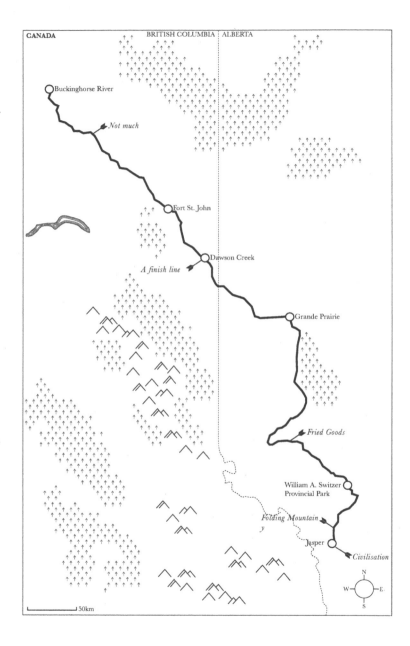

CANADA

BRITISH COLUMBIA | ALBERTA

Buckinghorse River

*Not much*

Fort St. John

Dawson Creek

*A finish line*

Grande Prairie

*Fried Goods*

William A. Switzer
Provincial Park

*Folding Mountain*
*y*

Jasper

*Civilisation*

50km

N
W   E.
S

## Day 29 – Buckinghorse River to some swamp just before Fort St John

I was by now close enough to civilisation for the nature to be unimpressive, but not close enough for anyone to actually want to live there. The scenery was all farms and no hills. What streams I saw were brown. I was sceptical of drinking the water. I stopped at an RV park to fill my bottles. It looked like a scene from *Deliverance*. There were two guys standing out front. One short and fat, one tall and skinny. They were missing teeth and holding cats. They stroked the cats. They cackled and told me they had no water. I nodded, smiled and backed away. I prefer my kidneys without teeth marks.

I stopped at another RV park. By this time, I was running out of water. The owner had no cats, all her teeth, and let me fill my water bottles. I was joined by two Australian motorcycle tourists. The hostess told us she would love to go to Australia, but was scared of the snakes. The Australians protested. I told her she didn't have to worry about the snakes, because the spiders had eaten them all. Her fear told me I'd done my bit for New Zealand tourism.

I lost one of the screws holding the cleat in my cycling shoe. There had been a noise coming from the pedal for days. With the attention to detail and conscientiousness lauded through my educational and professional career, I assumed it was some dirt in the pedal. I didn't check it. When the cleat started to rotate, and I couldn't unclip my right foot, I stopped and investigated. No screw, no spares. I pedalled with one foot loose. Only 100km to Dawson Creek. I hoped the bike shop there had the right screws. If not, only 600km to Jasper.

I also suffered from an inability to dress myself. The weather was bipolar. It started to rain; I put on my wet weather gear. The rain stopped; I took off the gear. I repeated this three times before I gave up and committed to get rained on. I got rained on. The rain stopped and the wind picked up. I delayed putting my jacket on too long and froze. These seem like small problems, but I took them to heart at the time. The wind continued to blow. The sky was wild. Clouds chased RVs up hills. Gusts from all directions attacked the bike. There was a five-metre drop below the highway. I reflected that this would be a poor place to break a leg. At least Canada had socialised medicine.

## Day 30 – Some swamp just before Fort St John to Dawson Creek

As population density increased, good places to camp became harder to find. I searched for 20km, and slept in a swamp. Signs on one side of the road warned: "High Pressure Gas Pipeline". Beyond the pipeline grew dense pine forest. On the other side was a decaying stream. I found a clearing in the pines and decided to take my chances with the pipeline. It wasn't great. Spring had arrived in this part of the country. My sanctuary was filled with half-metre-high grass and spiders not much smaller. I flattened an area and put up the tent. The spiders resented the invasion, but retreated without putting up serious resistance. I was thankful my tent netting had no holes.

During the night I learned why towns ask trucks to not use engine brakes. Engine brakes are loud. It was a long night.

As I rode the final 110km into Dawson Creek, every second car that passed me was a truck, and every second one of those was accompanied by a 'wide load' pilot vehicle. The trucks gave me a careful berth. Unless there were two trucks, in which case they didn't give a shit about me and I dove for the shoulder. By the time I arrived in town, I was covered in road grit and very ready to not be on the bike.

Dawson Creek is the end of the ALCAN. I took the mandatory photo by the 'Mile 0' sign. One month of cycling, 3,000km done, seventy percent of it on one road. Maybe I should have done more research on the road beforehand. When I planned this part of the trip, I thought to myself, "Good to get the isolated part in early, get some big miles on the bike, learn to camp where there is lots of space." Well, there was lots of space alright, and certainly lots of miles.

The bike shop had my screws though. As a celebration, I took myself out for dinner at a sushi restaurant, 1,000km from the nearest ocean. After the trucks, nothing could scare me.

## Day 31 – Dawson Creek, BC to Grande Prairie, AB

On the way out of Dawson Creek, I stopped in at the art gallery. It was the first cultural institution I'd seen since Whitehorse. It was also the coolest building in town: twice the size of anything else, a red wooden barn with 'ART GALLERY' painted in white block letters. Inside was a collection of photos showing the construction of the ALCAN in 1942. 2,000km+ of highway in the last frontier of North America was built in eight months to transport war supplies to Alaska to fight an Axis invasion that never came. The army had to explain the need for speed to the native tribes. One Chief asked, "But why does Hitler want all this land. Won't he be dead too someday, like everyone else?"

Out of town, the cycling was as interesting as the day before. I felt unmoored no longer being on the ALCAN. I spent a lot of time looking at the map.

In the afternoon I crossed into Alberta. A sheriff's deputy cycled on a standing bike on the side of the road. I pulled over to chat. Joan was checking boats for invasive fish and plants. She got about three boats a day, so decided to bring a bike.

The slogan for Alberta was "Wild Rose Country". This was two steps less ostentatious than the Yukon's "Larger Than Life", and ten steps less than British Columbia's "The Best Place on Earth". BC had really upgraded its sense self importance since replacing "Super, Natural British Columbia". I imagined the heads of the territories and provinces getting together when BC introduced that gem: "Yeah, yeah, you're right, we all agree, fuck BC."

The road passed through a string of small towns. It was hard to know what to do with all this civilisation. There were shops, cafes, places to sit. I missed the mountains. Between the towns, ranches covered the landscape. The last obstacle before Jasper was a 180km stretch with no water. I filled my bottles in the outskirts of the last town and found a place to camp by the highway.

# Day 32 – Grande Prairie to Smoky River

I woke up to discover my campsite infested. Mosquitos swarmed. Worse than Alaska, worse than the Yukon. I bundled myself into my wet weather gear. As I packed my tent, they bit my nose. Pursued to the road, I got stuck in a mud rut, couldn't unclip and fell over into a marsh. A truck honked its appreciation of my agility. An auspicious start.

A welcoming sign greeted the day's ride: "No Services Next 170km". With no services, I expected the road to be empty. It was not. All the Canadian industries were represented: oil, logging, mining, road building. The sun beat down, the trucks flew past, the hills didn't stop, and a heady mix of road grit, sweat and sunscreen accumulated. A truck kicked up a rock the size of a golf ball. That it didn't hit me in the face was a stroke of luck. As it was, it hit my arm as I wiped the grey sludge from my eyes.

70km in, I stopped at a trailer advertising "Fried Goods!" The goods, as advertised, were fried. I chatted to the owner about the area. She said at night it was lovely. It looked like there were little cities in the forest, lit up with the occasional gas flare. I admired her optimism. A trucker asked me how I was enjoying the riding. I told him it was shit, but at least the trucks scared the bears away. He was amused. "The trucks don't scare them bears at all," he said. "There's a big old sow grizzly with three cubs up the top of the hill feeding on a moose carcass." Oh, good.

It took me an hour to find the moose carcass. By this time, being eaten seemed like an agreeable way to go. At least there would be no more trucks. A van crested a hill and a man yelled out the window, "There's a grizzly up there with three cubs." There was real fear in his eyes. He didn't stop and I rode on. My earlier assessment that the safari section of the tour was over seemed premature. A middle-aged Canadian couple watched the dead moose from their car. They told me the bears had been out to feed three times. They told me I should stay and watch. Their car looked a safer viewpoint than my bike. I pushed on.

That drama done, the evening riding became sublime. I crossed a mountain pass, rode past the final factory, and the sun slipped behind a cloud. A doe jumped out into the road, a shock of white for a tail, spooked, then followed me down the hill. I joined the Smoky River Valley which led into the National Parks around Jasper. I found a truck-free campsite and took a shower with my water bottle before turning in, confident that the worst was done.

## Day 33 – Smoky River to William Switzer Provincial Park

A sign advertised one kilometre to Grande Cache. What it didn't mention was that it was one vertical kilometre. I crossed an old wooden bridge, the last remnant of the old highway before the discovery of oil, and then proceeded to climb. And climb, and climb. It was 8am and the road was cool and quiet. I felt aggrieved at the aggressive start to the day. Then the sun came out, the temperature soared and a truck roared past. It could have been worse.

The road after Grande Cache entered mountain territory. I was up to 1,500m. It still wasn't photo worthy, but I could feel that I was getting closer to something worth going to, rather than going through. Outside of oil country though, and the road was total shit. It was either under repair or in desperate need of it. I sensed scepticism as drivers weaved around me, or slowed so passing roadwork trucks didn't crush me. I went over a pothole too fast and lost my backup water bottle. This was a problem. The groundwater was still too polluted to drink, and I was on the margin to get to the next town.

As I considered my situation, a guy pulled up alongside and offered me water. Darren was from Dawson City in the Yukon (distinct from Dawson Creek in Alberta; Canadians do love a Dawson). When I told him I was from New Zealand, he replied his last name was Cruden, and his cousin was Aaron Cruden, the All Black. Good chat. We shot the breeze for a while about the ALCAN. His childhood memories revolved around the road. We laughed about how pleased the Army boys building the road must have been to find Liard hot springs. 2,000km of chopping roads through pines, then, out of nowhere, heaven-sent relaxation.

Dehydration evaded, I stopped at William Switzer Provincial Park and took a hike before stopping for the day. A 3km track looped through the forest around a lake. It felt great to get off the bike. After no rest days since Whitehorse, I was very ready to not be cycling. At 8pm, I was alone on the trail. Evening light filtered through spruce and birch branches. The path was lit by a molten, golden glow. I basked in the sun and the knowledge that the worst of the road was done. I would be in Jasper tomorrow. The mosquitos were still bastards and still everywhere. I arrived in my shorts and left in my rain jacket.

I camped at sunset in the forest, perched on a lush garden of moss. I thought I'd struck campsite gold. Tent up, sun down, I discovered the woodpeckers. They were miniature versions, but that didn't affect their volume. They nibbled the trees around my tent until they found a bug. Then they drilled.

# Day 34 – William Switzer Provincial Park to Jasper National Park

On the way into Jasper I passed Folding Mountain Brewing. The brewery was nestled into the mountains outside the National Park. These gave the first hint of the beauty of the area. Blocks of grey slate erupted from pine-covered foothills. It was 11am, but I'd almost reached civilisation. You can't drink all day if you don't start in the morning. I stopped for a beer. I was transported to another dimension. It was the brewery's birthday. There was a crowd. This was more people than I'd seen in a month. Old school rap was playing. High ceilings, exposed brick and cool people. The beer was the craftiest of craft: peach cobbler cream ale, black forest birthday cake porter, blood orange Gose. I tried to decide how many beers I could drink before cycling the last 60km. The bar staff hassled me to fill up my CamelBak. I hassled them for samples.

The ride in to Jasper was spectacular and chaotic. As the brewery bartender told me, "It's all downhill, but you go into the wind a little." She drove a Jeep. It wasn't all downhill, and the wind was so strong it almost knocked me off my bike. Oh well, I thought, it could be worse; it could be raining. Or, I could still be in Fort Nelson. Or, I could live in Fort Nelson.

The road followed the Athabasca River into the mountains. Proper mountains, with snow on. The granite ridge looked like a set of teeth in the green gums of a forest giant. I took fifty photos. Every change in perspective presented a new, more exceptional aspect. Smooth vertical cliffs, greyscale sedimentary bands of colour, tiered faces of grey rock eroded to terraces. Plenty of other people were enjoying the view. For the first time since Denali I felt the dense presence of other tourists. They were mostly interested in the wildlife. Three scraggy goats caused a traffic jam. Hordes piled out of cars to capture the moment. The goats were nonchalant. I now understood the prominent 'Don't Feed the Wildlife' signs. These people needed to be told.

I'd never seen people outside of New Zealand so excited by livestock.

I got to Jasper later than planned, delayed by wind, goats and beer. It was exciting to be in a place worth going to. It can't all be rainbows and candyfloss, but the road after Fort Nelson had held little appeal until now.

# Day 35 – Jasper

I woke up early and found a cafe. The possibility of coffee that wasn't purchased from a gas station was exhilarating.

Caffeinated, I went to the visitor centre to check if it was possible to camp on the road from Jasper to Banff. On the way into Jasper, I saw a lot of 'Campground Full' signs. Camping without a permit in National Parks felt a bit too much like stealing from the taxpayer. One of the staff was excited to meet a cyclist. Vicky told me about her son, a pro mountain biker. She'd been on tours. She had a few suggestions. In between stories of her trips with her son and his mountain bike crew to Nepal, Mongolia and Tasmania, questions about New Zealand and my ride from Alaska, Vicky organised the next two weeks of my life. She interrogated John's plan for Idaho. It passed muster. By the time I left, there were impatient tourists queued out the door, but I had a plan.

Waiting for me in the entrance to the visitor centre was a friend from London. I almost fainted. What are the odds? He laughed. Nick had thought he'd recognised me in the visitor centre and waited the thirty minutes it took for Vicky to plan my trip. He was on a road trip with his girlfriend, Turku, from Vancouver to Calgary. We talked about my trip. Nick had done something similar after deciding to quit his job and start a business, driving across the American South. We discussed the mental reset a journey could provide. I had been thinking a lot about the holiday-adventure spectrum from RV cruising, to sailing across the Antarctic. We agreed that to get yourself out of the grind, the journey doesn't have to be off the deep end. In fact, it's probably better if you aren't fighting for your life. As he described it, some parts of the South were familiar, and some were very different. The parts that were different inspired new ideas, whereas the parts that were the same gave you mental space to reflect on those ideas. We agreed to meet for dinner.

It proved easy to do nothing all day. I hung out at the hostel and met the staff. A German named Konrad had lived in Raglan, in New Zealand. We bonded over being shit at surfing. The owner of the hostel was a French Canadian named Jean. He was a cyclist. We chatted about the routes around Jasper and he recommended I go up to Maligne Canyon and do a hike. The French influence was visible in the hostel kitchen. There were cooking stations, sharp knives, and notices telling the dirtbag backpackers to eat their food from plates like humans.

In the evening, I went out to dinner with Nick and Turku. We got wrecked. After a month on the road, it was great to hang out with friends again.

# Day 36 – Jasper

Hungover, I faced the cloudless sky and told myself I'd feel better outside. After caffeinating to within an inch of cardiac arrest, I embarked on a hike. I crossed the Athabasca River and set out for the Old Fort Point. This was advertised as the easiest hike in Jasper. It was a sharp hill in the hot sun. I sweated. Children passed me. Halfway up, the coffee started to work. I regained composure. I overtook an elderly couple. The top of the hill presented a 360-degree view of the Jasper valley. South, back across the river, Jasper town nestled into the lower slopes of Pyramid Mountain, the red and grey slopes contrasted against the forest and the river. East, I looked upriver to Geraldine Peak, striped in ice and granite. To the north and west, slate grey peaks ranged into the distance.

Inspired by the success of my half-hour hike, I continued. I wandered at random down the hill and ended up in the Fairmont Hotel. Guests canoed on a placid lake and lounged on sun decks. I had my bear spray strapped to my pack. Better to have it and not need it than need it and not have it. There were signs warning of aggressive elk. I dismissed these as litigious North American fearmongering. A full grown bull elk wandered down the trail. I bolted cross country to the amusement of hotel guests armed with telephoto lenses.

I followed train tracks back to town. One of the freight trains exporting Alberta's mineral wealth passed. Shipping containers in every colour of a rust were stacked in twos on each rail car. I gave up counting the cars at seventy. These shared the track with the passenger rail. Some of the hostel crew tried to catch a train to Vancouver the previous day. It was delayed fourteen hours. I recorded this as a win for the bike.

In the evening I hung out with Nick and Turku. We went to Miette Hot Springs. These were commercial hot springs, buried under pool tiles. These were baths. There are few things more awkward than going for a bath with a couple. Thankfully, my friends shared my limited patience for group baths. We decamped to Folding Mountain Brewery. Nick's rental Toyota Corolla (the undisputed king of cars) provided a new perspective on the 60km back to town. I didn't drink all the beers, but I tried.

## Day 37 – Jasper

I woke up at 6am to cycle up to Maligne Lake and do a real hike: the 'Bald Hills'. It took me an hour to leave. I was sucked into the maw of Bear Paw bakery, a Jasper institution. Jasper had one McDonald's but two Bear Paws. In a fit of hungover early morning indecision, I spent $25 on baked goods for hike provisions.

The overcast skies and forecast rain meant I was alone on the 50km road up to Maligne Lake. Without bags, without sun, without rain, without wind, without traffic, this was the best cycling I'd done all trip. The 700m climb knocked out the cobwebs and almost justified the baked goods. The minor lakes on the way up were mirror smooth. They reflected the Maligne Range, the ridge defined against the sky like a razor blade slicing through clouds.

Wildlife was out in force in the grey summer dawn. As I left town, a family of elk lounged beside the road, unconcerned with passing cars or camera-happy tourists. Two of the more intrepid family members wandered across the road for breakfast and munched on hotel hedges. On the lake road, mule deer pranced. Shocked by my arrival, they bounced in unison into the forest. By mid-morning, I'd been joined by the tour buses. This was a daunting prospect on a road with a cliff for a shoulder. I arrived to a lakeshore packed with tourists, each wearing a name tag, the sure marker of a rube. I set out on foot up the Bald Hills.

The hike did not start well. The sun had risen, and it was hot. The heat would not have been an issue, except I was wearing my rain jacket to ward off the mosquitos. I had forgotten my bug spray. I sweated, they swarmed. Every few minutes, I would turn and attack the trailing cloud. This achieved nothing, but I felt it my duty to not let the bugs eat free. As I gained altitude, the pines shrunk and the view back down the valley emerged. I looked down at tourist boats cruising across the lake, chased by the dark clouds of a squall. At the top of the track, I realised why the hike was called the 'Bald Hills'. The rest of the lake was ringed by sharp peaks. The hill I had just climbed was capped by a rolling alpine meadow. I was high enough now that summer snow patches still dotted the meadow. At altitude, the mosquitos had abated. I set off to wander. Between the snow patches were yellow wildflowers and pines dwarfed to miniature Christmas trees. The weather had scared off most of the tourists. A solitary eagle circled. I reached an outcropping and clambered towards the edge. The local marmots were unfazed by my presence. One monitored my approach and prepared to move if it proved unavoidable. I took a photo. He decided I wasn't an eagle and continued to eat. At 2,400m, I stood eye to eye with the peaks across Maligne Lake. I felt small among the mountains. I had spent the last two weeks riding through the Rockies, but this felt like the first time that I had seen them. I resolved to do more hiking. The mosquitos chased me down the fire road.

I zoomed back to town. The only cycling better than uphill in the morning is downhill in the evening. I finished the day with a couple beers with some of the guys in the hostel. Max and Pierre were French, twenty-three, and travelling around Canada following a general theme of "nature and beers". Pierre told me his brother had cycled across Canada eating nothing but peanut butter and jelly sandwiches. He had some gnarly health problems when he got back to France. I remember it as scurvy, but I was a few cans in by that point. I reflected that touring on no money is easy to say and hard to do.

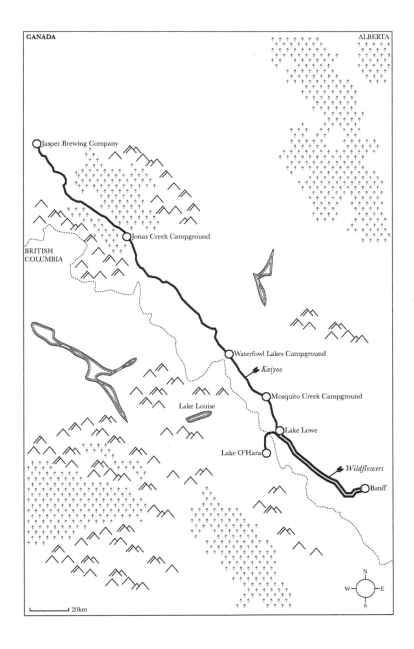

CANADA
ALBERTA

Jasper Brewing Company

BRITISH
COLUMBIA

Jonas Creek Campground

Waterfowl Lakes Campground

*Kaiyoo*

Mosquito Creek Campground

Lake Louise

Lake Lowe

Lake O'Hara

*Wildflowers*

Banff

N
W — E
S

⌞⎯⎯⎯⌟ 20km

# Day 38 – Icefields Parkway: Jasper to Jonas

I bid farewell to Jasper with a final Bear Claw cinnamon roll. I avoided spending $20 on extra baked goods this time, which I counted as self-control.

The day was excellent, bright blue skies and a light breeze. I had been looking forward to riding the Icefields Parkway since the Canadian border. The initial miles did not disappoint. The road followed the Athabasca River upstream through a valley surrounded by peaks. The mountains provided constant fascination. They evolved as I cycled past, a few degrees providing a fresh view and temptation to stop for a photo. To the east, sheer cliffs slanted away from the road at a sixty-degree angle, like one plate had sheered off and risen across another. Rifts between peaks had formed where the rock had been eroded away by rivers, glaciers or time.

I met more cyclists in a morning on the Parkway than I saw the two weeks to Jasper. None of them were all that weird, but they were all enjoying themselves. I met two Canadian brothers from Edmonton. This was the fifth time they had ridden the road. Each had more stuff on their bikes for a week's tour than I did for three months. I dreamt of the luxuries possible hauling thirty kilos of gear. I met an Australian couple doing a six-week trip. They had also started in Anchorage. I asked them whether they took the ALCAN or the Cassiar. "Aha, we cheated a bit," they laughed, "we took the boat and skipped the long stuff." I told them I was jealous. Hard rides and long distances were a great learning experience. Short rides, piles of gear and spectacular scenery seemed a more civilised way to tour.

I had four days to do the 320km from Jasper to Banff. I had planned to have an easy day: 80km to a campsite called Jonas, where I could do a hike. My body geared for longer days, I got in at 2pm. The campsite had walk-in sites for cyclists. To get to these, I had to carry my gear, and push my bike, up a steep hill into the forest. The result of this work was that I was the only one there. I pitched my tent serenaded by no passing trucks. I could hear nothing but a nearby stream and the wind swaying the birch trees. The hike went out the window. I lay in the sun and read a book.

## Day 39 – Icefields Parkway: Jonas to Waterfowl Lakes

The morning was cold as a witch's tit. I don't know how I could have foreseen this. Maybe, the fact that the road was called the 'Icefields Parkway'. Or, that my first stop of the day was the Columbia Icefields, a collection of glaciers so large it had grown a tourist industry. In any case, I didn't get the hint. I wore all my clothes as I cooked breakfast. Needing the warmth, I was up and attacking the climb by 7am. The 500m ascent up to the icefield was spectacular. The sun rose over the mountains in the east, suffusing the peaks and pines with a pale light. I was joined by the local Lycra brigade. What a place to have for a gym. The Lycra lads weren't as friendly as the cycle tourists. My waves were not returned. I waved more ostentatiously. I reached the lodge at the icefield around mid-morning. There were tours. They looked shit. The rubes wore matching jumpsuits with their name tags. I sat around the cafe making the most of the free refill coffee and chatting to tour bus oldies. A month of solitude can make you very friendly.

The afternoon's ride followed the North Saskatchewan River, glacial grey. The view down the valley rewarded the morning climb. Rows of the mountains faded into the distance, from full definition to pale blue shadows. The nearest peaks towered over the road. Any picture I took was of the sky, the dot of a distant snowcap poking out the bottom of the frame.

I set up camp next to a trailhead. Its proximity left no room for excuses. I set out down a forested path. Moss covered the ground and trees covered the sky. In brief clearings, the mountains popped their heads through the treetops to glance down at the trail. The trail notes at the start of the hike read: "Often very muddy". It's been sunny, I thought. This was irrelevant. The notes didn't say "Muddy when it has rained". It was muddy. The hike was described as "To a lake". This was misleading. A more accurate description would have been "through a swamp, to a swamp". A glacial-fed swamp ringed by vertical walls of granite, but still, a swamp. I considered writing a letter. Taught a lesson by my experience on the Bald Hills, I had put on mosquito repellent. I had, however, neglected to bring it along. Fool me once, etc. That's also what the mosquitos thought when they found me on my return journey. The opportunity they had been denied on my way out was pursued to the hilt on my way back. My bug spray had a two-hour efficacy, evidently. Still, it was nice to do something with my legs other than spin them round and round.

That night I struggled with route planning. After the simplicity of Alaska and the Yukon, I was confronted by infinite choice. My uncle recommended I cut back north to Yoho National Park and a place called Lake O'Hara. He described it as "The finest mountain gem in the Rockies." If anyone should know a gem it would be him: he'd spent two cumulative years of his life climbing mountains here. Going north would complicate the route south though. I was stuck between two competing thoughts. The first, "Don't waste time hanging around – it's a journey not a holiday." The second, "Do whatever you want – it's a journey not a race. And it is a holiday."

## Day 40 – Icefields Parkway: Waterfowl Lakes to Mosquito Creek

I have seen the future and his name is Kaiyoo. Just out of camp in the morning, I passed two cycle tourists sporting matching sets of yellow panniers and towing buggies. We exchanged greetings. A furry face emerged from one of the buggies and barked hello. Kaiyoo, Kai for short, was a malamute-husky cross and was having a grand old time. Kai's buggy had a covered section where he could lie down, and a space out front where he could sit up and take in the view of Pete and Mary struggling up hills. All the touring with none of the pedalling. Pete expounded the joys of travelling with a dog as he puffed and pedalled to keep pace with my first gear and I struggled to keep my bike in motion. As we approached a short hill, Pete slowed. "Here's where we fall behind," he said. "Kai is forty-five kilos." Love had a cost.

I climbed the last major hill of the Parkway. I got to the Bow Summit Lake early enough that the wind hadn't risen and the surface was glass. It was the best photo of the trip so far. The lake was encircled by granite peaks, bands of snow collected in terraced white wreaths. Their reflection in the lake was so perfect I could turn the photo upside down and not notice the difference. I met a lady from Massachusetts admiring the view. We chatted for a while about the crowds at Lake Louise, my next stop. "If you love it here, you'll hate it there," she said. She gave me some raisin bread and encouraged me to keep moving.

I arrived at the next campground at 12pm. It was full. Kaiyoo and his bearers arrived and were also without a campsite. Confidence comes with company. We pitched our tents on the Ranger's lawn. I decided I wouldn't wait around for Parks Canada to come kick us out. I paid my campground fee and went for a hike.

I cycled back up the road towards Bow Lake to find the trailhead for the Lake Helen hike. I based this selection on a route guide note which said: "Kilometre marker 35, Lake Helen: recommended hike." What it lacked in detail, it made up in brevity. After the swamp adventure of the day before, I was glad to follow any direction. Lake Helen though turned out to be phenomenal. When I got back, I described the hike to Pete, in a daze. He smiled, "They're all like that, you're just not used to the Rockies."

The hike started with a long stretch through a valley. More miles of pines. Two miles in, I decided that one hike here above the treeline was worth ten below. For some reason, endless pines, muddy paths, and voracious mosquitos don't do it for me. As I got above the treeline, the rest of the valley came into view. I walked along the side of a long valley, divided by a river a hundred metres below. Pillars of sandstone formed a ridge which ran back down the river valley to the horizon. I continued to the top of the valley and Lake Helen, which fed the river. Over the lake, stood the now familiar granite peaks. To the right was a ridge, 200 metres of beige and black boulders and broken rock. A trail led over it to another lake and river valley. I'd planned to stop here, but the temptation to go to the top of the ridge was too high. I scrambled up and along the ridge. At the end of the ridge I looked down to the two lakes on either side, and back along the valley towards the trailhead, 10km in the distance. I perched on the crest of the ridge, a near-vertical drop on three sides. 200 metres above the lakes, 300 above the river. I shared the view with two other hikers. The cult of saying hello to people on the trail in Canada is strong. Not here. We said not a word.

On the return hike, I met a Canadian family: Danny, Patricia and their daughter. We started chatting and Danny told me about a Japanese tourist they had met the day before. "She asked us if we had seen any bears. She said she really liked them, tons of enthusiasm. Then she showed us a selfie with her and a big grizzly five metres back off the trail. Honey, you met the only vegetarian griz!" They were pumped about my trip. I told them I was disappointed to miss Vancouver. Danny was amused: "Why would you want to go to Vancouver? You'll get no stories in Vancouver." He laughed, "We went for sushi and talked real estate. Afterwards we went for cocktails. Cool story, man. Go somewhere real." They had just come from Yoho and gave me excited descriptions of Takakkaw Falls, the Iceline

Trail and the brewery in the town, Field. Their enthusiasm was infectious. Together with the recommendation from my uncle, I resolved to cut back and go to Yoho and Lake O'Hara.

*A view which would become familiar: miles of shoulder, miles of pines.*

*Followed by my first experience camping without the protection of civilisation.*

*My first bears. You'll have to trust me. They are halfway up the hill.*
*I wasn't getting any closer.*

*I should have left the lentils at the entrance.*

*Don't like the weather in Alaska? Don't worry. Wait ten minutes. It'll get worse.*

*And then better.*

*Puppy therapy in Fairbanks with Mary Shields.*

*An inspirational lady: "I'll be back on the sled by the end of the year.
Easily ... Just keep going."*

*Some less relaxing wildlife photography.*

*My first roadside repairs. Spot the bear.*

*Paul says safety first.*

*Morale rescued by friendly Germans.*

*And a spell in the sun behind Jan and Kim.*

*Fort Nelson Hotel: all Tiki, no Piña.*

*The joys of the open road into Dawson Creek.*

*Stoked to be done with that one.*

*Airport rules.*

*That's a 'first day off the bike in two weeks' smile.*

*Making new friends over Maligne Lake.*

*With time to appreciate the view on the way back.*

## "The Icefields Parkway is the best road in North America." *p.10*

*Into the Icefield. Looks warmer than it was.*

*Kaiyoo: Why have we stopped?*

*The view back down the ridge between Lake Helen and Lake Katherine.*

*Welcome to O'Hara. If you haven't booked, don't bother.*

*Stay off the grass, Dave, you dickhead.*

*The author, embracing nature.*

*O'Hara from above.*

*Takakkaw. It is magnificent.*

*Electric blue in Kootenay.*

*Goodbye, Canada*

*Hello, Freedom!*

*Looking over the Spiral Highway down into the Snake River Valley.*

*Johnny Idaho's house in Lewiston. Apparently it sold. Apparently the buyers said, "The exterior paint job was meticulous". Please direct all paint job requests through my agent.*

*From Lewiston to Missoula. There are many rivers, but this one is mine. At least when it's dark and cool enough to think.*

*Brad and Olive.*

*Baseball in Helena. I think the mammoth is mandatory in the minors.*

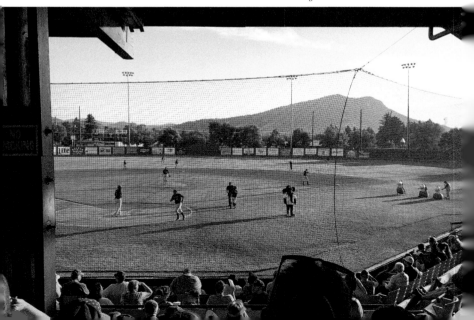

# Day 41 – Icefields Parkway: Mosquito Creek to Banff

I got up at 5am. I was determined to give Lake Louise a genuine go. At the visitor centre in Jasper, Vicky had described it as "the sacrificial lamb of the National Parks. The one that had to die, so the others could be free." I imagined it teeming with selfie stick wielding tourists. My Massachusetts friend from the day before told me she was on the trails by 6am to beat the crowds. At 5am, I ate her raisin bread for breakfast. It had rained in the night and my tent was wet. I packed it with stiff fingers as the sun started a slow climb over the mountains. I cycled the 30km to the lake in record time. It didn't help warm my fingers, but at least my legs were ready to out-hike RV people. My goal was one of the two hike-in tea houses. I'd been informed that this was the thing to do at Lake Louise. Both by people, and by the *Lonely Planet*, which advised that they had scones. An Asian couple I'd met over dinner the night before liked the tea houses so much they did both the one at Lake Agnes and the one at the Plain of Five Glaciers. 20km of hiking for tea and scones. They had a fight about which one was better. The wife was doing their cooking. She had produced four courses on a two-burner gas stove. I went with her recommendation.

I arrived at Lake Louise at 7am. Not nearly early enough to beat the crowds. The lake itself was glacial green and reflected the surrounding mountains, like every other lake along the Parkway. The Lake Louise Lodge towered over it like the Soviet Ministry for Natural Beauty. I took the obligatory tourist photo and set off up the hill. The tea house was a 3.5km hike up a ridge overlooking the lake. The path was steep and covered in horse shit. There were no horses, but the manure from the morning expedition had already been trampled to a fine green sheen on the trail. I studied my fellow aspiring tea house guests. There were the 'early risers', already coming down and all fitter than me. There were the 'selfie stickers': no viewpoint between the trees too small, no pose too ridiculous, no opportunity for self-documentation overlooked. There were the 'vastly over-equipped': bear bells, two hiking poles, and matching outfits. There were the 'dad made us', happy families all. Finally, there were the 'where's the cafe' people. These people had not been forewarned about the gradient of the climb. They were struggling.

I got to the top of the hill and fought for a place at the tea house. The crowds swarmed. I was reminded of something my raisin bread friend had said. In her Massachusetts accent, she imitated the stronger Massachusetts accent of her father: "They are out there, there are a lot of them, and they are enjoying it. That's great! Nature! Good for them! Find the positive in it. If you don't like the crowds, go somewhere else and stop bitching." The scones were great. I stopped bitching, paid my money, took my photo, and headed off back down the hill. As I left, a crowd of people were taking photos of a chipmunk with their iPads.

Back at Lake Louise, I tried to call and secure a space at Lake O'Hara. Access was restricted. I was greeted by an answering machine message: "Hi! You've reached the Lake O'Hara reservations line. Reservations open the fourth of April at 8am. Reservations can be made three months in advance of your visit. Reservations usually book out within one hour of lines being open. Thanks!" Oh, good. I waited on hold to see whether there were any cancellations. There were not, but the lady at the information centre in Field told me I could call back every day between 10am and 10:20am to see if there were any for that night. She didn't think it was likely. When I asked whether I could just bike and skip the crowd, she sounded offended: "Oh no, we can't allow that, it would just be too much ... too much." Of course, the restriction heightened my desire to go.

From Lake Louise to Banff, gone was the mellow two-lane road of the Icefields Parkway. I was back on the highway. I arrived at the hostel in Banff sweaty, hung my tent to dry all over the dorm room and wandered around the town eating ice cream. The town was packed with Indian tourists. My moustache got a lot of compliments.

# Day 42 – Banff

After the crowds of Lake Louise, I looked for an empty hike around Banff. Sunshine Meadows was a 15km journey from town, which I felt would discourage the casual. I rode back along the Banff highway then up a hill. Climbing forested hills on the bike was more fun when I reflected the alternative was climbing through the pines on foot.

Sunshine Meadows wasn't exactly a deserted paradise. There was a gondola. Still, there were serious hikers with serious equipment for multi-day trips. A group of Italians in their fifties arrived at the trailhead at the same time as me. Each had skin so tanned and weathered it could make a decent pair of Italian hiking boots. We said our hellos. They set off, gesticulating away, at a cracking pace I was unable to match. I caught up with them again at midday as they were having lunch. They greeted me with a languid "ciao" from behind their antipasto board.

The start of the hike was the typical slow ascent through the pines. It seemed more pleasant than usual. Maybe because I was alone on the trail. Maybe because it was the first time I had remembered to bring bug spray.

After 8km of wandering through the trees, I popped out into an alpine meadow. There were no glaciers, lakes or granite peaks. This looked like something out of *The Sound of Music*. Mt Assiniboine, the 'Matterhorn of the Rockies' stood in the distance. The faint view of this peaky peak made me wish again for more appropriate long-range hiking gear. After a few hikes and many hours on the bike to fill with day dreams, I'd had ample opportunity to plan my gear purchases. A backpack I could fit my tent in would be nice, as would a T-shirt with sleeves. The real issue though was the cleats on my mountain biking shoes. If I hit the cleat at the wrong angle on a rock, it would slip off and send me flying. This wasn't an issue on the trails, but rock hopping across streams presented a problem. I crossed them on hands and feet, in a sort of downward-dog shuffle from rock to rock. There were lots of streams. I tried to cross when no one was watching.

The views of the mountains were stunning, but by now familiar. What was new about this hike was the flowers. I wouldn't have thought I would be so enthusiastic about flowers. Nature does strange things to people. Exploding magenta fireworks, bluebells, multicoloured daisies. I discovered the 'portrait' mode on my phone. I took lots of photos of flowers crouched down, lens inches away. I was glad it wasn't an iPad.

At the top of the meadow, I looked out over the ridge to another valley. On the opposite side sat a two-tiered lake, connected by a waterfall. I was drawn to explore. After descending three miles and getting no closer to the lakes, I realised I had no map, no tent and no food other than a pack of supermarket muffins. I turned back to the ridge. Back at the top, I stopped to eat lunch and met two hikers. My muffins were only mildly embarrassing. Jan and Beth had each spent a year travelling New Zealand. Jan told me proudly that he had done 11,000km, mostly on a motorbike. Beth scoffed. She had done 18,000km. New Zealand is 1,600km from nose to tail. They had seen it. They laughed at me for not wanting to spend the night in the valley: "It's summer, just sleep under the stars!" Jan gave me a serious look: "The Rockies are endless. You can just keep going. If you fly up to 12,000ft in a little plane, you can hit the horizon 4 times before you run out of mountains." I contemplated this as I headed back to Banff. I had no idea what he meant, but it sounded great.

# Day 43 – Banff, AB to Lake O'Hara, BC

By the time I cycled out of Banff, I still hadn't managed to secure a booking for Lake O'Hara. I had tried calling at the allotted time, begging, booking online, calling outside of the time, more begging. I was tempted to skip Yoho altogether and head straight down to Idaho. As I rode back north to the turn-off. I resolved to make a final decision after calling O'Hara one last time.

After yesterday's hike, I noticed wildflowers everywhere. The clearings by the side of the road provided almost as good an environment for them as the alpine meadows. Elsewhere, the mighty pine conquered all. On the highway out of Banff there were too many varieties to describe. They grew in patches, fighting their way through the roadside grass. I threw out my flower identification guide in Dawson Creek, so most of them were daisies, multicoloured, multi-shaped daisies. There was also a grass that looked like shiny purple wheat. It grew in thick rows by the side of the road. When a truck or an RV passed, the wind rippled through, an iridescent wave. Enthused after the hike in Sunshine Meadows, I told myself that I was going to get off the bike and take photos of all the flowers. This resolution didn't survive the reality of stopping on the verge of the four-lane highway.

Otto wins! I placed what could have been my tenth call to the tourist information centre in Yoho. The lady kept me on hold for fifteen minutes, then told me that there was one cancellation at Lake O'Hara. There were rules. I couldn't bring my bike. I could only bring one bag on the bus up. I couldn't bring a cooler. I couldn't bring my dog. Okay lady, sure, can I pay? I was standing on the side of a motorway with two bars of cell signal, fumbling with my credit card. I managed to part with my money and secure my space. After I hung up, I realised I knew nothing about this place aside from that my uncle liked it, and that it was difficult to get to. Anyway, I was in. Off I went.

I cycled up to the car park at the bottom of the Lake O'Hara road. There were three signs. The first detailed why the park was so good: its network of trails, the meadows, the lakes, the waterfalls. The second covered why and how it was being protected: the historical overuse, the subsequent limits on numbers, the bus-in system. The third sign covered what to do if you turned up without a reservation: "There are lots of great hikes in the Rockies! Some of them are less than an hour's drive from here – ideal for a day trip!" That's how you say fuck off in Canadian.

I locked my bike to a tree in the car park and packed bagels and a bag of trail mix into one pannier with my tent and sleeping gear. There was no way I could fit my cooking gear, so it was going to be a cold culinary camping experience. I was hanging out by the sign eating leftover muffins, when I met the Ranger. Jessica told me she had lived in New Zealand for a year, split between Piha and Wanaka. I told her she had good taste in places. She looked around us at the mountains: "I don't pick shit spots." Jessica told me I could leave my bike in a disused bus rather than locked to a tree: "What are you even doing? Ridiculous." She gave me a grin and went to get the bus driver. The driver was pumped about my trip. She looked like she could pull the bus up the road. I asked her for hike recommendations for O'Hara and without hesitation she replied, "Lake McArthur tonight and Alpine Loops tomorrow. Done." She looked me over: "You've biked here, you should be able to do it." That said, I was sorted, if slightly intimidated. After thirty minutes on a dusty, corrugated gravel road I was rather glad they didn't let me ride up.

As we arrived at the campsite, Ranger 'I-don't-pick-shit-spots' Jessica gave an intense conservation talk: "Don't step off the trails. If you want to pass someone, get skinny, go from rock to rock. If you step on a blade of grass, it might not recover this season, it might not ever recover." These were serious nature people.

I met a sixty-year-old guy on the bus who also wanted to do the Lake McArthur hike. Dave and I agreed to set up our tents and push off quickly to beat the sunset. The hike there was unremarkable. I wondered whether I was getting used to the Rockies. This feeling disappeared when we reached the lake. Ranger Jessica had described the lake as "Powerade blue". A bowl of peaks and glaciers layered with concentric rings of grey granite reflected on the surface. I explored the edges of the lake, careful not to step on any blade of grass. There was still a slight wind, so the reflection was not quite perfect. Dave kept exclaiming, "It just needs to mirror up! God damn it! Mirror up!" We hung around for another hour waiting for the photo to get marginally better. Dave took his photos to heart.

On the way back to camp, we talked about packing light and crashing bikes. Dave had done a lot of motorbike touring and talked to me about intermediate pilot syndrome. The worst pilots are the ones with medium experience. The ones with no experience know they are bad, the ones with lots of experience know they are good, but the ones with medium experience just think they are good. There are cocky pilots and there are old pilots, but there are no cocky, old pilots. That made sense. By my third warm-up trip, I thought I was getting good at cycling. I took too much speed into the bottom of a hill, lost my nerve, touched the brakes, then lost the sleeve on my shirt and all the skin on my arm.

Back at camp, I met two guys who had food in my locker. The food lockers were supposed to be one per campsite. When I asked what happened to their locker, they said something got messed up with their reservation. This sounded like clear bullshit, but the tentsites were big, and my tent was small, so I offered them half of my site. They had hiked up and hoped for a cancellation. "I'm not coming all this way and not coming to O'Hara," Sam said. As we pitched the tents, we chatted trips. Luke and Sam had spent the last year in South America. We were at similar places in life. They both worked in consulting and quit at thirty to go hiking. Their tent looked well used. Sam was writing a book. I joked that a year in South America didn't help him sort out his life plan very much. "Oh no, I'm deeply aware of this," he replied, "but failing the possibility that I write the next great American novel, what's the alternative? If I go on any more holidays society won't let me back in." They were doing a different hike the next day and invited me to come along. After four hours of Dave, I was keen to hike alone and do the Alpine Loops. The bus driver didn't seem like someone to turn down a recommendation from lightly.

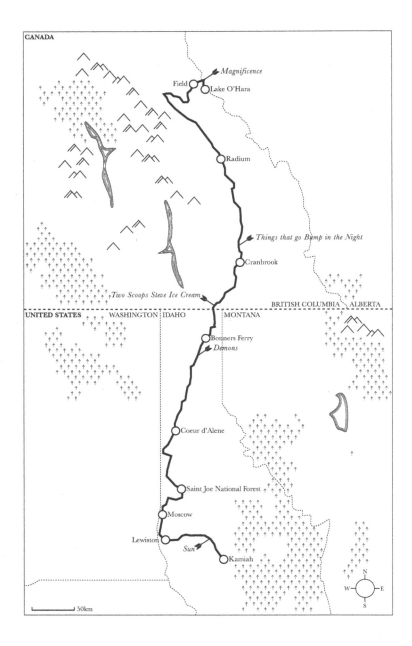

CANADA

*Magnificence*

Field ◯ ◯ Lake O'Hara

◯ Radium

*Things that go Bump in the Night*

◯ Cranbrook

*Two Scoops Steve Ice Cream*

BRITISH COLUMBIA : ALBERTA

UNITED STATES    WASHINGTON : IDAHO | MONTANA

◯ Boriners Ferry

*Demons*

◯ Coeur d'Alene

◯ Saint Joe National Forest

◯ Moscow

Lewiston ◯

*Sun*

◯ Kamiah

50km

N
W — E
S

## Day 44 – Lake O'Hara to Takakkaw Falls

I set off on the Alpine Loops early. It started strong, 500m of elevation gain in 2km to a saddle. The dawn raid mosquitos were fierce. I was reluctant to drench myself in DEET so early in the morning. I hid in my rain gear. This seemed like a great idea until I was 300m up and covered in sweat. I told myself that once I got to the saddle, I'd be above the trees and the mosquitos would abate. This was incorrect. I got to the top pursued by a hungry horde. There must not be much wildlife in O'Hara. Trying to coat myself in bug spray and change clothes at the same time, I danced on the ridge. The mosquitos attacked. I swatted my shoulder and got three at once. Three bugs, one swat. Other than the mosquitos, the view was excellent. From above, I could appreciate the unique appeal of O'Hara. A bowl was formed by a ring of blocky peaks, all crumbling towers of stone. These stood 1,000m above the valley floor. The bowl was dotted with glacial lakes, each a different shade of turquoise, on different levels and connected by streams and waterfalls. The Loops ran around the outside of the bowl, across the mountainsides around O'Hara. It was good.

The crumbling towers of stone translated into difficult hiking. The route picked its way between fallen boulders. More wildflowers clung to rock faces or nestled beside streams. A lilac flute, a pale-yellow orchid and a white bell which grew on a red stem out of samphire moss. It was tough to stop long to admire the flowers below the fifty-metre cliffs, evidence of their structural security the boulders strewn across the valley floor below.

After navigating the second of the loops, I arrived at a lake. Two people were chilling in inflatable kayaks in the middle, with another three sitting on the shore. I went over to say hello. Emily was a professor, researching the changing levels of mineral content in the lakes and what it was doing to the ecosystem. I told Emily she had an amazing gig. She laughed, "No doubt about that, my husband is in the kayak. We come up here every summer and hang around the lakes." I asked a bunch of inane questions. What is the bluest lake etc.? Emily didn't have much to do, and took my questions in good humour. The clearest lake in the world was officially in New Zealand. She couldn't remember what it was called. "Either blue lake, or clear lake, something like that," she said. Classic Kiwi creativity. They had evidence, however, that a lake in BC was clearer. They weren't going to publish though; clear lakes aren't science. Victory by default! New Zealand retains the crown! The kayak team returned. There was work to do. I pushed off.

My favourite character from O'Hara was a Chinese guy. I first passed him as I came down from the saddle. He asked me to take a photo of him. In between swatting mosquitos, he struck victorious yoga-girl poses. I photographed. We parted ways. He found me again as I chatted to the researchers. He asked me to take more photos. The path was thin, and the college crew was in-shot. He didn't mind. He struck more poses and I took more photos. The research interns looked on in fascination. I passed him a final time on the route up to the last loop. I arrived too late to photograph him. Deep into tree pose, his camera was set up on a rock, on a timer. I wanted to ask for his Instagram but couldn't interrupt.

The final loop was the 'All Souls Route'. The other loops were named for geological points. All Souls was named for the fear. By this point, my legs were jelly. A drop down the face of the scree would mean the rest of my body would join them. I struggled halfway up a peak and along a face of loose rock. As I reflected on the joy of the challenge, I heard steps behind me. The bus driver jogged past me. She exhorted me to hurry up to make the 2:30pm bus and was off. I was rewarded for the risk of death and damage to my ego with a full 360-degree view of the valley. I'd seen O'Hara from every angle and it had just gotten more impressive. I ran down to avoid disappointing the bus driver. I bought a piece of carrot cake at the lodge and relived the views of the last seven hours.

Leaving O'Hara, I coasted down a long, gentle hill into Field. Danny had recommended the Iceline hike and the Field Brewery. After O'Hara, I felt like this would be a good send-off to the Canadian Rockies before I departed for Idaho. I parked up at the brewery and recovered from the Alpine Loops with a burger and a pint. Three pints, if I'm honest. I then discovered that the trailhead for Iceline was 30km back up the hill to O'Hara.

Up to this point, I had had the feeling that all the little decisions I had made on my trip had worked out well. Route choices, hostel choices, hike choices, all good in the end. I was willing to admit that a burger and three beers before cycling 30km up a hill in the sun might not have been one of those decisions. But, it went swimmingly. There was some sweat, but no blood and no tears. After turning off the main road, my route followed the Yoho River upstream towards Takakkaw Falls. Because I wasted so much time in the pub, the sun had time to dip behind the hills and I was in the shade for most of the ride. As the burger started to hurt, I rounded a corner. There were the falls. Takakkaw means something like "it is magnificent" in the local Cree language. They weren't wrong. A thin stream ran 20m down a cliff. There, the stream hit a ledge and exploded into a fire hose. The plume of spray shot out ten metres from the cliff face and arced 200m to the river below. You could see the falls from the hostel. I remarked on them to the hostel manager, Joel. He gave me a deep look: "Takakkaw is a mystical place." Joel lived ten days here with no cell reception, then four days off and back again. He had bonded with Takakkaw.

I shared a bunk room at the hostel with four English lads. They had just gotten back from a five-day hike in Kootenay and were on their way to O'Hara. We swapped mosquito and bear stories. Harry was the first person I met who had used his bear spray in anger. The first time he used it was their first night in the US. He set it off in their hostel. The spray cleared the place out. People emerged from their rooms coughing while Harry stood in the corridor and apologised. "We didn't make any friends there," one friend said. His friends all started laughing. "Tell him the second one, you massive dickhead!" The second time Harry used the spray was on the hike. They were sitting down to make dinner and were attacked by horseflies. At the end of a long day of hiking, Harry was at the end of his rope. He attacked the horseflies. "Fuck off you dirty great bastards!" He mimed emptying the canister, spraying wildly. He got the spray all over his legs. They were still burning. The bear spray fixed the horseflies though.

## Day 45 – Takakkaw Falls

In the morning, I asked Joel for a little local hiking knowledge. He added 10km to the Iceline Trail. Thanks, Joel.

The trail started with switchbacks through the forest opposite the falls. With each corner Takakkaw became more impressive. It was over a kilometre to the other side of the valley. The thunder of water on stone rumbled through the pines.

I popped out of the forest at Yoho Lake. The path skirted the shore. A lone peak stood above the lake, its round base of scree tapered to a thick white collar of snow. A square totem head of bare rock pushed skyward fifty metres from the collar. I followed a dirt path around the bottom of the lake. The path started out fine. It had rained the night before and the leaves of the trees and shrubs were coated with water. The path narrowed. I pushed branches aside to pass, collecting water. I started to curse my local knowledge. A little knowledge is a dangerous thing. The path faded to nothing. I'd lost the path a few times the day before in O'Hara. There it reappeared if I pressed on. I pressed on. I collected more water. By this time rather wet, I looked at the map. The trail should have been where I was. Maybe it was above me? I bushwhacked up the hill. This was a bad idea. The hill was soaked, and the path was nonexistent. I slid down the hill, admitted defeat and backtracked. I proceeded to collect whatever water was left on the branches I had pushed past half an hour before. Not a particularly auspicious start to the hike. But, I thought, it could be worse, it could be raining. Onwards.

Thirty minutes going the right direction and I was back to praising my local knowledge. I could now see Takakkaw Falls and the glacier that fed them. A river of ice stretched as far as I could see behind the falls. The falls pummelled down, thousands of litres per second, all summer long, all fed by the melting glacier.

I arrived at the Iceline plateau. A moonscape of fallen rocks bounded by tan coloured cliffs. Glaciers nestled into the cliff faces. Small waterfalls and streams coursed along the plateau and down into the valley below. I now saw the full scope of the icefield that fed the falls. It extended to the end of the valley and around, feeding waterfalls that coursed down into the Yoho River. The glacier curled in to fill the end of the valley, a mountain of black and blue ice oozing towards the river head.

By the time I got to the end of the valley, I'd walked 15km. My feet were still wet from the misadventure around Yoho Lake. Squish, squish. I climbed the ridge. At the top, the river ran out of the glacier beneath my feet, and over the edge of a cliff, 200m below. Back down the hill and I found the bottom of the falls. The river had found the path of least resistance around a big boulder, splitting the fall in two. I soaked in the spray, a rainbow above me between the Twin Falls.

Wet shoes had sated my appetite for nature. My feet were finished. The hike, however, was not. The last 8km were spent counting the steps and skipping photo opportunities. Local knowledge served me well, but it hammered my feet. My mountain biking shoes had ripped holes in my socks then holes in my heels. I covered these up with band aids, then with blister patches, then with tape on top of blister patches. Soaking this mess at the start of the day was not a great opening move.

I whinged to Joel about my bushwhacking adventures around Yoho Lake. He commiserated. He had once packed out a freezer full of meat someone had left him at a hike-in cabin. He took a wrong turn, didn't notice, and walked two miles before he realised he was lost. He then realised he was wandering around with a freezer full of defrosting meat on his back. Bear bait. That put my stroll in perspective.

## Day 46 – Takakkaw to Radium

As I set out for Idaho, I reflected that I had barely scratched the surface of the Rockies. I told people the story of the plane flying at 12,000ft hitting the horizon four times and not running out of mountains. No one had any idea what it meant, but everyone agreed it sounded impressive. It gave a sense of the infinite possibility to get lost in the wilderness here.

On the highway back to Banff, I met another touring cyclist. Dave was puffing away towing a trailer. He was in his sixties and training to ride from Banff to Mexico. Dave had come down from Jasper over four tough days. He had struggled. I told him I'd come from Alaska, and the hills were still brutal. Dave laughed, "Son, I walked up them, don't try to make me feel better." He asked me what I was doing with my life. I told him I hoped I'd figure it out on this trip. Dave had moved from London to Yosemite in the 1970s to rock climb. He laughed again, "The only thing this adventure is going to teach you is that you want to do more adventures." He was right. After six weeks on the road I had no clarity, but lots of trips planned.

I left Dave at the Kootenay turn-off and headed up Storm Mountain. True to the name, a thunderstorm surrounded the hill. Purple clouds contrasted against the bright sky behind me. I stopped to chat to a hitchhiker sitting by the side of the road and gave him some water. His name was Aidan. He was about twenty, had been playing guitar in Banff and was headed back home to Calgary. As I rode off, lightning struck ahead of me and rain started to fall. It was a shit day to be hitchhiking, especially with a guitar. I turned around to give him some trail mix. Karma secure, I continued into the storm.

A road worker at the top of the hill screamed as I passed her, "That thunderstorm was aaaawesome!" Over the crest, the sun shone through storm haze. The thunder, the lightning and the screaming combined to a wild atmosphere. The emotion peaked, the storm passed, and I coasted down into sunny skies.

The Kootenay was destroyed by fire in 2001. A forest of burnt trunks stood bare, new trees pushing up around them, the saplings light green. The river was electric, jumping, almost too bright to be natural. The blue rapids accentuated the vitality of the new forest.

The National Parks turned on a fauna display for my last day. White-tailed and mule deer grazed by the road. A stag froze as I approached, then bolted up the hill, crashing through new forest growth. The final goodbye came 150km into the ride. Legs finished, I trudged up a 300m climb. A brown bear foraged for berries three metres from the road. By the time I saw him he was beside me. We exchanged glances. The bear went back to his berries. I tried not to make 'injured prey' noises as I climbed. After what felt like an hour I was past him and stopped to look back. His full attention was on the berries. Bear don't care.

I left the Rockies behind and shot out into the Columbia River Valley. I found my first free campsite in weeks. I had missed the freedom of finding hidden campsites. Perched above the valley, hidden from the road by a line of trees, I watched the sun sink behind the hills.

# Day 47 – Radium to Cranbrook

It was hard not to feel a sense of loss after leaving the Rockies. I got up and rode along the Columbia River Valley, with the Kootenay foothills on one side and the valley on the other. It was OK. The OK hills were small and the OK river was brown. The OK towns were geared towards family holidays. Signs advertised paintball, escape rooms, petting zoos, par three golf, zip lining, hot springs. A full selection of OK activities.

Out of the mountains, I was back in the people. There were shops. There were farms. There was real estate for sale. Billboards advertised new developments. Columbia Hills. Valley Lodges. Mountain Meadows. Prices started at $62k. Wait, sixty-two thousand dollars? Canadian? Are you kidding? You know what you get for that in London? Dinner. The best part though was the estate agent billboards. Headshots and an inspirational slogan. Nothing inspires trust like a billboard-sized picture of a face. A father-son team shared one double-sided board. On one side they were in suits, businessmen doing business things. On the other side they held snowboards. The slogan read, "It's your holiday, own it!" Cool. A lady with a six-inch ginger perm wore a purple Angela Merkel suit and posed in her best impression of Rodin's *The Thinker*. My cousin is a real estate agent. I wondered how much billboards cost in Auckland.

My post-mountain mood was not helped by a headwind. The road followed the river, the wind followed the valley, the wind followed me. I stopped at a turnout overlooking Columbia Lake. A kite surfer flew over whitecaps. I wondered how high whitecaps needed to be before they classed as waves. Now, I'm not one to complain about a headwind. Although I have previously, bitterly, and at length. However, this wind did dominate the afternoon's activity. I prayed for passing trucks and the brief boost of turbulent assistance they offered. 100km/h speed limit signs mocked me. Drivers flew by, encased in their windproof sanctuaries. Trees hunched over under the assault of the gale. I stopped at an RV park to fill water and drink a litre of Gatorade in record-breaking time. It was twenty-six degrees. I felt like I was in an oven on fan-bake. A fellow cyclist approached. He said he had passed me riding the other direction. Then his wife came and drove him back here. Apparently, he had a great time. Apparently, it's never like this. Apparently, I just got lucky. What to do? Onwards.

In the afternoon, I met two heroes of the human race. I was spreadeagled on top of a rest stop table, regretting whatever past decisions had brought me there. Jack and Logan stopped their journey north to give me a beer: "Hey bud, we thought you might want this." Big grins. They were mountain bikers, headed out for a weekend rip. We talked shit about the wind, swapped trip stories and adventure film recommendations. They were from Kimberley. The town had a fantastic billboard posted outside the rest-stop. The turn-off for Kimberley headed straight, the main road to Cranbrook, left. The bright red billboard had two arrows. Straight: "Good Times". Left: "Everything Else". Jack and Logan loved their town. I reassessed my morning negativity. They were an hour's drive to the Rockies. Their Friday afternoon activity was to strap a campervan on to the back of a pickup truck, load up the bikes, load up the beers, and head off to the mountains. They insisted I visit Kimberley. It was an extra 10km, 300m up a hill. I told them I would. I one hundred percent could not be bothered. They left, and I set off the direct route to Cranbrook, pleasantly anaesthetised.

## Day 48 – Cranbrook, BC to Bonners Ferry, ID

Things that go bump in the night. I was woken at 3am by an animal noise. Half squeal, half grunt. The squeal wasn't so bad, but the grunt sounded big. It repeated for half an hour. I had time to study the noise, to build a picture of the animal making it. In the darkness outside my tent, the squeal would build to the guttural crescendo. It sounded like it was getting closer. I lay still. I didn't want to get out of the tent to look around and alert the beast to my position. I was tormented by visions of a bear ripping apart the tent, or an elk stomping on me, forcing me out of my warm sleeping bag. I clutched my bear spray. I Googled: "nocturnal animal noises Canada". This was useless. I couldn't play the noises. One of them could have been a mating call. It took a long time to get back to sleep. It was probably a squirrel.

I passed through Cranbrook on the way to the US border. The heroes of yesterday had thrown shade on Cranbrook. So did *Lonely Planet*, which called it, "a strip mall of a town". I was familiar with those. I hoped for a cafe and a place to fill water. I saw a sign for a farmers' market. Strip malls in southern BC are a lot more middle class than in the Yukon. What better way to spend the last of my Canadian cash than purchasing more bougie groceries than I could carry. I bought beef jerky from a man with a moustache. We swapped moustache compliments. I fought to buy the last two cinnamon rolls from a fat woman (never trust a skinny baker). I bought spinach from real farmers wearing real farmer clothes. I bought sourdough bread from some lesbians, also wearing farmer clothes. They described their bread as 'experimental'. I felt at home. I left well equipped for the ride south. The *Lonely Planet* writers were probably from Kimberley.

The only event of note on the way to the border was ice cream. I stopped at a place called Two Scoop Steve's. If you are ever going south from Cranbrook, stop at Two Scoop Steve's. It was great. My last day in Canada was decadent.

I crossed into the USA. Immigration gave me the third degree, such as it was. I didn't expect it, but I should have. I was wearing a T-shirt with no sleeves. It was so sweat encrusted that I could lift it over my head without it changing shape. I had covered a rip in the front with an iron-on patch of mountains and bears. I had a curly moustache, Lycra and weird tan lines. I smelled like a zoo enclosure. The guards radiated suspicion. I was taken into the main office building. It was filled with taxidermy animals. There was a cougar, an ibex, a selection of deer, and a moose head with a little stuffed toy beaver resting in the antlers. The officers had written on a plaque below 'Rocky and Bullwinkle'. I laughed. One of the guards was excited that I got the joke. I had established rapport. They established I wasn't a criminal.

The guy behind me did not have such a pleasant immigration experience. I had seen him at a gas station before the border. He looked like he was going to smuggle drugs. If there is one thing I have learned from watching *Border Patrol* on TV, the people who get arrested smuggling drugs look like they smuggle drugs. Caught with seven pounds of weed strapped to your chest? Maybe you should have shaved the dreadlocks and lost the tie-dyed shirt. A briefcase full of cocaine? Next time, forgo the pencil moustache and matching crocodile skin belt and shoe combo. *Breaking Bad* quantities of meth? At least get some false teeth. The officers searched his car next to where I re-packed my panniers. They were excited. One drew his finger across his throat and said, "He's going downtown." I thought they only said that in movies. I was reminded of *Fear and Loathing in Las Vegas*. "Imagine what it is like inside of the possessed mind ... a dope fiend refers to the reefer butt as a 'roach'. Because, it resembles a cockroach." The officers argued over whether a glass pipe was a crack pipe. One exclaimed, "Angel dust!" over and over again, ecstatic. I considered offering the man my services as his attorney. But, who has time for that shit.

## Day 49 – Bonners Ferry to Coeur d'Alene

It is a buzz crossing borders. Last night, I rode down a hill into Idaho. I looked across the river valley to a line of hills. The valley was covered in crops. The early evening light and the yellow fields stretched away into the distance in between the hills. I was out of the mountains and into farming country. This morning, the air had no chill. The road signs that had warned drivers of moose and bears now warned of cows.

There was a marked difference in the culture over the border. The no trespassing signs were back, posted on fences. I was greeted in Bonners Ferry by a huge American flag. The town had 10,000 people. It must have needed them all to hoist this thing. It was bigger than the largest building. The American 'Live Free or Die' ethos was alive and well. It found its true expression in the automobile. The men driving wore cowboy hats. I saw Jeeps with the doors chopped off, classic muscle cars, and a plethora of raised pickup trucks, one painted in camouflage, one driven by a thirteen-year-old boy. He smirked at me. It was Saturday, and there were lots of men with great facial hair, wearing leather, riding motorcycles. I tried the Whitehorse waving game. No response. These were Americans. None of the riders were wearing helmets. No helmet on a motorcycle struck me as the implausible outer limit of individual freedom. There were more churches than in Canada. I guess if you don't wear a helmet on a bike you want to be damn sure of an afterlife. Bonners Ferry Adventists advertised "Demonology 101" (Luke 11:24-26, if you're looking for talking points). What a fun way to spend a Sunday.

After a morning riding through farms and churches I got to Sandpoint. It looked like Brooklyn with fewer homeless people. I Googled "coffee roaster" and was directed to a reclaimed barn filled with tattoos, round-frame glasses and creative facial hair. People were too cool to pay me any attention. Idaho was a state of contrasts.

As I cycled out away from the cafe, I met a cyclist called Max. He saw me lost, looking for the path which crossed the lake outside Sandpoint. He offered to show me the way and I followed along. We turned off the road. Suddenly, my back wheel locked, the bike went sideways, and I crashed all over the path. My rear mudguard had lost a screw and gotten stuck under the tyre. I was going walking pace, but crashes with four panniers look drastic. We chatted as I struggled with the bike. Max lived in Santa Cruz, but his dad lived in Sandpoint. He was starting to get into cycle touring. We chatted about gear and routes. It felt strange to be the expert. I pitched him the Icefields Parkway, and he invited me to stay at his house in California.

Houses dotted the lakeshore. As I rode the bridge over the lake, the town was out playing with their boats. It looked like a good way to spend a Sunday. Instead, I cycled 80km down the highway at full speed in the sun to Coeur d'Alene. There isn't any other way to cycle on a highway than at full blast. By the time I got to the city it was 2pm and I'd done 120km. I took the scenic route through town. Coeur d'Alene was enjoying Sunday as much as Sandpoint. Anything remotely seaworthy was in use. Boats, jet-skis, paddle boards, rafts, inflatable flamingos. If it floated, it was in the lake, if it burned, it was on the grill. In the park by the lake, legions of identical blonde kids played volleyball. I learned later that Coeur d'Alene and Sandpoint were the home of the Aryan Nations and Richard Butler (shit people). I knew it was too perfect.

The road out of Coeur d'Alene wrapped around the lake. I was now on the route set by Johnny Idaho. I tried to follow the directions he had given me with Google Maps. For the first time this trip, I got Google Maps'd. I was familiar with this concept after being digitally directed to ride through a golf course on my way from London to Brighton. The idyllic road I had been following out of town ended. The Google Maps route continued, it just ceased to be a road. The route led under an Interstate overpass. Three teenagers with motorcycles hung out under the bridge, smoking. I approached, wary. Youths. This was Idaho, they were very helpful. You might even say they were ... Idahelpful. They told me it was a dirt bike track. They thought it would be marginal on a bicycle. Well, it was track or backtrack, so track it was. After fifteen minutes of swearing and hand-lowering the bike down drops, I was deep into the track. I tried not to think about what it would be like to get back up if I had to turn around. The track ended. I was in a driveway. Off I went, up a gravel hill. After eating dust for half an hour, I rediscovered the lake shore road. Boats criss-crossed sunbeams. The ride was great, the only downside was the desire to be on a boat.

## Day 50 – Coeur d'Alene to Saint Joe National Forest

I woke up in a clearing cut for power lines, hidden from the road. I looked out through the treetops over the lake through the tops of the trees. I was proud of my campsite huddled amongst the lakeside villas. I reflected that the more populated it got, the more creative I would have to be with camping.

I passed the south end of Lake Coeur d'Alene and dove back into farming country. In the valley the sun shone, and hay was being made. I observed two schools of hay bale stewardship. First, there were the farmers who built colour-coordinated, orderly structures. As children, they'd built Lego from the instructions. Then, there were the kids who left Lego landmines around the house for parents to step on. These farmers left their bales scattered over the field, wherever the baler spat them out. They were probably more fun.

The sun was making its case as the fourth horseman of the cycling apocalypse. It was thirty-two degrees. No clouds. I had planned to do 160km to get to Moscow and a bed at John's place, but by midday I was drenched in sweat and re-evaluating this and other life choices. I'm no expert on demonology, but they couldn't be operating much hotter than this.

I stopped at a diner for Gatorade. Cinnamon rolls and hot coffee had lost their appeal in the sun. Gatorade was my new vice. I chatted to the owner. Judy was a spry sixty-five and originally from upstate New York. Her husband had trained as a gunsmith. She told me she loved Idaho because her and her husband liked to "recreate". I asked what this meant, mind running. Our eyes locked in miscommunication. "Recreate," Judy said, "like recreational activities: quad biking and hunting." An image flashed of Judy blasting at a fleeing herd of deer with a .44 Magnum from her quad bike. Judy was excited to have someone from New Zealand at her diner. She pulled out a guest book that had last been signed in 2016. I told her about the Norwegian tradition of writing a holiday report in a cabin book, and that some cabins I'd visited had books with notes from the holidays fifty years past. She loved this. I realised I had fated all future foreigners to sign the guest book.

I sat down at a large table in the diner. A group arrived. One tried to order a beer that the other thought was socially beyond him. "Hey, you haven't gone all hoity-toity on us now, have you Sam?" I laughed and got a grin. A middle-aged couple came in. The owner introduced me to Bob and Evelyn and told my story. They were originally from Bakersfield, California, but they had lived in Idaho for thirty years. No one is more zealous than a convert. The conversation started poorly. "You're going down to Mexico? Why are you doing that? You're going to get killed!" Bob said. I smiled, "It's probably more dangerous in some parts of the US." I'd wanted to chat to people about gun control. "Probably in Chicago," Bob replied, "but that's just blacks killing blacks," he thought for a moment, "and blacks killing whites too. The gang violence down there is terrible." After a few weak protests, I lost my nerve. I didn't stand up and leave, I didn't tell Bob to go fuck himself. I just said, "Uh-huh", and the conversation moved on. We talked about the individualism in small towns. I got the standard spiel on the sense of community, how people liked their freedom, but came together in times of need. In the end, Bob offered to buy me dinner. I left and wondered what this trip would have been like if I was black.

That afternoon, I had my first awe-inspiring moment since the Rockies. I rode through the Saint Joe National Forest. White pines lined the road. The trees grew right to the shoulder, so close that their roots sometimes broke the asphalt. Each trunk was 50m tall and towered me. There were no cars. I rolled down the middle of the road in the silence and the shadow of the trees. I found a campground nestled in a grove. Evening set and I communed with the trees.

# Day 51 – Saint Joe National Forest to Moscow

I started the morning at Codi Jo's Wagon Wheel on the way to Moscow. The waitress had a tramp stamp, there were Big Buck Hunter game machines in the corner, and country music played on the radio. There is nothing that separates heartland America from the coasts like country music. It was everywhere. A contender for my favourite song was playing: 'The Farmer's Daughter' by Rodney Atkins.

*I'd be on the tractor she'd be on my mind / with that sun beatin' down on this back of mine / Just when I thought it couldn't get no hotter / I fell in love with the farmer's daughter / We got married last spring / Woah and there ain't no better life for me*

Rodney is a lyrical genius. The best bit of this was that they got married. It didn't even take half the song. It happened in the second verse. That doesn't happen in rap. This was bible music. Thirty million views on YouTube.

Riding out of the diner, Rodney crooning in my head, I saw a canary yellow biplane. It was crop dusting. The farms in this part of Idaho were not industrial scale operations. It was too hilly, with too many steep-sided valleys. Up these hills and down these valleys the yellow biplane flew. It cut so close to the tops of the hills that I thought it was remote controlled. It was not. It was just some fly boy farmer having a great time on a sunny day. I haven't seen enough crop dusting to know if this was usually how it was done. If so, that's nuts. Every time the plane dived into a valley I expected to see a fireball. Instead, the plane bobbed its yellow head back up and banked hard for another pass, clearing power lines by metres. Between the motorcyclists without helmets, Judy telling me she liked to recreate, and the aggressive 'no trespassing' signs, I now viewed everything through the lens of "Live Free or Die". No government is going to tell me how to fly my damn plane!

Since Coeur d'Alene, the towns had fitted my stereotype of

heartland America. Gun shops, 'game processing' for hunters, car mechanics, diners and no-nonsense bars. No creperies. I was curious to see Moscow, Johnny Idaho's town. The town sign on the way in was encouraging: "Moscow, Home of the Arts". Riding through, it was like being back in Sandpoint. There were wine shops, cafes, camping stores and an organic supermarket. I bought 'hoity-toity' beers and headed for John's house.

John was not going to be back before late afternoon and told me to make myself at home. I explored. A green truck and two dirt bikes sat in the driveway. In the garage, two road bikes and a bike trailer hung from the ceiling, and four sets of skis and a surfboard from the wall. There were two barbecues. John had the right toys for Idaho. I made myself a coffee and settled into a couch covered in animal furs.

John came back a couple hours later. He had been working on another house he owned in Lewiston, thirty miles away. We talked about my trip so far and discussed the vagaries of camp cooking. John had done his share of cycling tours, as well as a seventy-day sea kayak trip down the coast of Baja California. I got the full tour of the toys. The green truck out front turned out to be a fully fledged escape vehicle. In addition to being a river guide, John had a biology degree and had worked variously for the Department of Fish and Game, the San Diego Zoo, and universities doing environmental field research. The truck had a bed in the back, a 75-gallon water tank, a water purifier and pump, a shower, power outlets, a fridge and a full pull-out pantry. John had built all this under a bed frame mounted in the tray. It was a setup to go anywhere, and to stay there. John seemed like a cool guy on the plane, and his route advice was turning out well, but now we were hanging out his stories were starting to blow my mind.

A safe the size of a refrigerator sat in the corner of the living room. It looked like it could hold a body. I had mentioned some of my impressions of Idaho so far: the motorcyclists without helmets, Judy hunting from the back of her quad bike, the prevalence of gun stores. John admitted to being "one of those Idaho gun nuts." The safe held the guns. I was just glad it wasn't a body. John guided hunting trips in the autumn for big-horn sheep and deer. He told me that you could kick the shit out of the guys on hunting trips much more than you could on river trips. "People come on river trips to have a good time," he said. "People come on hunting trips to be pushed." John laughed, "Shut the fuck up, Brad, we are trying to be stealthy. Now move, fat boy, get that hill!"

John had organised a dinner at home with a few friends and his girlfriend, Kassie. We had a couple of beers, chopped vegetables and John put on some country music. No one here was immune. The friends showed up. One was the sister of my rafting guide in Iceland, another an ammunition engineer at a gun factory in Lewiston. Kassie was a potter. It turned out she was a workaholic potter, with three jobs that I never got straight, a teaching studio, a market stand, a university affiliation, and eighty-hour work weeks. John cooked dinner on the gas grill outside on what he referred to as a "disco". The disco was a flat wok, two feet wide. I asked about the name. John said it was a copy of a thing he used when he lived in Chile. He made it out of an old plough wheel that he had found buried in a field. John patched it, then welded handles. "Three dollars and a couple minutes welding time," he said. Of course. Over dinner, the ammunition engineer invited us to go paddle boarding on the Snake River. John had not finished doing some painting he needed to get done on his Lewiston house. I offered to skip the paddle boarding and help him out finishing the work. Manual labour? I'd clearly had too much to drink.

The dinner party wound down and we headed to bed. I slept on the couch covered in furs. One was a reindeer fur smuggled from Norway on the flight we were on to Seattle.

## Day 52 – Moscow and Lewiston

We got up at 6:30am, coffee and out the door. On the drive down to Lewiston, I felt it appropriate to mention my facility with manual labour: "I just want to set your expectations here: I work an office job." This got a laugh, but I don't think John understood the gravity of the risk he was taking by letting me loose with tools.

We arrived, and John handed me a tin of touch-up paint. He instructed me to cover white spots he had missed on the first coat. A clear task, ability-appropriate, I thought. I set out with expectations of success. At first, the paint looked different when I put it on. I mentioned this to John: "Nah, don't worry, it changes colour when it dries," he said. Ok mate, you're the expert. It turned out the paint was indeed a different colour. It wasn't much different, but it was different enough. John discovered this when he emerged from the other side of the house where he had been painting the eaves. By this point, I had finished destroying the other three sides. The house looked piebald. John took this better than I would have. We went and got more paint, the right colour this time. I was able to finish the job with the walls looking no worse for wear than if I hadn't been there at all. Things could have gone worse. I deejayed, so I'd like to think I made a net positive impact. We went and got milkshakes and took a swim in the river. On the way, John told me a story about the years he worked as a carpenter. He worked with a guy, Dave, that had gone to the Berklee School of Music for Mandolin. Dave was a mandolin prodigy. He wasn't much of a carpenter. Whenever he screwed up, the boss would say, "Dave, you're one hell of a mandolin player." It took me a while to catch on, but I think in that story I was the mandolin player.

After the swim, we showered, had a few beers in town and played ping-pong. I won. Confidence restored. At least I was better at ping-pong than painting.

## Day 53 – Moscow to Kamiah

In the morning, John got ready to go to Salmon to work on another house, and I got ready to get back on the bike. Kassie and John were excited about my ride to Missoula and through Montana. They kept finding new places for me to stop. Hot springs were suggested. It was forty degrees in Lewiston yesterday. Centigrade, real degrees. I said I'd think about it. Kassie suggested I check out a minor league baseball game. "Ten bucks, cold beers, real America," she said. That sounded more my speed. There was a game in Helena, the state capital, the following week. We discovered it would be Disney Day. We spent half an hour trying to find characters with good moustaches. Only Jafar, apparently. I wondered what sort of people I would meet in Helena turning up to a baseball game in a red robe with a talking parrot.

Procrastination opportunities exhausted, I set off out south to Lewiston. John gave me a rural route off the highway. The farms along the route were at their full potential. It made for beautiful riding. Each field was a block of colour on the hills, yellow wheat, green garbanzo beans and mustard barley. The horizon was unbroken by a single cloud. Farmhouses sat back from the road in copses of trees to keep the sun at bay. Machinery sat close, ready to be unleashed on the fields.

The route down to Lewiston was a historic road called the 'Spiral Highway'. It was built in the 1850s by a railroad engineer. It was an engineer's road. A creative assortment of corners kept the grade a constant five percent all the way down. It was a long way down. Moscow was at 800m elevation on the hills above the Snake River. Lewiston was in the river valley, at 200m. From the top, the road looked like someone had drizzled a line of molasses across the hills. I didn't do the road justice, coasting down heavy on the brakes. John had done no-brake descents, of course.

I'd already been sweating Moscow. In Lewiston it was now

forty-two degrees. The prospect of August at sea level was frightening.

After a coffee and air conditioning stop, I set off east towards Missoula. Highway 12 followed the Clearwater River upstream through Nez Perce National Forest to Lolo Pass. The pass separated Idaho and Montana. Over the next three days, the highway regained the 500m I lost in twenty minutes on the Spiral Highway. I cycled along the river, winding through hills covered in sun-baked grass. The riverside alternated between rolling hillsides and vertical canyon walls. Neither provided any escape from the heat.

For the last ninety minutes of the day the sun abated. I started to appreciate the surroundings again. The tops of the yellow hills turned pink. Back to the west, the river glowed between the hillsides. The moon rose full and yellow, reflected on the surface of the river. With sunset, I traded the view for safety. Trusting cars to see you at dusk is a decent bet each time but you only need to lose once. Even so, there weren't many cars and it was finally cool enough to enjoy the ride. I pushed on.

John had suggested I camp in a park in Kamiah. Due to my late start, and my inability to pull myself away from the air conditioning in Lewiston, I arrived late. There were fifty people watching a movie on an outdoor screen. It was too dark to continue. If dusk riding was marginal, night riding with no street lights and no shoulder was crazy. I shuffled past the crowd to the back of the park and the bank of a river. It's difficult to be inconspicuous dragging a touring bike with four panniers.

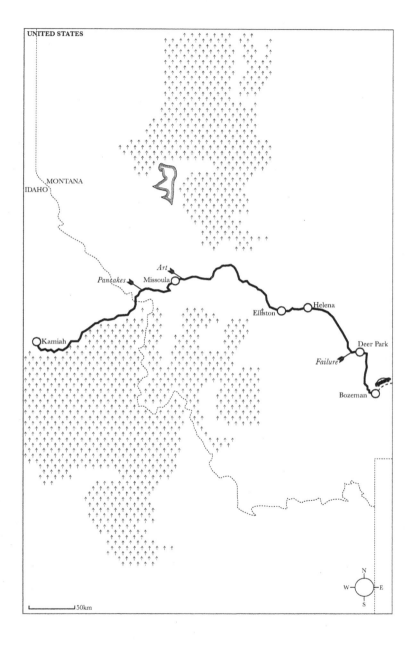

## Day 54 – Kamiah to Nez Perce National Forest

I set off from Kamiah after breakfast by the river. The timber mill that had kept me company through the night was still crashing, sawing and crunching away. Urban camping had its flaws.

On the way into the last town before the National Forest I stopped to give a cyclist water. Andy sat by the side of the road with the front wheel off his bike, trying to get a lift up the pass. We started chatting. Andy made fun of me for having such a fast bike and so much gear. "You smoke herb, man?" he asked. "What do you need to go so fast for? Enjoy the view. What you got in there, a tent? Man, a tent, what do you need a tent for?" He gestured to his schoolbag-sized backpack. "I've got this. Anything that doesn't fit, doesn't go. A hatchet and a mosquito net, that's a pretty good tent. Some pine boughs and some needles, that's a pretty good mattress." He delivered this speech with a monk's smile. I told him maybe next time and headed into town for coffee.

I ran into Andy again 200m down the highway. He was properly baked, by sun and herb. I stopped to offer him some more water and get another lesson in minimalist camping. Andy was glad to oblige. "You have to learn the plants and berries that are edible and carry cans of tuna," he said, "then you can make a tuna salad with sunflowers." He offered me some plants that definitely weren't sunflowers. He left me with a benediction, "You'll learn son, you'll learn, you just have to do the work. God bless you."

This was the first time I had followed a single river for so long. It was interesting to watch it change from an ooze through Lewiston to a stroll at the start of the forest, to a rush halfway up the hill. I felt connected to it. I was reminded of Alastair Humphreys when he walked along a river in India: "There are other rivers, but this one is mine." I had been here two days, so I might have been getting ahead of myself, but I could see what he meant.

It was hot. So many crystals were forming on my skin that I considered selling them as table salt. I skipped the hot springs. Instead, I found a new best campsite of the trip. I dragged my bike down an unmarked trail over fallen trees. An oasis emerged. A sandy patch of clear ground for the tent, a wide river bend for a swim. The sun sparkled on the river. I luxuriated in cleanliness.

## Day 55 – Nez Perce National Forest, ID to Missoula, MT

I set out from my idyllic river beach campsite at sunrise. The dawn sun filtered through the pines. With the recovery of altitude, gone were the sun-dried yellow hills of the previous days. The sun reflected off the river as the road bent around it. It blinded and amazed by turns.

The first goal of the morning was Lochsa Lodge, another of John's tips. He recommended the breakfasts. I had two. The waitress was suitably impressed and disgusted. During the first course, she came over and asked me, "How are the first few bites of your breakfast?" It was obviously her go-to line. It didn't fit here, as the breakfast was gone. I smiled through squirrel-packed cheeks and ordered pancakes. Two, American-sized, huckleberry pancakes. After missing the springs, I felt good about doing justice to this recommendation. I was also extremely full. Cycling was unappealing. As I basked in a post-pancake, pre-indigestion glow, I remembered there was still a 200m climb to the pass into Montana. Maybe the pancakes were unwise.

I was wrong. There was 600m of climbing left. The breakfasts stopped hurting and started helping just in time for the roll down the other side of the hill.

After a 40km digestive glide, I found my way to Missoula. I'd been trying to book into the one hostel in town for a couple of days. I'd heard it was a nice town and had planned to kick around for an afternoon and wander. The hostel was full. I called. I emailed. I played the cycling card. I mentioned I'd happily crash on a couch. I'd even pitch a tent in the living room. No dice. The next best option was a bed and breakfast for $175. It looked good. It was tempting, but the antithesis of frugal touring. I talked myself out of it and decided to go to a brewery, have a few beers and then cycle 20km out of town to find a place to camp the night. Save $175 on the room, spend

$30 on the beer, come out $145 ahead. I was making money.

Missoula was indeed a cool town. I rode in through leafy suburbs and took myself on a tour of the University of Montana, quiet in the summer. After Sandpoint, Moscow and Coeur d'Alene, I was getting the sense that university towns were the place to be in the US. Missoula was founded as an Old West trading post on the Clark Fork River, Hellgate Trading Post. It had gentrified since then. A cycle path followed the river through town. It was Saturday and the sun was shining. The town was enjoying it. Families picnicked by the river. Kids jumped off a bridge. There was a standing wave where a river kayaker and a surfer competed for cheers. A Celtic festival was in full swing in the town park. A shirtless man with a ginger ponytail, a kilt and Celtic tattoos strolled the hills. It was his best day.

I headed for a brewery. There were plenty to choose from. Montana liquor licensing laws made it cheaper to open a brewery than a bar. Each brewery could only serve you three beers, and had to shut at 9pm. Missoula had 75,000 people and sixteen breweries. Even if you toured them all, you'd be in bed by 10pm. You'd also be dead. It was all very civilised.

The one I chose, Draught Works, had nineteen of its beers on tap. They were adventurous. Pineapple IPA, tomatillo sour, blood orange Gose. The inside was covered with art. A local artist, Tim Nielsen, had done portraits of people he admired. Revolutionary figures: Malcolm X, Florynce Kennedy, Fannie Lou Hamer, as well as local people. There was a poet that the artist had played football with in college, a high school teacher, and a singer who was an inspiration to his niece. The best part were the captions. Florynce Kennedy's started with her line: "My main message is that we have a pathologically, institutionally racist, sexist, classist society. And that niggerisation techniques don't only damage black people, but they also damage women, gay people, ex prison inmates, prostitutes, children, old people, handicapped people, native Americans." This was not the Montana I was expecting.

I decided on a beer and went to stand outside. The brewery had large fans spraying water. I could have died happy. I went to get a refill and met the bartender. Audrey had done some long-distance hiking and cycle touring and was keen to chat. I was in front of the bar and in the way. Audrey handed a beer to a customer over my shoulder and continued talking. A second bartender came over. She was from Alaska. I told her I loved it. She handed me another beer. This was getting even better.

Audrey and I discussed the relative merits of hiking and cycling. I told her my plan to find a place to camp on the road to Helena. Audrey was from Helena. She gave me brewery and coffee recommendations. Then she looked down the bar and had a brainwave: "You have to meet Brad, he'll give you a place to stay and he has a dope house," she said. Audrey pulled me down to the other end of the bar and introduced me to 'The Dude' from the *Big Lebowski*. He was leather-tanned, with straight shoulder-length grey hair and a beard. He was in his fifties, but with tattooed biceps stretching the sleeves of his T-shirt. Brad greeted me with a grin and invited me to take a seat. Audrey introduced me as cycling from Alaska and told Brad that I was headed to Helena. He offered me a place to crash. I told him I liked the art in the bar. He told me he organised it. This was a good start. We got chatting and Brad told me his story. He joined the Coast Guard after high school and was there for 25 years. He had spent time on ice cutters in Antarctica, the US base in Okinawa, and the Aleutian Islands which stick out from Alaska towards Russia. After retiring, he moved back to Montana and went to law school in Missoula on the GI bill. Now he spent his time supporting the local art scene. As we chatted, the Alaskan bartender gave me more free beers. I loved Missoula.

Brad and I said our goodbyes and then headed to another brewery where he had to make an appearance. I briefly thought this was too good to be true, then shoved my cynicism aside. Everyone seemed to know Brad at the next brewery, and the walls were covered with more art that he had supplied. I got the tour. We headed outside to check out the band and chat to the locals. I wondered how hard it would be to move to Missoula. Did they have office jobs here? We sat down with Brad's crew and they asked about my trip. I said I was headed to Yellowstone. Everyone was excited. We were close enough now that everyone had Yellowstone stories. They also had one unanimous recommendation: the Beartooth Pass. It's hard to resist a great name. The pass was on the eastern edge of Yellowstone. That was significantly further east than I had planned to go. Local knowledge never shortened a journey.

After the brewery shut, we headed back to Brad's house. Audrey had alluded to the fact that it was a sight to be seen. The entire house was a mural. It was also home to about forty pieces of local art. Also, a pug, Olive. Brad told me she was his third pug. He just loved the breed. There was a magnet on his fridge that said, "I Love My Pug". I got a full tour of the mural that was a house. Brad planned to cover every wall in every room, including the ceilings. Each room had its nature theme. The basement was a cave. On the first floor, one room was the rising sun, another the sky, another the setting sun, another the forest and mountains. The art pieces were all colour coordinated to match with the different colour themes of the rooms. With the air of the obsessive, Brad was in the process of coordinating the light fittings and other detailing. The project had the feel of one that would never be completely finished, but always improving. I slept in a room Brad referred to as 'The Big Lebowski Suite', and reflected on my surreal afternoon.

## Day 56 – Missoula to Elliston

We got up early and Brad took me for breakfast. The Mountain States don't mess around with breakfast. We had steak. This was accompanied by three fried eggs, biscuits and sausage gravy, grits and fried apples. I felt like I could build a house (not well). Brad got on the phone to Audrey to find me a place to stay in Helena. Back at the house, I said goodbye to Olive, and Brad gave me a lift out of town. It was a beautiful drive and we got carried away chatting. We went fifteen miles. It took twenty minutes in the car but would have been an hour and a half on the bike.

The route from Missoula to Helena followed the Blackfoot River for the first 80km. At each bend, there were middle-aged men in waders fly fishing. I passed a retired couple cycle touring. They were headed up to Glacier National Park. They used to live by Yellowstone and were excited that I planned to ride the Beartooth Pass. "Plenty of hills, plenty of bears," the husband said. I came down from Alaska, I said. I've got my bear spray on quick-draw. I demonstrated. They both laughed, "You'll be fine." As they turned off to Glacier, the husband shouted back at me: "Happy trails man ... Love, peace and chain grease."

The road climbed and left the river. Out of the forest, Montana was shade-free. I stopped at a roadside diner to get out of the sun. It was called 'Trixies' and dead animals hung from the walls. The waitresses chatted to the customers, the customers at the bar chatted to each other, and the pie was homemade. I tried all the pies. Ice cream is good for heat stroke.

The road continued uphill through ranch land. It was fenced on both sides and there were no trees. Camping looked challenging. There were access roads on the map to the National Forest or to creeks, but they were miles off the route on loose gravel. I resolved to push on to a place where the National Forest came closer to the highway. This took me to 145km on the bike for the day. I found an access road to the

National Forest marked on my map. It was unmarked and went through driveways. The sun was setting. I decided to chance it. After selecting a spot past the driveways, I got halfway through dinner. Pasta-smeared, bags askew, I was caught in flagrante delicto by two large men. They had big beards and were walking bigger dogs. I tried to start out on the front foot. "Hi guys, nice evening to be walking the dogs," I said. "Yes, it is," they replied, "and what are you doing?" I considered bullshitting and decided against it. "Looking for a place to camp." Camp was the magic word. They got excited. They told me to head two miles further up the road where I could get right by the creek. I thanked them. The campsite was excellent.

## Day 57 – Elliston to Helena

Brad had laughed about a tough hill on the road to Helena. It was indeed a curly one. Back up to 1,950m I went. And right back down. I rolled down the hill into town at 10am and beelined for Audrey's coffee recommendation. It was legit. It had a treehouse. The fridge behind the coffee bar had stickers saying, "A Woman's Place is in the Resistance" and "Protect the Oceans". I'd started to appreciate how diverse America was. In Alaska, Idaho and Montana it was easy to go from a roadside diner draped with flags and guns, to a town with cafes and bars that wouldn't look out of place in London.

I had some time to kill until the baseball game. It was too early to go to the brewery. I asked the barista what else I should check out in Helena. She recommended the Archie Bray, a ceramics studio space at an old brick factory.

The Archie Bray was a crazy space. There were the old brick making facilities and three generations of kilns. Instead of being replaced, they had been built around and had become part of the space. The old buildings were now sculptures in their own right, halfway between historical monuments and works of art. There were supposed to be thirty artists in residence. At 2pm on a Monday, I wandered around alone. I found a sign saying everything was closed for 'Bray Day'. I searched the internet for what this was and came up blank. I'm sure they just made it up. The studios were open, so I gave myself a surreal self-guided tour. I cruised through taking photos and stealing things. Kidding.

After my art appreciation afternoon, I went to buy my baseball tickets. The minor league stadium in Helena, Kindrick Field, seated 2,000 people. When I showed up, the box office was open, the lights were on, but no one was home. I waited. Then I went in and wandered around the stadium. This was becoming thematic. A guy in half a uniform asked me if I needed anything. We returned to the box office and he talked me through the shade characteristics of the seating plan. I went for the $9 deluxe option: maximum shade.

I still had an hour before Tony and Ciara, the people Brad introduced me to, finished work. Where else? It was five o'clock somewhere. There is something about drinking at a brewery that feels like more of a legitimate activity than drinking at a bar. I was supporting local commerce, Montana entrepreneurs, the lifeblood of the community. It was still $5 a glass and if I drank six my bike would stop working.

I met Tony in front of his house just outside of central Helena. He opened the garage to store my bike. It had company. Along with five mountain bikes, there was a bike stand, a full workbench of tools and an array of spare tyres. The garage was so full there was nowhere to put my bike but on the stand. I could tell we were going to get along. We went inside for a beer and then off to another brewery. Tony was a buddy of Brad's from law school in Missoula. He was equally enamoured of Brad. "You got Brad's seal of approval, that's enough for me," he said.

Tony was a lawyer. He ran a non-profit mountain biking club with his buddies on the side. They built trails and put on events. As Tony talked about it, I started to realise it was a serious organisation. They ran the highest prize money event in enduro mountain bike racing. I felt that, as a cyclist now, I should be able to appreciate mountain biking, but I had no idea what enduro was. Tony described it to me as, "Like downhill mountain biking, except you have to bike to the top." It sounded hard. Tony showed me some photos of their most recent race. It looked hard. One photo was of one of Tony's friends going face first into a dirt track, at speed. During that race one woman lost the seat from her bike. She stuffed it down her cycling shorts and finished the race. She won. Like a boss. They were running an event in two weeks in Jackson, Wyoming and Tony invited me to come along.

We met Ciara at the baseball game. Tony and Ciara welcomed me into their crew. As we walked into the stands they saw some friends. We ditched my seats and commandeered space around the group. I was introduced, and Tony moved me to the middle. It was a perfect small town America scene. Their friends had their young children in tow all dressed in their Disney outfits for the game. I was glad I didn't come as Jafar. The friends chatted, drank beer and half watched baseball. The children played in the stands. At half-time the stadium ran competitions for the kids. A highlight was the fish slingshot. This was exactly what it sounds like. Two people manned a slingshot and fired a trout thirty metres into the air. A kid had to catch it in a net. What a concept. The sun set, the kids played, the game wore on, the parents finished their beers.

After hot dogs, monkey nuts and probably three too many beers, we headed back to the house. Tony offered to tune up my bike. While he worked, he gave me his mountain bike to play around on. I zoomed around the neighbourhood in the dark wearing flip flops, over people's front lawns and driveways. The mountain bike was fast. I tried to imagine what running one of these down a 45-degree angle was like. I decided to go to the race in Jackson.

## Day 58 – Helena to almost Deer Park

I woke up a little dusty after the beers. Tony cooked breakfast and he, Ciara and I sat around talking. Tony headed off to work. Ciara settled down to work on publishing the papers from her PhD. We procrastinated, chatting while I packed. It took me until midday to get on the road. By this time, I was firmly committed to Jackson. As I rode off, I reflected on how small decisions could change the direction of the journey. Talking to John on the plane brought me to Idaho. Meeting Audrey in Missoula had transformed my trip through Montana. Now, Jackson.

A haze had settled into the valley. There were forest fires further west. Tony had said that if I had tried this trip last year, I would have been breathing soot. As it was, the road from Helena to Bozeman ran through flat farmland on a wide highway. The haze dimmed the hills to shaded suggestions in the distance. Motivated by monotony and by the difficulty of camping in wheat fields, I decided to take myself on a DIY Google Maps tour of rural Montana, cutting out a section of highway.

Over a wooden bridge, through a one pub town and onto an open country road. The asphalt turned to gravel, the gravel turned to dirt, and the road turned to a track. I consulted my digital assistant to see whether I had taken a wrong turn. No, this track was the correct track. As the road got worse, the scenery got better. The farms gave way to open hills. The road followed the early headwaters of Missouri River, then diverged up a gravel hill.

I had been defeated by no hills on this trip. I was defeated by this one. My road touring tyres slipped in the loose dirt. The tyre slipped once. I thought, "She'll be right." The tyre slipped twice. I did not unclip. I fell over. I pushed my bike up 100 vertical metres through sand. In Montana, no one can hear you sweat. Google told me this was the only real climb, so I decided to tough it out. On the other side of the hill, my loaded bike skidded alarmingly in the loose grit as I tried to coast down. I hung on to the brakes with both hands, one foot trailing loose to arrest slides.

After this bastard of a hill, the road levelled out. The track was still garbage, but I was alone. The early evening sun bathed the hills in gold. There was no noise of car engines. The only sounds were the flow of the river and the screams of eagles overhead. I congratulated myself on adventure achieved. The sweat had been worth it. Then, a 'Bridge Closed' sign. The sign had been there so long that grass had grown over the gravel track up to the bridge. Thanks Google. Over the bridge, the road was fenced off with a five-foot gate. It was covered in 'no trespassing' signs. I considered fording the river and hopping the fence. The backtracking avoided weighed against the risk of becoming a gun violence statistic. There seemed to be no other option than retracing my steps. No wonder there were no cars here. I retreated. It hurt. Mentally, physically, emotionally. Do you know what I like less than pushing a bike up a hill? Pushing a bike up a hill I've just ridden down. As a consolation prize, I found a campsite on the summit with 360-degree views, pitched my tent and watched the sun set. The eagles screamed and the river flowed.

## Day 59 – Almost Deer Park to Bozeman

It was a beautiful start to the morning on top of the hill. I cooked breakfast as the sun spilled into the valleys. Then I started riding. The easy option was retracing my steps to the highway. Google advised a more experimental route. This looked similar to yesterday's. The possibility of another dead end after 30km of gravel, sand and sweat defeated me. The journey back was my penance. I ricocheted down the hill. Teeth rattled, sit bones bruised. I regained the tarmac to discover that the jolting had dislodged my last water bottle. 50km to the next town and no water.

It might be an obvious thing to say, but lack of water really affects one's enthusiasm for the landscape. I suppose I could have stopped and knocked on a farmer's door, but I had decided my recompense for not taking the gravel road less travelled was fair. Farmland crawled by.

I passed the gravel road that I might have come out of if I had taken the adventurous route. This event weighed on my mind for miles before it happened. I hoped for it to be a driveway. A rutted gravel driveway. A driveway locked by gates and guarded by dogs. It wasn't. I probably could have made it. I wasn't curious enough to go back and check.

I stopped into a diner at the first town to get water. The owner saw my bike and came out to have a chat. His name was Nick, and he had immigrated from Switzerland. I asked him how he ended up here. He told me he was working as a chef in Germany and one of his Indian dishwashers asked him to call the American embassy about some sort of youth mobility visa. They told him the Indian dishwasher couldn't have one, but the Swiss chef could. He got on a plane and thirty years later he was running the diner in Belgrade, Montana. Nick had a moustache and rode a motorcycle; he had assimilated. I reflected that when I got back to reality, I was going to miss people coming up and talking to me whenever I sat down with my helmet on.

I arrived in Bozeman after what felt like an endless day. I had high expectations for Bozeman aka 'Boze-angeles' (so named for its invasion and subsequent improvement/destruction by Californians, and possibly its self-regard). I didn't see anything remarkable on the way in. Endless American-perfect suburbs. Tree-lined streets, flags flying in front of three-car garages, two and a half kids and two and a half kayaks. I checked in to a hostel and generally got my shit together. By the time I re-emerged to find some food, Main Street had turned into "The Largest Dinner Party in Montana". There were food trucks packed shoulder to shoulder on both sides of the street for half a mile. I got ready for some serious eating.

## Day 60 – Bozeman

Bozeman got less micro-manicured as I got further away from the town centre. I spent the morning at the Museum of the Rockies until it was overrun by RV people. I learned lots of things that had nothing to do with cycling. Half of all the water used in Bozeman in summer was used on people's lawns. The museum encouraged residents to plant native gardens. From what I could tell, these would be made out of rocks. The region was essentially a desert. The English landscaper I met in Whitehorse, Matt, liked to point out that putting grass on our lawns was a strange pursuit. He referred to it as "asserting humanity's dominance over our environment through the planting of an imported and naturally unsustainable mono-crop." Matt had planted a lot of grass in his day. While I was there, he had turfed the hostel's lawn. It looked like hard work. No wonder he was ambivalent about grass.

I rode over to a coffee roaster on the north side of town. It was too cool. No one wanted to talk to me. I enjoyed my perfect coffee in silence. Over the road there was a gallery in an old mill. It was too early for the breweries, so I went over to check it out. The gallerist sat in a single room, alone. We started to chat. I'd kept my sticker from the Museum of the Rockies to mark myself as a rube, and was ridiculed. Liz gave me a short tour and we talked travelling. She'd done a year backpacking with her husband in 2000 around Kenya, India and South East Asia. They'd stayed in a lot of brothels: "If you don't use the services they are cheap places to sleep. Gross, but cheap." We swapped wildlife stories. Liz told me she'd met a mountain lion while mountain biking in Colorado. They came over a ridge and surprised it. It spat and hissed. They jumped off their bikes and lifted them up to look big: "I know you're not supposed to run away and look like prey, but we went back down that trail pretty damn fast." They had taken their two kids rafting on the Salmon River when they were three and five: "That was one of those things where if everyone had died, people would have said we deserved it." Now their kids were older, Liz and her husband tried to take them on vacations off the standard middle-class trail, "To show them that not everyone is rich, white and owns a canoe." Liz recommended that I go to a rodeo. It was the thing to go to in Wyoming. "The smaller the better," she said. I told her that was deeply in my corner. I'd find one.

I went out for a beer in the evening with a friend of a friend and his stepdad. Connor had gone to law school with Vic, a friend I hadn't seen in ten years. He instantly welcomed me: "There is a festival in town for the next three days, come hang out with us tomorrow. My cousin, Nick, is here, we are planning to go on a hike in the Beartooth Mountains," he said. "It's going to be awesome. It's called the 'Beaten Path'. We have been trying to do it for years. You should definitely come along." Before I knew it, I was scheduled to hang out with Connor and his family for the next week. The conversation moved on. We chatted about beer and fishing and my trip so far. We got back on to the topic of our mutual friend. "So, how do you know Vic?" Connor asked. I had to admit the connection was tenuous. To his credit, Connor didn't visibly recoil from the fact that he'd just invited some random guy to spend a week with his family, with three days alone in the wilderness. His stepdad grinned into his beer. We had a few more beers while I tried to convey that I was fun, or at least safe to go to sleep around.

Afterwards, there was live music on Main Street. It was a great small town affair; people meeting on the street and catching each other to chat. Connor's stepdad knew half the crowd.

It was still early by the time I got back to the hostel. I found a buddy and went to explore Bozeman by night. Scott had started his own business working for medical device companies organising surgeon training of new devices on cadavers. I took my drink with me to the bathroom.

# Day 61 – Bozeman: Sweet Pea Festival

I'd come to Bozeman at the right time of year. A music festival started at 3pm. I spent the morning at another cafe where people were too hip to chat. I mapped the route south from the Beaten Path and the Beartooth Pass. Over the pass in Wyoming, I found a town called Cody. Cody advertised itself as the "Rodeo Capital of the World". There was a rodeo every night of the summer. It was either a horrendous tourist trap, or the people in Cody just really liked their rodeo, or both. In any case, it seemed like a good idea.

I was the first non-volunteer to arrive at the festival. The volunteers were there well ahead of the crowd and had staked out the best seats. By staked out, I mean that people had moved their homes into the park. No one does lawn furniture like Americans. There were fold-out armchairs, inflatable footrests and fridge-sized coolers. I sat on my rain jacket and felt underprepared, not for the first time.

Connor and his family arrived. I joined them at the main stage. They had been coming to the festival long enough to have worked out the optimal strategy. They had blankets, and the older generation had smuggled in Moscow Mules in thermoses. Connor, Nick, his cousin and I had to settle for beers in the tent at the back. The festival was a multi-generational affair. Young kids in tie-dyed T-shirts with long blond hair and bare feet jumped around with grandparents in tie-dyed T-shirts with long grey hair and bare feet.

## Day 62 – Bozeman: Sweet Pea Festival

Before the festival today there was a fun run and a parade. Connor and the whole family got out to run. The 7am start time from clean sheets deterred me. The parade was a step up from Fort Nelson's. The town turned out and packed both sides of the street. Pickup trucks towing floats and groups of dancers and singers cruised down the street. The local fire department brought out their engines and sprayed the hoses. Little kids ran out in the street to play in the water. The Agricultural Research Association tried a similar trick. They had attached a sprinkler to their float. It sprayed the crowd sitting on the side of the road. People scattered in chaos.

I wandered down to the festival and read my book beneath a tree while the early bands played. Connor, Nick and the rest of the family turned up in the afternoon. We hung out all day drinking beers, watching the bands and investigating the food stands. The Sweet Pea Festival had gotten so famous that it attracted successful bands from out of state. To give the local bands a chance to play when the town was at its best, another festival, SLAM, had started over the road. There was free whiskey tasting. We went to investigate. The whiskey makers were grain farmers that had diversified and set up stills on their properties. We tried all of them. At least Montana makes good beer.

After plumbing the dark depths of Montana's whiskey culture, we returned to Sweet Pea and listened to the last few bands. The festival peaked, finished, and we headed into town to another brewery. Some of Connor and Nick's friends from Bozeman joined us. One of the guys was the head brewer at one of the local breweries. We talked about his rise from helping out to taking over as the head brewer. He had taught himself from textbooks and now the brewery was exporting across the US. I asked if they were hiring. After too many beers and two days of music, I was looking for any excuse to immigrate.

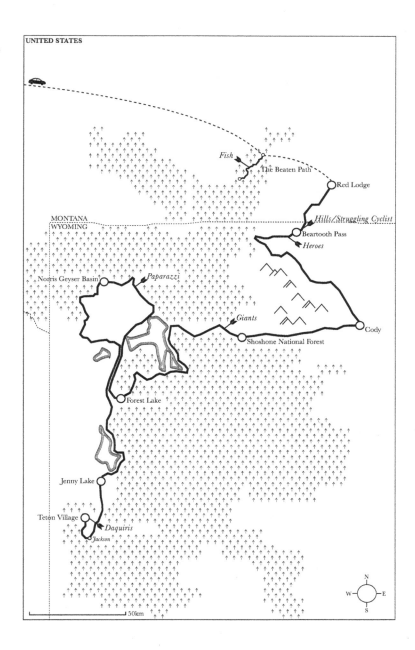

UNITED STATES

*Fish*

The Beaten Path

Red Lodge

*Hills/Struggling Cyclist*

MONTANA
WYOMING

Beartooth Pass

*Heroes*

Norris Geyser Basin

*Paparazzi*

*Giants*

Shoshone National Forest

Cody

Forest Lake

Jenny Lake

Teton Village

*Daquiris*

*Jackson*

N
W E
S

50km

## Day 63 – Bozeman to the Beartooth Mountains

In the morning, I went to buy my fishing licence. Nick and Connor had offered to teach me to fly fish. I had the impression that the hike was going to be a little about the walking and a lot about the fishing. The guys in the shop were excited to sell me my first fishing licence. Brad had recommended the book *A River Runs Through It* to learn about Montana. The first line was: "In our family there was no clear line between religion and fly fishing." Montana took its fly fishing seriously. The author, Norman Maclean, had once turned down an actor for a movie adaptation because he showed up to fish without a licence. I wasn't going to make the same mistake.

Hike prep filled the rest of the day. We borrowed a pack for me from one of Nick's friends, shopped for food and bought missing bits of kit from the camping store. Bozeman had an REI and a Sportsman's Warehouse next door to each other to cater to the two distinct segments of Montana outdoor consumers. REI for the yuppies, and Sportsman's for the Republicans. We spent an hour in REI. I popped into Sportsman's for price comparison and wandered past the magazine rack. It was filled with such gripping titles as: *Doomsday – Nuclear Attack: Escape Strategies and High Risk Areas*; *Offgrid – Modern Family: Expert Advice on Protecting Your Family from Today's Threats*; and *AR-15: Built for the Hunt*. I purchased some light bedtime reading.

We headed back to Connor's mum's house and packed. Connor had talked about going huckleberry picking over the last week. A pie on the counter looked like it had taken days to fill. I commented on it and was offered a piece. I was stuck being rude to refuse and rude to eat so much of other people's labour. I tried to take a small piece and failed. It was delicious.

We set out and drove down to the Beartooth Mountains. For dinner, we stopped for American-sized burgers and beers in a heartland diner. Perfect hike preparation. We turned off the highway and drove through ranch land towards the mountain range. The foothills were interlaced with streams. Nick and Connor exclaimed with growing excitement at each one: "Delicious ripple ... right there, look at that, just look at that ... I bet there is a monster lurking in there ... perfect hole." I had no idea what they were talking about, but it seemed fishing related and I was starting to catch their excitement. We got out and inspected one of the streams. The boys leant over a bridge, trying to catch sight of their prey in the fast flowing water below. Heavy weather hung over the mountains. We watched a red and orange sunset glow below looming clouds. I tried to remember whether red at night meant shepherd's delight or sailor's fright. By the time we found the trailhead, a dense fog hung between the cliffs. The sun had set, and the dark mountains looked foreboding. We camped at the base of the valley and prepared ourselves for a wet morning.

## Day 64 – Beartooth Mountains: The Beaten Path

The mountains shaded us from sunrise. Sunlight filled the valley opposite, leaving us to shiver and watch warmth spread slowly down the mountains across the fields towards us. The tents were wet with morning dew. Nick and I flapped them around and hung them in trees to dry. By the time we finished the last preparation and procrastination the sun had just touched the tents. They were no drier. We packed them away wet and resolved to stop early and put them up to dry.

After the ominous mist of yesterday, the sky had completely cleared. The weather was perfect. Blue skies and light breezes. We set off, confident we were not in for three days in wet tents. The climb was relentless. Granite cliffs towered over the trail. We stopped to sample the local flora. Berry bushes were in full fruit. Wild raspberries, huckleberries and thimbleberries. The segments of the small raspberries came apart easily. Juice covered our fingers. The huckleberries were the pick of the bunch, the flavour something like a blueberry. Everyone I met from Montana insisted they were better. They stained your hands the same colour purple. We ended up with blotchy palms. The bears liked them too. The evidence of this greeted us in the middle of the trail. It looked like someone had put a stick of dynamite in a huckleberry pie. We exchanged nervous jokes about meeting a bear along the hike. At least they had lots of berries to eat.

The hike led up a river. This river flowed down from Fossil Lake on the Beartooth plateau by way of ten intermediate lakes. The air was still and the sun beat down. At each lake we came to, the pink and grey cliffs surrounding the valley reflected in the still surface. The reflection was broken only by bubbles as fish fed at the surface. Nick and Connor pointed these out excitedly, "Rise ... rise .... oh, oh, look, look, a big rise there." We didn't last much longer hiking. Anticipation stoked driving past the streams yesterday, the boys could take no more. At 11am we found a lake and broke out the fishing rods.

Connor instructed me on how to set up the rod. The first step was to snap together the segments. This was easy enough. The next was to feed the line from the reel, through each eye, up to the tip of the rod. This proved more challenging. Each time I lost hold of the line, it flowed back down the rod, slow enough to see, too fast to catch. Supporting the rod, pulling the line through each eye and holding the line in place made me feel like I had one too few hands. The perfect trout fisherman would have three hands, each with seven needle-thin fingers. By the time I succeeded in assembling the rod, the boys had flies in the water and were in their own world.

Connor and Nick caught fish. I caught the rocks behind me. I did start to appreciate the meditative properties of standing on the shore weaving a line back and forth. At its best, the line flowed out in a graceful arc, the fly floating down to kiss the surface, only to be whisked away after a fleeting instant of insecurity. I never achieved this, but I was sure it would be nice. Connor alternately encouraged me and berated me to keep my wrist straight, to not dump my line into the water, to not scare the fish. My back cast was too short, the most mundane of beginner errors. My line drifted out in a lethargic wiggle. One cast in ten would hint at the serenity of line in motion. I spent more time with my line in my hands than my fly in the water. I broke for lunch. The scene was idyllic. As I sat on sun-warmed rocks, the boys continued to fish, lines flowing out into space. A waterfall cascaded into the far end of the pond, glittering across the pink granite cliffs. As Connor said, most of fishing was being here.

After lunch we walked. We ran out of lakes before we ran out of energy, onto a plateau of marshy ground. Then we ran out of energy. Our planning had been flexible, which is another way of saying that we hadn't done any. Our maps didn't show distance or available places to camp. The marsh was not ideal. It was covered with lush forest fed by the lakes above, but infested with mosquitos and without access to running water. We decided to push on to the end of the plateau and the climb to the lakes above. Connor and I were showing our desk jobs and were tiring. We hiked in silence. Nick led the pack. He had spent four years working as a contractor in Bozeman and rock climbing. He was at home in these mountains. Head down and feet forward, Nick kept sufficiently ahead of Connor and I to drag us onwards. Never too far to let us give up, but never too close to let us slow.

We passed a campsite already colonised. The group encouraged us with news of a campsite further on. As we left, one laughed, "I hope you like heights." We hiked up a waterfall. In the heat, it looked like the world's best one-ride-only waterslide. One final push over boulders and up a hill and we were above it. The campsite barely had space for our two tents around a fire pit and sat directly next to the trail. It was heaven. On the opposite side of the trail from the fire pit was a flat expanse of rock and the stream running to the head of the falls. We dropped our packs and edged to the lip of the slab. Below, the waterfall dropped thirty metres down to a lake. We gazed back down the valley. The sun set between the cliffs. They glowed. The fast flowing stream and a light breeze kept the mosquitos at bay. We built a fire, smoked too much of a medical joint, and sat in exhausted and meditative silence. The expanse of stars lit the Montana sky.

*Camping to the screams of eagles between Helena and Bozeman.
Following defeat by sand.*

*In Montana, there was no clear line between religion and fly fishing.*

*Nick performing a morning rain dance.*

*Nick, from behind. Another view which would become familiar.*

*Connor, pointing at fish*

*The author, attempting to find them.*

*The best thing about switchbacks is you can see them all the way down.*

*Cody. Wyoming. America.*

*Cody Rodeo. Looks fun. For the horse, at least.*

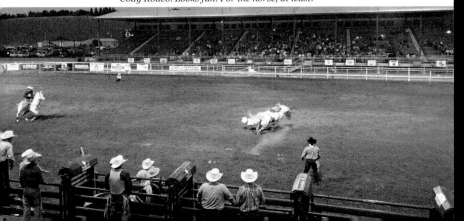

# Yellowstone

*Buffalo at dawn in Yellowstone.*

*The park paparazzi.*
*These people need to be told.*

*"It looked better on the postcard."*

*The first view of the Tetons.*

*Better up close.*

*Tony, pre-daiquiri*

*Pretty sure this is legit. Thanks, Google.*

*Cool campsite. Probably not worth losing my bike for.*

Welcome to Portland.

Cape Lookout. Cape is a four letter word for hill.

The first sunset into the Pacific.

*Corners, coastlines.*

*Redwoods!*

*No pigeons in California.*

*On the road out of San Francisco. "You should go in. It's dark and wild."*

*Fog.*

*Another coastline. Some more fog.*

*Lycra locusts.*

*Roadside fashion show, on the way to Oceano.*

*Well ventilated wine tasting.*

*The Camino Del Cielo into Santa Barbara. If it's good enough for Lance, it's good enough for us, Tucker.*

*Surfboards and sunshine.*

*But mostly, suburbia.*

# Over the border

*Top tamales.*

*Tip-top tacos.*

*I should have started in Mexico.*

# Day 65 – Beartooth Mountains: The Beaten Path

We had ambitions of rising early, catching the dawn across the valley and setting off for the top of the Beartooth plateau. We go up late and basked in the sunny morning and strong coffee. Shirts off, we cooked breakfast on the rock slab overlooking the waterfall. Passing hikers, up, breakfasted and on the move, surveyed our disarray with disdain. We had another coffee. There was no rush, the fish would wait.

We decided to keep our hard won campsite at the top of the waterfall and set off up the trail with daypacks and fishing rods. After half an hour, we stopped for the first fish. Connor and Nick gave me the best spot, perched on a boulder by the lake, clear of grasping rocks. I repeated my fumbling with rod and line, like the virgin I was. I caught nothing. We pushed on.

The second stop tested our commitment to our campsite. Each new lake seemed more incredible than the last, surrounded by peaks, linked with energetic streams. This lake had islands. Nick, the mountain goat, hopped from island to island. He forded shallow streams too far to jump, leapt over streams too deep to ford. Connor followed carefully, and I reluctantly. My mountain biking cleats slipped on the smooth granite. The biggest fear of a man hiking with men is not to be able to keep up, or worse, to need help. Nick island-hopped to the opposite bank of the lake. The last obstacle was a two-metre gap (adjust for exaggeration) of fast flowing mountain current. On the far side, a welcoming flat boulder to land on. On the near side, a 45-degree angle. Nick took one step down the face and launched himself to the other side, space to spare. Connor and I exchanged looks. Connor jumped, heel splashing the water on the opposite bank. I followed, cleats clacking on the rock. Success. Getting out is always the easy bit. The opposite bank was a perfect campsite. Secluded from the trail, sheltered from the wind, an expanse of flat boulders with patches of soft grass inviting tents. Nick made plans to camp. I thought of jumping over with the gear. We decided to continue up the path, fish and make a final decision in the afternoon. Nick and Connor leapt back across. I scouted for an easier crossing but found none. The longer you consider an obstacle, the higher it becomes. I shut my mind and jumped, landing with both feet and hands. I grinned to the guys. No problem. I considered how to avoid changing camps without being a drag.

We passed a group of fishermen. They were from Alabama. One wore camouflage pants, tucked-in grey T-shirt stretched over his skinny frame. I wasn't sure how the camo helped with the fishing, but he looked like he meant business. Between the accent and the jargon, I understood nothing. The best thing about trout fishing is the jargon. The chance to hike through remote wildernesses is nice. The battle between hunter and hunted is fine. Being able to live off the land is good. The jargon is phenomenal. Thousands of different flies, each with their own names: Woolly Bugger, Stimulator, Parachute Adams, Bunny Leech. These together with descriptions of the fishing spots in terms that only meant anything to fishermen, the Alabamans and Connor and Nick were speaking a new language. We continued and I asked them to translate.

We meandered up the path, fishing at will. The plan to push for the top of the plateau was sidelined. Each new lake had a new stream feeding it to investigate. Every new stream had new holes to explore, new ripples to assess. We turned from the main path, following Nick and Connor's sixth sense for fishing spots and our loose interpretations of our inadequate maps. We followed a stream up to the base of a tumbling waterfall. The stream stopped and pooled in pockets, then cascaded over pink boulders. We spread out along the banks, Connor and Nick excitedly directing me to new spots. Crowded by the steep banks of the stream we roll cast. Without room to swing the rod fully back, we took a shorter length of line and flicked it on to the surface, letting it flow down the stream like a trapped bug. Trout lurked in the clear water, waiting to be tempted to the surface. I met my prey. It watched, it waited, it thought about not striking, it struck, I panicked. I caught my first fish. The feeling was electric. I reeled it in and displayed it to the guys, shouting back to cheers. Victory! They were having equal luck and taking advantage of it with more skill. My fish was full of life, brilliant patterns of red and gold decorating the silver of its belly, flashing in the sun as it battled to get back to the water. I dislodged the hook from the trout's mouth and let it slip back into the stream.

We stayed on the trail into the early evening, hopping from spot to spot along the riverbank. We headed back down to camp. The guys were still ecstatic with the fishing, stopping at new holes missed on the route up and re-examining old ripples for fresh signs of life. Exhausted by the catch and our adventures up the trail, Nick dropped the plan of moving the campsite. I said nothing and hid my relief. We retired to camp and another evening spent contemplating the infinite.

## Day 66 – Beartooth Mountains to Red Lodge

On the last day of the hike, we still didn't manage to get up for the sunrise, but we did catch a lot of fish. With a long hike back, we decided (or the boys decided, and I followed) to fish the river near our campsite. We walked up river and worked our way back down. At the first hole, the guys took the hard spots in the middle of the river and I parked up on the bank, secure. I picked a patch of calm water after a rapid. A small waterfall drained into a pit. I stood so close I could reach the tip of rod over the hole and drop the fly in. Each time I did this a fish came up. The only thing stopping me from catching twenty was the fact that I got my line tangled every second cast. Tangled in the rocks. Tangled in the trees. Tangled in the line itself. If there was a way to tangle a rod, I found it. Every time I looked over at Nick and Connor they were pulling a fresh trout out of the river.

Each fish we caught we released. This was the done thing in Montana. The experience of pulling the hook out could be traumatic. Doubtless it was more so for the fish. I couldn't get the hook out of one determined mouth. Inexperienced, it took me a few tries to locate the hook. The fish gasped for breath. After these exploratory manoeuvres, he started to bleed from the gills. This didn't help my squeamishness, but did increase the sense of urgency. Fingers in throat, the hook released. He slipped back into the water. I washed the blood from my hands and wondered whether I had killed him.

Nick and Connor continued to pull fish from the river by the silver fistful. Connor and I stuck to the banks. As we meandered back towards camp, Connor caught fish, and I learned the full set of knot permutations that a fishing line can achieve. Each time I felt my roll casting was getting better, I'd flick the line forward only to discover I'd caught a tree branch behind. Fly fishing rewards arrogance quickly. The guys assured me that this was par for the course. I started to feel guilty about losing so many of their flies. I went to increasing lengths to fish them from the river and from trees. My proudest moment of the fishing was a fly retrieval operation from three metres up a pine tree. Three metres isn't a big climb, but when the pine bends over a river which turns into a thirty-metre waterfall after the next set of rapids, it's big enough.

The proximity of this waterfall didn't bother Nick. He walked down the middle of the river, hopping from stone to stone through the rapids. Nick fished all the way back to our campsite, catching a twelve-inch trout where we had washed dishes. After this hole, the river bounced once over a set of rocks then disappeared over the lip of the fall. We set off from camp. Nick looked back at the falls. We hadn't seen the sharp end of the falls since two nights earlier. He considered the precipice he had been clambering over: "Huh."

The walk back was long and the midday sun hot. Each time we recognised a cliff from the hike in, it reminded us how far there was still to go. The huckleberries proved irresistible, no matter the rush. The bushes had recovered from our assault on the way in. If anything, they looked even more laden. We ate berries, talked shit and dreamt of beer.

We arrived back at the car at 7pm, dropped packs and removed shoes. Feet luxuriated in freedom. Connor and I inspected blisters. Nick was unaffected. Connor hadn't seen the back of his feet in two days, having left his socks on to keep blister bandages in place. They weren't in great shape. At least the hike was worth it. We showered in the river and headed off to Red Lodge for the long awaited beers. Red Lodge is a 5,000-person town famous for being the start of the Beartooth Highway. Being a highway entrance isn't usually associated with quality. Typically for Montana, it still had a brewery that would be a weekly destination for me if it were anywhere close to London. The brewery was the perfect end to a great few days in the mountains. The sun went down, and the beers disappeared. The boys dropped me at a motel with a teepee and set off on the drive back to Bozeman. I reflected on how lucky I had been to meet them.

## Day 67 – Red Lodge, MT to the Beartooth Pass, WY

I woke up in my teepee in Red Lodge. The Beartooth Pass awaited. I talked to my parents while getting ready. I told my dad I had been in the mountains for three days and hadn't investigated the climb. He looked at the map: "It's 1,600m straight up," he said. What? Fuck, that's a long way. "Oh, no, no, my bad, you're at 1,600m now, it's only 800m." This seemed more reasonable but was still a long way up. The sun was shining, and the sky was blue as I set out. I looked forward to getting back on the bike after a week of sitting around at Sweet Pea Festival and hiking. I would have looked forward to it more if my legs weren't so sore from the hike. My knees made reproachful noises as I rolled out of bed. I finished packing and cruised through Red Lodge, fuelling up on coffees and breakfast burritos to push me up the hill. Onwards.

I saw my first big snake dead on the road. The prospect of rattlesnakes looking for a warm home at night had worried me for weeks. I had started to check my shoes. We met a local hiker at the end of the Beaten Path. He told us that one of the cabins there was owned by two brothers. They hated each other and couldn't decide what to do with the house. They hadn't been in it in years. It was now infested by rattlesnakes. I asked how many rattlesnakes was in an "infestation". One snake was infestation enough for me. I learned that infestations can get more serious than that. During winter, rattlesnakes crowd into balls. Hundreds of fat rattlesnakes slithering over each other, in your living room. Be nice to your siblings.

The first part of the road followed Rock Creek. After three days fishing, the river looked different. No longer was it just flowing water, I viewed it with more interested eyes. There seemed to be trout hiding in every bend. The river was picturesque, glittering in the morning sun. Or, as I should describe it in my new trout fishing lingo: it was gin clear, a delicious ripple with exquisite holes. There was a monster hiding in that eddy, I'm sure.

I passed 800m of climbing halfway up the first set of switchbacks. The feeling that I was crushing the climbing and would soon be done was replaced with a growing realisation that I had no idea how high the pass was. The public support I got as I started cycling should have tipped me off. The more thumbs up at the bottom of the hill, the further to the top. After the tenth switchback I decided the worst thing about switchbacks was that you could see them all the way up. There was no hiding from them. The Beartooth Mountains topped out in a plateau. Matchbox-sized cars above reminded me what the next hour of my life was going to be like.

Near the top of the pass, I met two more heroes of the human race. At metre 2,950 a girl yelled out a car window at me, "Yo, you want a beer?" This was not an offer to be turned down. Firstly, because I liked the concept, and secondly because I hadn't talked to two girls my own age in as many months. Cycle touring was not a great way to meet women. Barb and Julia were from New Jersey and gave me an IPA. Barb had done some cycle touring, which explained the beer offer. I resolved to always carry beer in my car for passing cyclists. Barb and Julia had built a caravan and were driving coast to coast over three months. We chatted, and I pitched Cody, the 'Rodeo Capital of the World'. Who could turn down an offer like that? They agreed to meet me there the following day.

After 1,600m of climbing, I arrived at the top of the plateau with a real sense of cycling achievement. The black highway stretched down the valley until it faded into the blue mist of the horizon. At each viewpoint people congratulated me. A group of large men in leather jackets riding Harley Davidsons with no helmets told me I was tough. I wish I had a photo of this moment. The lads were in full biker kit, complete with American flag bandanas. I was wearing my Lycra and sleeveless uniform. We all had great moustaches. The peak of the climb was 3,338m and it felt high. From the plateau, the surrounding peaks were at eye level, and still covered with snow.

The best thing about switchbacks is that you can see them all the way down. The descent went by quickly. The road coiled through green alpine meadows covered with wildflowers and dotted with clear blue lakes. I should have stopped to take more photos. I flew past, spending my altitude with reckless abandon and delighting in speed without effort.

## Day 68 – Beartooth Pass to Cody

The route from Beartooth Pass to Cody was a quiet highway called the Chief Joseph. It was named after the chief of the Nez Perce Indians. Everyone I met the day before told me it would be much easier than the Beartooth. I should have known by now to trust nothing said about roads by people in cars. The hills were smaller, but there were more of them. I still climbed 1,400m. After the hills, I dropped down into the Wyoming plains and the temperature shot up to thirty-seven degrees. I ran out of water. There were no streams. There were no gas stations. My planning was unimpressive. After glorious cycling the day before, I arrived in Cody defeated. Approaching an intersection leading into town I crested a hill, legs burning. I slowed to turn, a moment of indecision and I toppled over in slow motion with my feet clipped into the pedals. 5,000km of cycling and still a rookie. Some days you ride the bike, some days the bike rides you.

I went to check in to a campground in town. The lady at the front desk gave me infinite recommendations of things to do in Cody. She gave me six pamphlets. I tried to ask where I could get water. She explained each pamphlet in detail as she handed it to me, on a roll. I waited for her to regain consciousness. The town was geared towards Wild West tourism. The Buffalo Bill Centre was the largest building, and included the gun museum, her favourite attraction. I couldn't be bothered with any of it. I went into town to get a new chain for my bike, had an American-sized burger, and prepared myself for the rodeo.

Just as I'd started to lose faith in my beer heroes, they called. Barb and Julia were already at the bar warming up. I joined them. Appreciating local traditions was best done with company. Especially if the company was from New Jersey and this was as foreign a country to them as it was to me. I had asked the campground receptionist why Cody had a rodeo every night. "People round here just love rodeo," she said. We headed down to the arena. The stands were not full, and this was clearly for tourists. No matter, bulls were to be ridden, culture awaited.

The evening started with a prayer. The prayer began with relatively vanilla Jesus material. Then the announcer thanked "The good Lord for horses, livestock and rodeo." Julia burst out laughing. This was not well received by our stand companions. After the prayer, followed the patriotism. First, a poem by Johnny Cash for the flag. A single rider walked a horse round the arena holding high an American flag. The poem played over the loudspeaker to a snare drum. This lasted five full minutes. Then, the national anthem. We were encouraged to sing. It was rousing. The final pre-rodeo anticipation was a strange interlude where a flag bearing the logo of each of the sponsors was run out by a horse and rider. This segment went on for longer than the prayer, the poem and the anthem combined. America loves advertisers, and advertisers love rodeo.

The first rodeo event of the night was bucking broncos. Each round, a man tried to ride a horse for eight seconds while the horse tried not to be ridden. The horses won all rounds. We sat just behind the enclosures. One of the cowboys, Wyatt, had "Ride for God, Live for God" embroidered on his back brace. We were told he had gotten three concussions and still wanted to get back on the horse. He wore a wide brimmed Stetson hat. I joked that Jesus was his helmet. That went down well in New Jersey. The other rider was not riding for God, he was Australian. He stood during the prayer and had a hang loose sign with the Australian flag on his denim vest. He fared no better with the horses.

Between the men riding horses and bulls were events requiring less of a death wish. Men lassoed a calf from a horse, ran after it and trussed it up. Women did the same, without the trussing. Mixed teams of two lassoed a calf, one around the head and one the back legs. There was barrel racing, where women rode horses at ridiculous speeds around a lap separated by barrels in the arena. It was the Wild West equivalent of drag racing.

The rodeo clown was the real star of the evening. He played MC. In between rounds, he told jokes and did magic tricks. During an intermission, he got every kid in the stands out into the arena. Eighty children, all hopped up on Mountain Dew. The kids each got a ribbon, and two calves were let out into the ring. Pin the tail on the bullock. The kids ran and the calves spooked. It was chaos. To help the kids warm up for the challenge, the clown took them through a stretching routine. Side to side. Up and down. "Now kids, sit down. Now lie down. Now make dirt angels. Oh yes, your parents are going to love me for that one. Last but not least, touch the sky. Now touch the ground. Grab two big handfuls of dirt. Put them in your pockets. A nice souvenir from Cody Rodeo!" The man was a genius.

The big bulls played the finale. Eight seconds, man versus bull. The bulls prevailed.

# Day 69 – Cody to Shoshone National Forest

I was hungover and my legs hurt. I took the morning off. I felt guilty about skipping the museum. I had no idea who Buffalo Bill was. Cody was set up by him and was still geared towards the legacy of his era. I wondered how the museum dealt with the genocide of the Native Americans. The last mountain pass into Cody was called 'Dead Indian Pass'. Signs related the story of the flight of the Nez Perce Indians. They were attacked by the US army after refusing to give up their land and be forced into a reservation. A wounded man was left on the pass and killed by the pursuing army. The Nez Perce escaped the valley, and almost made it to safety in Canada. Almost.

Buffalo Bill's name was William Cody. Up to 1869 Cody was variously a herdsman, a buffalo hunter, a messenger, a soldier and a military scout. In the early 1870s Cody began a stage career and played the persona of 'Buffalo Bill'. Cody merged with the persona. He looked like Giovanni Ribisi with a better moustache and flowing locks of brown hair. Apparently, military scouts of the day all wore their hair long. "We who wear our hair long have let nature have her way in the matter and profit by it," he said. "Those who cut it short have all manner of health problems." Following success as an actor, Cody expanded the vision of the Wild West productions as a director. He organised 'Buffalo Bill's Wild West', an outdoor performance with hundreds of cowboys, Indians and animals. These turned into a global phenomenon. He toured the world, he performed for royalty, he met the Pope. In later life, he returned to Wyoming and did old man things. He founded Cody, gave it his name and built the main hotel. The campsite host recommended their 'Wild West Gun Show'. I skipped that and felt no guilt.

The Plains Indian wing of the museum was more a celebration of culture than an account of a genocide, with handicrafts and images of Indian life. One wall outlined the factors in the death of the Indians and their culture: disease, settler encroachment, buffalo extinction. The buffalo extinction was treated differently than in the Buffalo Bill wing. A plaque there read: "The decline of the buffalo was the result of human interaction with a complex, dynamic system." In the Plains Indian wing, there was another story: a picture of 40,000 pelts piled high, the meat left to rot. In the words of an Indian woman: "The white men hired hunters to kill buffalo ... sometimes there would be a pile of bones as high as a man, stretching a mile along a railroad track." The population of Plains buffalo fell from sixty million in 1840 to 1000 in 1886. This was both for profit from pelts (they did make undeniably dope coats) and to eliminate the underpinning of life for the Plains Indians.

In the gun museum there were indeed lots of guns. 7,000 guns in glass cases. Pistols, rifles, shot guns, other guns, more guns. On the way out of town I passed a shooting range that advertised "Kids eight and up can shoot!" America.

The temperature as I left read 92 degrees Fahrenheit on a motel sign. I'd given up trying to do the conversion to Celsius. First, because the math was hard, and second because every time I was interested, the answer was: too hot.

It was indeed too hot. The landscape was interesting though. Gone were the granite cliffs. A river ran through parched hills. Lush trees along the riverbanks stood in stark contrast to the yellow land. Ranches scattered across the countryside, just out of eyeshot of one another. Sedimentary rock formations jutted from the hills in all varieties. Single boulders, jagged pinnacles alone or in groups, improbable spires, and whole hills of layered cliffs. I couldn't face crossing another mountain pass into Yellowstone for the third time in three days. I set up camp in the afternoon in a National Forest surrounded by RVs. I sweated in the shade until the sun went down. Then I sweated in the dark.

# Day 70 – Shoshone National Forest to Lake Campground, Yellowstone National Park

I got an early start to the day. By yesterday afternoon it was too hot to appreciate the scenery or really anything other than the three litres of water I drank when I got to camp. Those were appreciated. At 7am the ride was more appealing. The road followed the river upstream into the National Forest. The hills closed in. Dark sandstone formations looked like the mounds of terrifyingly large termites. Boulders and spires were pitted with two-foot-deep caves where the giants lived.

In the quiet cool of the morning, the animals were out in force. I now resumed the safari portion of the tour. I startled two falcons. They screamed, circled and threatened to dive-bomb until I got out of reach of their nest. I'm going to call them falcons, but I didn't have my glasses on, so they could have been aggressive pigeons. A white-tailed deer provided the next excitement, crossing the road with her three fawns. They crossed at a roadworks traffic light, like it was there for them. The mother led, and the spotted fawns trotted in line after her. They stopped in the middle of the road to have a good look at me as I coasted up, then startled as I unclipped to take a photo. I didn't get a photo of the next little family. A momma grizzly and her two cubs were taking a stroll by the road. These National Park celebrities were being harried by the paparazzi. Telephoto lenses stuck out of car windows. One enterprising chap got out of his car with a tripod. Momma bear wasn't hungry, so meandered on through the bushes.

In Yellowstone the geology and the scenery changed again. It got worse. I was expecting to climb the hills, cross the pass, and drop down towards the lake to be overwhelmed by the beauty of the famous Yellowstone caldera. After the pass, I was back to Yukon-style hills and pines. Pines and hills. Wildfire smoke obscured the view. I pushed on and found my campsite. The site was full at midday, except for the hiking and cycling spaces.

Something like four million people a year visit the park, mostly in July and August. Even compared to Banff it was a zoo. The one bright spot of my arrival was a ten-point bull elk. He was having the same reaction as I was to the heat and crowds. He'd decided it was time for a swim. I stopped by the side of the road to observe. I was twenty metres from him through the trees. He turned and gave me a long-suffering look, then went back to his bath. He was used to the attention. In the closest turn-off, the paparazzi had gathered, blocking one lane of the road. The swarms piled out, snapping on camera lenses and frothing at the mouth.

In the afternoon I went on two hikes that weren't worth the mosquito bites. Yellowstone Lake was massive, calm and covered with smoke. I hiked up switchbacks through pines. The blue lake faded into the blue haze. I headed back to camp. The wildlife provided distraction from the smog. Another bull elk wandered into my campsite for a snack. Ten metres from my tent, he seemed relaxed. I was less relaxed. Up close, he was huge. A car door slammed. He sneezed, and scratched his nose with his back leg like a puppy.

# Day 71 – Yellowstone National Park: Lake Campground to Norris Campground

I was on the road before dawn. The paparazzi were already out in force, slamming screaming children into cars. I followed the Yellowstone River through Hayden Valley. The river was fed by hot spring tributaries. In the cold of the morning, it steamed. Beside the road, vents exhaled clouds of steam and filled the air with the smell of sulphur. Buffalo roamed the valley. I passed one unmolested by tourists. He surveyed the river, his head resting on his front legs and the dawn sunlight glinting on his back. Another buffalo stood on the road. Steam rose from his back. He gave me a long look as I rode past, and I tried to appear non-threatening. It's easy to tell when a buffalo is watching. They turn their entire front section towards you. A buffalo is mostly front section, so you have about 900kg of buffalo pointed at your soft bits.

I set out for a hike along the Grand Canyon of the Yellowstone. The road followed the canyon, and the hike followed the road. At 8am people packed the trail. The canyon was still beautiful. 150m-high clay walls painted shades of beige, yellow and red by volcanic action. Vents in the cliffs spouted steam. The river painted a thin blue strip between the cliffs. The sluggish, steamy flow of the Hayden Valley was channelled into the narrow canyon. Rapids frothed as they bounced through. I could see why this is one of the main attractions of the park, but with no way to beat the RV people by hiking, I beat a retreat.

Back onto the park roads. Traffic rolled, sun roasted and RVs passed too close for comfort on the narrow highway. I stopped off at the 'Artist's Paint Pots' for a break from the road madness. The walk from the car park to the pots was uphill. I watched drivers who had just rushed by me on the road struggle up the half-mile track, obese, sweating. The Paint Pots were pits of boiling mud, in different textures and colours. A fizzing spring gushed out of a rock bed covered in dark red algae. I imagined the magma pulsing metres beneath our feet. Since this was America, there were signs everywhere telling people not to step off the walkways into the boiling mud. As I passed one, another tourist remarked, "We should just take all these down and let natural selection run its course." Harried by the crowds, I was in a similar frame of mind.

I searched for a way to escape the seething mass of humanity and found a hike labelled "strenuous". At least this was certain to discourage RV people. Also, 'Monument Geyser Basin' was an impressive name. I stopped at the trailhead, and a car pulled up and a girl got out. I locked my bike to a tree and we started the hike together. Kelly was a physical therapy student driving home to Missouri from Wyoming. Kelly had done even less planning than I had. She had slept in her car the night before after failing to find a campsite. We hiked and chatted up through more switchbacks and more pines. I learned all I need to learn about physical therapy grad school. At the top of the hill she took a picture, "To prove to my parents that not everyone you meet when you travel alone wants to kill you." We looked back across the river valley. It was filled with pine trees. 'Monument Geyser Basin' consisted of three anaemic steam vents. They would have been fine if I wasn't expecting monumental geysers. Kelly was enthusiastic. She told me it was a symptom of being from the Midwest. The key to happiness is low expectations.

After sweating down the switchbacks, I cycled to a campsite full of touring cyclists. My neighbour was an odd guy from Kentucky. He was fifty and riding a carbon fibre bike and no gear. Bill described himself as "slap-packing". He had a chair, but no cooking pot. With no jacket, he used his stove to warm his tent. This was not advised by the manufacturers. The rest of the crowd were more normal. There was a French guy about my age that had also come down from Alaska. We swapped jokes about Kentucky Bill and complained about the crowds. Bertrand told me he met a motorcyclist the day before who arrived, saw the traffic and turned around. By now, I was considering doing the same. The last group was two couples. Carlos and Vega were from San Sebastián, and their friends were from Bilbao and Moscow. They were in their late forties and had both been travelling for more than four years. I had started to feel I was becoming a cycle touring veteran. I had been travelling for fewer months than they had years. They were each carrying four panniers and a big drybag on the back of their bikes. When I joked that most touring cyclists tended to optimise rather than accumulate, Vega laughed at me: "When you are doing a short trip, you know, six months, a year, you can put up with anything," she said. "When you are doing serious travel, you need the little things."

I convinced Carlos and Vega to come with me on a hike called 'Purple Mountain'. It turned out to be what I was now discovering was a typical Yellowstone hike. Endless switchbacks through pines. I had a captive audience to interrogate though. Before starting to cycle tour, Carlos and Vega had spent a year backpacking through Africa. They travelled by local public transport, down the west coast and up the east. After spending yet another night stuck in the bus queue at a border crossing, they decided to get bicycles. They had exceptional stories. Meeting people in Australia that had done eighteen laps of the continent in their RVs, swimming in a lake of Jellyfish in Indonesia, being abducted by a mob in India and forced to come to a wedding party, cycling through Mongolia in winter. They joked that they could forget whole countries: "How was Mongolia?" "Umm, good. Yes, Mongolia was good." "How was the food?" Vega laughed. "Um, yes the food in Mongolia was good." Not many people would be able to forget a Mongolian winter. We achieved the peak, gazed over a hazy, pine-filled valley, and agreed to tell the group the hike was great. I resolved to get the fuck out of Yellowstone.

## Day 72 – Madison, Yellowstone National Park to Jenny Lake, Grand Teton National Park

I fell off my bike again. I pulled up to an intersection, forgot to unclip and toppled over like a felled tree. I thought when I bought these shoes that eventually I would become an expert in their use. There would be a period of adjustment, sure, and that might entail some falls early on, but at some point these would stop. Not so. It was an inauspicious start to the day.

I spent my morning trying to beat the crowds to the 'Grand Prismatic Spring'. This was the last iconic Yellowstone site I wanted to see, an alkaline pool filled with a rainbow of geothermal algae. The view was great, but what really made the experience memorable was hearing someone dressed as a full-grown adult man say to his wife, "I expected the colours to be more vibrant. They were better on the postcard." Tourists are terrible. Goodbye, Yellowstone.

On the road out of the park, a hiker flagged me down and asked directions. Steve was hiking the Continental Divide, 5,000km from Mexico to Banff. He looked like a marine. He asked what Yellowstone was like. I told him it was packed with smoke, RV people and the hiking was shit. He laughed. Steve had done some cycle touring. We discussed the relative merits of cycling and hiking. "You have to get off the bike man, cycle touring is Russian roulette. Hiking is the way to go." Steve had a clear opinion. "I once biked the length of Japan with my ex-girlfriend. She got hit by a drunk driver. He snapped her bike in half." "Oh, so she was ok then?" I asked. "No man, she was fucked," he replied, "broken bones, five operations, it was terrible." I thanked Steve for his fun chat and cycled off.

The rest of the ride was uneventful. By evening, I couldn't remember a single mile of the road out of Yellowstone. There were pines, they lined the road. There were hills, I climbed them. It all looked the same. The Tetons were a different story. As I crested the last pine hill, Teton Lake appeared. Over the

the faint outline of a trail up one face. We asked some hikers passing the other way whether they had attempted it. The wind was too high and the drop too far. The potential for a 360-degree view of the mountains was too inviting. It was a scramble. We clambered over boulders, dislodging stones which fell to the valley below. It was worth it. At the top we looked back down the neighbouring canyons. At 3,330m we were at eye level with all but the largest peaks, the chaotic power of the tectonic forces that created them still visible. Mountain faces of bare rock were covered with jumbled lines where plates had been shoved upwards. Over the back of the peak, Idaho farmland extended into the distance. Faint outlines of yellow fields faded away below the smoke horizon. Someone had formed a sleeping hollow in the broken rock on the top of our peak. I imagined the sunrise would be a breathtaking, freezing, experience.

We descended another canyon across patches of snow painted red by rock dust from the peaks. Erik was slow descending, so I picked huckleberries and quizzed him about his time in the Dutch army. He'd worked as a combat engineer for six years, and served a tour in northern Afghanistan. Erik told me they had accomplished nothing. He said the mission was pure theatre; a checkbox exercise for politicians. They trained policemen to play the role that community police play in Europe. The policemen told them they wanted to keep the Taliban out of the town, not hand out speeding tickets. After Erik came back, he saw a news report showing Taliban soldiers strolling through the town square. Erik said it was an eye-opening experience. "People here and in Holland live in heaven," he said. "People there live in hell." Erik quit the army and got a corporate job.

By the time we reached the bottom of the canyon, our legs were finished. We hitched a lift back along the road to Jenny Lake. There we got the obligatory post-hike ice cream and headed back to camp.

## Day 74 – Jenny Lake

I spent the morning procrastinating in the campsite. Teton National Park was at the nexus of the Continental Divide and TransAmerica cycling routes. Following these set routes was a more social experience than touring alone. I chatted with a crew of three that had met along the TransAmerica. Two guys from Malaysia studying in Philadelphia, and a guy from Lawrence, Kansas, called Jeff. The Malaysians were about to graduate and were struggling with the prospect of moving back to conservative Muslim families after spending four years "smoking, drinking and chilling." Jeff had just returned from living in Costa Rica on a grant from the Department of Defence to learn Portuguese, "To keep an eye on those pesky Brazilians," he said. "I applied to learn Portuguese in Costa Rica and they went for it," Jeff laughed. "The US Government, eh?" We chatted about mountains and hikes. An appreciation of natural beauty unites touring cyclists. While we chatted, an elk wandered through the campground. We fell silent and watched it meander towards the lake. After having what Jeff termed a "social morning", the boys headed off to Yellowstone and I set off to hike Avalanche Canyon.

Avalanche Canyon was advertised in the *Lonely Planet* as one of the better hikes in the Tetons. At the trailhead, I noticed that the hike was not marked. I decided to follow the *Lonely Planet* directions and push on. A hike called Avalanche Canyon was hard to pass up. I walked around a lake. The summit of the Grand Teton wavered in the ripples. After a brief climb, I located the turn-off to Avalanche Canyon. The turn-off was unmarked, but looked well worn. I headed down it, skirting dead trunks that had fallen over the path and pine trees whose branches had colonised the free space. There were footprints on the ground. I decided people must be using the trail and ignored its unkempt state. The bush got thicker and darker. I continued the climb up the canyon. The trail petered out as the people with my

2013 version of the *Lonely Planet* gave up and turned around. I encountered a huckleberry explosion of bear shit. It was so fresh as to be still steaming. I decided discretion was the better part of valour. I jogged back, bear spray in hand, fingering the safety. If you are listening for bears, a red squirrel sounds disturbingly similar. As I re-joined the trail, I encountered a group of hikers. They stared at my unholstered bear spray. I sheepishly returned it to its side pocket.

After this debacle, I wandered around Taggart and Bradley lakes. This was also supposed to be a good day hike, but without an evocatively named canyon to climb, I'd lost momentum. I spent most of the afternoon meandering off the path to pick huckleberries. I was in my swim shorts. This wasn't doing much for my image. Bent over bushes, moustache stained purple, in a singlet and pineapple printed shorts, families gave me a wide berth.

On the way back to the trailhead, I met a couple of National Parks workers improving the trail. We chatted for a while and I told them I'd tried to head up Avalanche Canyon. They had a good laugh at my pineapple shorts: "That is a serious bushwhack. Maybe next time try wearing pants." That felt like a good time to end the expedition.

## Day 75 – Jenny Lake to Teton Village

Jeff and one of the Malaysians had hiked a peak called Static Mountain. They said it was excellent, the toughest hike you could do in the Tetons without ropes. I'd planned to have a leisurely day making my way the 30km to Jackson. After my abortive expedition yesterday though, I felt like I needed to do another hike to give the Tetons their due.

I got up at 6am to make sure I had time to do the hike and get to Jackson early enough to find a campsite, and go meet Tony before the mountain biking competition. When I finished breaking down the tent and packing the bike, the sun was just starting to drape its pink blanket on the mountains. It had not warmed the air. I had lost my gloves, and my fingers froze. With the sun low over the horizon, my shadow stretched for miles. I was in a rush to get to the trailhead, figuring I'd have to be off and running at 7:30am to make it to Jackson in time. The prospect of 1600m of climbing at pace was daunting but exciting. As I cycled, I assessed and reassessed my estimate for how long it would take based on my speed on previous hikes. After a cold 10km I reached the turn-off. The road was closed. I rode down the highway to a cafe and had pancakes for breakfast. Maybe next time.

In Jackson, I learnt that the road was closed because of grizzly activity. The lady in the visitor centre smiled, "Not because the grizzly was doing anything. He was just minding his own business. They closed the road because of the traffic jams people cause. Bear jams." My pancakes felt validated. I asked about places to camp. "No camping here, honey," she laughed. "This is civilisation. You have to pay for civilisation." I cycled out of Jackson to Teton Village. It turned out that Tony and the crew were staying there as well. Once again, luck made up for poor planning. We met up in the evening for drinks. Frozen huckleberry daiquiris. God bless America.

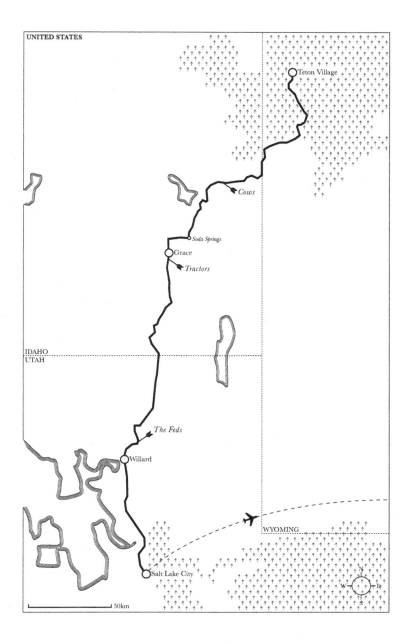

UNITED STATES

Teton Village

Cows

Soda Springs

Grace

Tractors

IDAHO
UTAH

The Feds

Willard

WYOMING

Salt Lake City

N
W   E
S

50km

# Day 76 – Teton Village, Montana Enduro Series

When I arrived at the mountain biking competition the guys were halfway through the check-in process. There were 150 riders kitted out and milling around. Everyone was busy. Tony was taking photos, his crew were checking people in, setting up timing bracelets and getting riders to sign injury waivers. The waivers were important. This was not an injury-free sport. One of Tony's buddies had broken both his neck and his back in separate incidents. He was still crushing trails. As was his son. Everyone had an injury story. Tony was proud of a time he had broken a rib going over a jump and stayed on the bike.

With everyone busy, I hung around the bottom of the course eating the sponsor products. I handed out goodie bags to the riders. There were few no-shows. One for the doctor, I ate their protein bars. Eventually one of the guys, TJ, gave me a lift pass and told me to go explore the course (aka to piss off). I headed up to the top of the first chairlift and the start of Stage 2 of the race. The race already had its first injury, a forty-year-old man with a broken hand. Mountain biking was a challenging sport to watch live. There weren't many places on the course that you could stand and watch more than one corner of the race. The most interesting thing that happened was a bear wandering across the course, stopping the race. Bear don't care.

I didn't feel that I was getting a good sense of the sport watching riders shoot through single corners. I headed down to the bottom of the hill. I met Tony at the organisers' tent and he offered to let me do a couple of laps on his bike: "That Taliban green weapon over there." Why not, I was a cyclist now, right? How hard could it be? I got back on the chairlift with the bike and headed up to try the stage that I had been watching riders cruise down all morning. It was described to me as "flowy" which meant there were no rocks or roots as obstacles and no major jumps. I did not achieve this flow. On the first corner I lost my nerve, grabbed the front brakes and went straight over the handlebars. I was fine, but my shorts were not. I managed once down the mountain. By the end of the course, I started to see the joy in the sharp turns through the trees. I was acutely aware though of the thin line separating me from going straight through one of those turns straight into one of those trees. Tony laughed at me when I said one run was enough. I went off to buy a pair of underwear so I didn't end up on a list.

The race ended. I helped pack up by going to buy beers. As the guys packed the equipment, various Jackson Hole staff came up and congratulated them on the event. It seemed like this was a big day for the resort and for Tony and his crew. It was great to be a part of. Tony loaded me down with the remaining sponsor treats that I hadn't managed to pillage in the morning. I had enough granola bars, protein bites and energy gels to keep me jacked all the way to Salt Lake City. As my goody bag filled, I ticked off breakfasts where I wouldn't have to eat oats. Everyone was in a great mood as we headed off for dinner.

## Day 77 – Teton Village, WY to Grace, ID

I left Jackson Hole needing to put some miles on the bike. Staying to watch the mountain biking meant that I had three days to go 450km to catch my flight to a family reunion. Having the hard deadline of a flight put a little pressure on. The wildfire smoke was the thickest it had been. There wasn't much call to stop and enjoy the view. I had a tailwind and I was on the downhill side of the Continental Divide. The road followed the Snake River downstream. I set out to do my first 200km day.

The hills were mild, the wind favourable, and the free protein bars delicious. 200km looked achievable. Google wasn't going to let me off that easy. At one point, I felt myself heading too far east. I checked the map. Indeed, I'd missed the turn-off. The reason that I had discounted that particular road as the turn-off was that it wasn't really a road. More of a track. There was no cell reception, so I couldn't check the length of the detour that it would mean staying on the highway. I had to make a decision. The track was marked with a road sign: "Snake River Cutoff". That sounded like a shortcut. The sign itself didn't bode well though, being battered almost beyond recognition. I decided to roll the dice.

After the first 5km of wrist-jarring, knee-rattling road corrugations I regretted this decision. I saw no cars. In the proud tradition of navigation by Google Maps, the track deteriorated as I got further down it. I dreaded another high gate, a 'no trespassing' sign and a long trip back. I saw no cars, but I did see a lot of cows. The whole area was open range, so the cows were not fenced in. I found something strangely menacing about the cows. It could be their size, the way they tended to stand in the middle of the road, or the way that they watched me as I rode past, slowly turning their heads in unison. The whole herd, staring, chewing, considering eating me alive. I finally passed a car coming the other direction. I watched him closely for a sign that I was in his driveway: shock, anger, drawing a firearm. I waved. He waved back. I celebrated.

The rest of the 'Snake River Cutoff' passed without incident. Google Maps, in a final act of deviousness, tried to take me down a mining road. It was beautifully paved, but guarded by signs with flashing lights saying, "Active haul road, no entry". I stuck to the gravel. As the road re-joined the main road, I pissed on the last of the gravel and resolved to stay on highways with numbers. My avoidance of the haul road was validated as I passed its exit onto the highway. It looked shit.

I'd bribed myself through the gravel with a promise of a good dinner and a good rest in the first town. This being Sunday and this being Jesus country, everything was closed. I settled for a burger and an American-sized milkshake from the local fast food joint. Now that I was past the gravel and within sight of my 200km goal, the goal took over. Normally, I left myself 20km to look for a campground. This went out the window. By the time I got to 200km I was absolutely done. I had no more energy or creativity to find a campsite. I caved and got a motel.

## Day 78 – Grace, ID to Willard Creek, UT

I woke up early. My knees were not in good shape and one part of me regretted the long ride the day before. On the other hand, there were now only 240km to Salt Lake City and my flight. It felt good to have put a serious dent in the total. I set out from my motel slowly. After yesterday's focus on distance, I resolved to stop and take more photos. The early morning sun shone down on potato fields. Rays piercing clouds gave halos to hilltops. It looked like a biblical scene. That explained the churches.

As the day wore on, smoke dulled the light and shaded the horizon. Photo opportunities focused on American Pride. The Pride was strong in southern Idaho. Grace, where I had spent the night, had flags flying from every lamppost. The steely glare of a bald eagle backed by the stars and stripes surveyed passers-by. My first photo was a farmer driving a large, John Deere-green piece of farming machinery. A metre-long exhaust pipe stuck up from the back of the three-metre-tall machine. The farmer had hung an American flag from the pipe. It was so large it almost reached the ground. I stared. The farmer caught me staring. I waved. He glared, like an eagle. The next photo opportunity was a bright red pickup truck. The driver had his Star-Spangled Banner flying from a pole he'd installed behind the cab. It flew back three metres, past the end of the tray. The installation looked professional, and permanent. I saw him coming out of a supermarket. I don't think he was doing anything special, just going about his normal day, celebrating America.

Cycling the long, straight country roads, I was reminded of Dave, who I met coming out of Yoho. Dave said the hardest thing for him was to enjoy each day at a time, not to focus on the future. During his first tour across Europe, he was distracted by how good it would be when they reached their destination. Their destination was Basel, so I'm not sure exactly what he was focused on. Dave said he didn't enjoy the last four days, "it was just Basel, Basel, Basel." Now I was obsessed with Salt

Lake City, which had about as much to recommend it as Basel. Maybe Dave was flying out of Basel.

I crossed into northern Utah. It looked very much like southern Idaho. In any case, at the first town I stopped for Mexican food. Two burritos and a taco. This was a great decision. For the eight minutes it took me to cover this trough of food in hot sauce and shovel it into my face, Salt Lake City was completely absent from my thoughts.

I'd planned to start looking for a campsite earlier in the day. Salt Lake City and its commuter towns extended north along the Great Salt Lake. The constant population looked like it would make it hard to camp. Before this, there was a 20km stretch of hills. I searched every inch for campsites. There were none. Utah landowners were fond of six-foot-high wire mesh fencing. These fences were meant to stop livestock from wandering onto the road. They also rather effectively stopped passing cyclists from finding somewhere to camp out of view of the highway. I popped out the other side of the hills and into the urban sprawl.

I considered my options. I could put another two hours on the bike and get a motel at sunset. I could look for an urban campsite, but chances seemed low. I was loath to skip camping for two nights in a row. I saw a sign for a State Park and turned off the road. They wanted to charge me $35 to camp. This wouldn't have been so bad, but it was the same price as an RV. I tried my charm. That failed immediately. I couldn't take becoming an RV person, so I left. I cycled south and looked for a route back into the hills I had just crossed. I spotted a gap in the houses where power lines had been built. I found a hiking trail coming off a dead-end side road. Perfect! I cycled up to the hiking trail, locked my bike in some bushes, and set off with my camping pannier. After fighting my way up the trail for twenty minutes, I scrambled up a ridge. A small camp-able patch of ground nestled between sagebrush bushes. The trail continued up into a red walled canyon. Back down the hill and over the town, the sun was a dark red balloon, settling into the Great Salt Lake. Dragonflies flitted from bush to bush, bright blue and huge. I set up my tent and sleeping gear, congratulating myself all the while. I reached for my phone to document this urban camp success story. I'd left it on the bike. It was a sweaty run down and back to catch the sunset.

## Day 79 – Willard Creek to Salt Lake City

I woke up to a grey sky after a long night. As soon as it got too dark to shift my campsite, the wind took hold of every piece of loose fabric. Snapping tent flaps sounded like machine gun shots. In the end I slept, I woke, the world turned.

I scrambled down the hill and discovered my bike was gone. This, of course, was to some extent my own fault. I'd locked the rear wheel to the frame, but there was nothing to lock the bike to, so I just pushed it into the bushes. I had done this too often in less populated places and had gotten complacent. I stood reflecting on my stupidity. After a minute of reflection, I wondered what the fuck I was going to do about my flight the next morning. I'd moved my passports from my backpack to my panniers when I went hiking in Grand Teton. This seemed like a good idea at the time. Less so now. I wandered down the road.

A lady walking a puppy called out a good morning and asked how I was doing. I told her all my problems at once. She offered to give me a lift to Salt Lake, and to call the police. This sounded better than what I had planned, which was nothing. After a few minutes on hold with the Police Janet decided to just text the local police chief, her buddy. She showed up in five minutes. Jean was in her mid-fifties, with short grey hair, and a grey T-shirt tucked into work pants. She had a strong handshake and didn't smile. Jean took over. Janet departed, wishing me luck.

Jean asked me a few questions about where I'd parked the bike, where I was camping, and what had been lost. We got in her truck and drove back up the hill to the canyon to "examine the crime scene." Crime scene! We parked and walked back to where I had hidden the bike. She inspected the bike tracks in the sand. As we walked back down towards the car from my hiding spot, she told me to stop. "Which set of tracks is from where you brought the bike in?" Jean asked. I showed her. "Ok," Jean walked along the tracks, pointing, "so here is where they dragged the bike out. Show me your shoes." I showed her my shoes with the pedal cleat underneath. "So, these prints here are yours," she said, "and the ones on the left of the bike track there are whoever took your bike." Police work! Jean got out her camera and took photos of the footprints. I filled out a list of the stuff that I'd lost and sent her photos of my bike. Jean gave me a lift down to Ogden where I could get a train to Salt Lake City. On the way, after 45 minutes on the phone, I was told I would be able to get on the plane with my driver's licence. I asked the woman on the line for a confirmation number. She didn't have one. I asked for her to send me an email confirmation. She re-sent my original booking reference. This did not inspire confidence. I asked for her name and employee reference number. "Sure thing! My name is Ashley, and my employee signature is "A-S..." I waited. "Is that it? A-S?" I asked. "Yes," A-S replied. Jean laughed, "It should be A-S-S." We were getting along. When we got to the train station in Ogden, Jean printed my police report and gave me her mobile number. She told me to call if I had any trouble at the airport.

I reflected that if Janet hadn't said hello and offered to help, I would have been in an Uber, without a police report, and trying to figure my shit out from Salt Lake after a $70 cab ride. Instead I got a lift to a $5 train, witnessed some real detective work, got a printed police report and the police chief's mobile number. Everything is fun once. At least this simplified bike transport. I had lost my clothes though, so now I was riding Utah public rail in a sweat-encrusted cutoff singlet and a pair of Lycra bike shorts. At least I still had my helmet and my pannier of camping equipment. I looked like a lost cyclist, rather than a hipster.

I got to Salt Lake City and, out of consideration for other passengers on my flight the next day, went to buy some non-Lycra shorts and a T-shirt with sleeves. I chatted to the shop assistant. She felt sorry for me and dug out some free clothes from the back of the shop, "To show you not everyone in Utah is a dick." I went to a supermarket to buy a new razor. It was called Rancho Market. Everyone spoke Spanish. Apparently Salt Lake City is twenty percent Hispanic and Latino. Who knew? There was mariachi music playing. A little boy looked at me and gave me a nod, "Cool moustache, mister." This improved my day immensely. I went next door for tacos and margaritas. They were legit.

# Day 80 – Salt Lake City to Boston

The police report and my driver's licence were sufficient to get on the plane. Well, sufficient along with a little "enhanced interrogation". It wasn't quite waterboarding, but I did get a thorough rub down. The TSA agent was Julio, a Latino man in his mid-fifties with a brilliant moustache. He led me through security and brought me to a stop behind a screen. With a long look in my eye, he said, "I will touch you." I thought he was joking. Julio was not joking. He explained in slow, graphic detail the search process. I'm not sure how this made up for me not having a passport, but I was sure glad I didn't have a kilo of meth strapped to my inner thigh. When Julio found out I was cycling he got excited. He was a keen mountain biker. As he searched my bags we talked about mountain biking. He loved the scenery. I felt like we made a connection.

In the airport there were crowds of young Mormons on their way to mission. They had the same suits as the Delta employees. The Delta employees looked unimpressed.

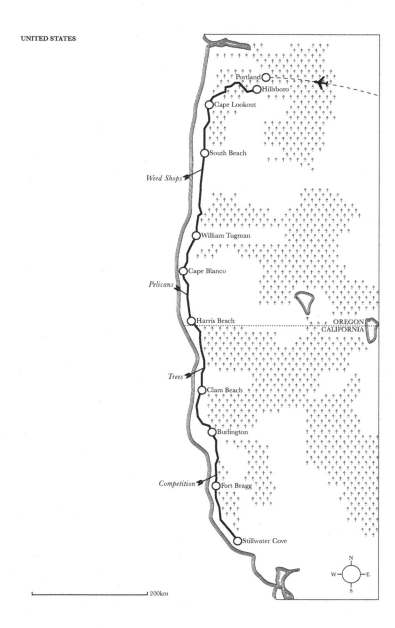

UNITED STATES

Portland
Hillsboro
Cape Lookout

South Beach

*Weed Shops*

William Tugman

Cape Blanco

*Pelicans*

Harris Beach

OREGON
CALIFORNIA

*Trees*

Clam Beach

Burlington

*Competition*

Fort Bragg

Stillwater Cove

N
W    E
S

⌐_____⌐ 200km

## Day 81 – Portland, OR

I had minimal interest in going south from Utah through Nevada or Arizona to get to Mexico. Six weeks in the desert? Hard pass. I skipped that shit and flew to Portland. It was a journey, not a race. After three months inland, I looked forward to the Pacific Coast. I almost made $500 on the way there. I agreed to give up my seat on my overbooked flight out of JFK and stood by the gate until everyone had boarded. Two people missed the flight and I was shown to my seat. That $500 would have gone a long way to replacing my bike. Such is life. In deference to my economic circumstances I took public transport from the airport to the hostel.

I woke up and walked across town to a bike shop. My plan was to either buy a new bike, or to build one at a bike cooperative. Portland was rich in bike cooperatives. The thought of building a bike was attractive. It was cheap. I also thought it could be handy to learn something more about bike maintenance than how to change a tyre.

Early on a Saturday morning, the sunny summer streets of Portland were filled with homeless people. There are roughly 15,000 long-term homeless people in Portland, a city of 700,000. To put that number in context, there are 9,000 in London, where the Mayor has called it a "national disgrace". London has 9 million people. Many of Portland's homeless had set up semi-permanent tent camps. Oregon closed the Dammasch State Hospital, a mental institution just south of Portland, in 1995 and released the majority of the patients housed there onto the streets. In reaction to growing homeless numbers, and a declining supply of shelter beds, the mayor of Portland passed a "Safe Sleep Policy" in 2015. This allowed homeless people to set up tents overnight on city sidewalks. The policy provoked a predictable reaction from residences with homes and businesses that served them. It was revoked in 2016. The homeless people, predictably, didn't disappear. They, and their tents, were still very much in residence, such as it was.

Apart from the slowly collapsing socio-economic structure, Portland was as hipster as advertised. Yuppies brunched, walls were covered in art, and shops displayed signs welcoming all customers regardless of race, sex, identity etc. They didn't mention Republicans. Or the homeless.

After that cheerful introduction to the city, I arrived at the bike shop and went for a test ride. It felt great to get back in the saddle. How quickly fades the memory of bruised sit bones and creaking knees. I chatted to the salesman about my plan to build a bike. Omar had done a lot of bike touring. He didn't think much of my plan. He wouldn't, I guess. I was still tempted to skip the comparison shopping. Financial guilt got the better of me and I forced myself to at least go check out the bike co-ops.

On the way to the bike co-op, I passed a man with a perfectly trimmed moustache. He wore suspenders and sat behind a typewriter with a sign saying, "Custom poetry: your poem, your price." Back to the other Portland.

I got to the bike co-op, took one look at the piles of assorted bike parts and decided to buy a new bike. Sick of slipping on rocks, I got some new shoes as well, without cleats. What are credit cards for, anyway? Play to your strengths.

In the evening, I went for beers with a friend of a friend. Bryan was my age and had won the tech startup lottery. He was now working on his jazz guitar. Portland is where young rich people come to retire, and a city of contrasts.

## Day 82 – Portland

I spent the morning on trip prep. On the way to the grocery store downtown, I passed at least fifty homeless people in various states of physical and mental disarray. I watched as people wandered into the road, disoriented, stopping traffic. This seemed to be common. No one got mad, this wasn't New York. Everyone stopped and a passer-by would try to usher the wayward person back to the sidewalk. I passed an ambulance with the slogan: "Meeting Every Customer's Needs." Conflating patients and customers seemed appropriate.

Prep done, I took myself on a bike tour. Coffee shops, breweries, food trucks and vintage stores. Kombucha on tap. Cat accessories. Artisanal donuts. In the leafy Portland suburbs, the homeless people thinned out and you could almost forget about them.

In the evening, I met two more friends of friends for dinner. Both were American-born Chinese and grew up in Portland. I asked how the city had changed. "It's just gentrified everywhere," Amy said. "There are no Chinese people left in Chinatown anymore. It's too expensive to live downtown. But, now we have artisanal donuts."

# Day 83 – Portland to Cape Lookout State Park

Omar had recommended I take the train out of Portland and follow the Nestucca River to the coast. Now I'd cheated and flown to Oregon, it could be a slippery slope for the cycle touring rules. The train was like any commuter train on a Wednesday morning. No one was smiling except the drunks. I wasn't sure it was worth the twenty free kilometres.

Rural Oregon looked a lot like rural anywhere in America. Pickup trucks, American flags, small farms. More of the trash by the side of the road was in Whole Foods bags. I crossed into the Willamette Valley, wine country. Interspersed between cornfields were now rows of manicured vines. At the start of September, the vines were in full fruit, ripe to be picked. One town had a public 'stomp' event. It was advertised with a picture of a man stomping on grapes in a tub. He looked like he was having fun. I wanted to stick around, but it was in a week. The vineyards reminded me that the worst thing about going on holiday was it just made you want to take more holidays.

Dreams of wine faded as I started to climb. The road was empty. I cycled uphill through a silent forest. The trees towered over me, the peace only disturbed by my panting. I was starting to really appreciate the forest when I saw a sign saying, "Tree Farm, Planted 1991". I was basically riding through a tall timber cornfield. I crossed the farm boundary into Nestucca State Forest. It didn't look different, but it felt more authentic.

Daydreaming, I veered onto the shoulder. The shoulder was sand, with a two-inch drop from the road. I weaved, out of control, into the middle road and came to a stop. I was upright, both feet planted on the road. This was a new experience. I appreciated my new cleat-free setup.

By the time I got out of the Nestucca River valley, I had done 1,000m of climbing. After two weeks off the bike, I felt it. I was now very grateful for the train. After crossing the hills, I was within 10km of the coast. I felt like the work was done. Not so. The last climb to the Cape Lookout State Park was a soul crushing 250 vertical metres. I read later in a route guide that "cape is a four letter word for hill." Cape climbed, I got my first view of the Oregon coast. It was worth it. The campground was on a long spur of land. From the top of the cape, I could see for kilometres along the spit. The sky was cloudless blue, and the afternoon sun shone off the sea. Orderly sets of waves the full length of the spit broke on clean white sand. I stopped to take a photo at a turnout. There was another guy there. He had stopped his car, pulled out a chair and sat eating muesli bars. He grinned at me, "It doesn't get better than this, does it?"

The campsite had a hiker-biker section. It was $8 a night, right on the beach and came with a shower. There were similar campsites all down the Oregon and California coasts. I might have camped by the side of the road for the last time. After the climbing, the sweating, and the beauty of the surf, I had ambitions to go for a swim. This lasted to the water's edge. Oregon is not California.

I camped next to a guy in a hammock with a camouflage tarp. It looked like a serious setup. Jean was from Montreal and was going down and around the Americas. That's easy to say and hard to do. From Oregon to Patagonia down the west coast, so far so normal. Jean then planned to ride north up the east coast. That route included the east coast of Brazil, French Guiana, Suriname, Guyana and Venezuela. I asked him if he was sure there were roads. He wasn't, he hadn't looked. He had sold his apartment and quit his job in Montreal though, so I guess he was going to find out. Where there's a will there's a way. Unless there's quicksand, then you're fucked Jean.

# Day 84 – Cape Lookout to South Beach State Park

I woke up to the sound of waves on the beach and the smell of breakfast on a campfire. No trucks, no hordes of bugs in the tent flap, no unidentified mammals in the bushes. I wondered if the route down the coast was going to be too comfortable to be interesting. It took me a long time to pull myself away from the campground. I had to climb back up the cape.

I did it. It wasn't as bad as I thought it was going to be. It's never as bad as you think it's going to be. There was a sea fog covering the coastline. At the top of the hill I broke through most of the fog. Sunbeams speckled through trees and reflected off wisps of clouds.

The bike route diverged from Highway 101 onto the old road south. Off the main route, the road was empty. One car passed me in 20km. The road looked like it had been deserted for years. Moss hung from the trees and covered the sides of the bridges. The surrounding forest was undisturbed by homes. Trees hung over the road and cut out whatever sunlight the fog had missed. My only company were blue jays. They resented the intrusion and squawked as I passed.

I appreciated the diversion from the highway even more when I rejoined it. It was a highway, and it was busy. I somehow had thought that 101 would be some sort of rural highway, unfrequented by cars. This was misguided. There were towns, and people were driving between them. The first major town I passed through was Lincoln City. Lincoln City proved the US could give the UK a run for its money when it came to faded, disused coastal towns. There was an outlet mall. I didn't stop.

The highway had signs every kilometre telling you were either entering or leaving a Tsunami Danger Zone. I loved these signs. What the hell are you supposed to do with that information? If a tsunami hits, you are one hundred percent finished. You can't drive away from it, it's a literal wall of water. The Cascadia

Subduction Zone runs down the full Oregon coast. If that went, this whole place would be ocean.

The fog persisted through the day. It could not hide the brilliance of the coastline. The cycle route followed the coast. Sometimes this was on the 101 and I had to share the experience, good as it was, with heavy traffic. Other times the path diverged, and a lane would cut closer to the sea. At one bend on the 101, a cliff fell away thirty metres from the roadside. At the bottom, a pack of seals basked. I stopped and rolled the bike back down the shoulder to get a closer look. This was poorly received by the traffic, but the seals were fascinated. Curious whiskered faces turned towards me. One treaded water beside the group. He rolled onto his back to check me out, flippers flapping. I passed more headlands. At another, I stopped to watch a pod of grey whales. They blew spray and dived, meandering down the coast. In between seal coves and whale watching headlands, creeks ran through wetlands into the sea. Herons abandoned fishing positions, launching themselves on white wings as I rode by. Oregon safari was less intimidating than the Yukon.

The road was well set up for cycling. The bridges, less so. In the afternoon, I crossed the worst piece of cycling architecture I had encountered on the trip: a 300m-long bridge across Yaquina Bay. No sidewalk, zero shoulder, less chill. A tennis ball-sized flashing light above the road was there to alert drivers of cyclists. It didn't work. If 'cape' was a euphemism for hill, 'historic bridge' was code for death trap.

The only thing more impressive than the coastline were the campsites. Hot showers! Free coffee! $8! There was a group of middle-aged cyclists travelling together. One came over and introduced himself while I was cooking dinner. I went over to the group to chat. They had come from all over the world to tour together down the coast for three weeks. One was from Canada, one from the UK, one from South Africa and a few from various states in the US. The guy who organised it, Scott, set up a route plan, put up an ad in various cycling forums and asked people to pay a $40 'commitment fee', which they got back if they turned up. Two people hadn't turned up and the group was spending their commitment fees on beer. We swapped touring stories. Riding down the coast seemed like it was going to be a social experience.

## Day 85 – South Beach State Park to William Tugman State Park

It was a cold morning in the campground. I had not replaced my jacket after the bike theft. California is warm, right? Oregon was not. I shivered as I set out in my long underwear. I recalled how ridiculous I thought the guy from Kentucky in Yellowstone was; no jacket, heating his tent with his stove. Now I had become him.

To warm up, I stopped for coffee in a town called Yachats. I have no idea how that is pronounced. The coffee shop was packed, vegan and sold hemp. You could get your fix in gummy bears, dark chocolate or one of their smoothies: "Cheech and Chai", "Snoop Dogg Herrrbal Latte", or "Get Toasted". They sold bright yellow stickers with an octopus in a top hat carrying a cane and the slogan "Keep Yachats Eccentric". Of course, it was too hip for people to take much interest in me. I was left to daydream about how eccentric Yachats was.

After the coffee the sun came out. The spiritual sun, as well as the actual ball of burning gas. The road onwards hugged the coast. It was tough to not stop every few minutes to take another photo of the coastline in the sunshine. Then it wasn't. I now had sufficient photos of waves rolling into long deserted beaches around rocky headlands. Only another 2,000km of this to Mexico.

I stopped for lunch in a pullout overlooking a pack of sea lions. I sat on a stone wall dangling my legs over a sixty-metre drop to the surf. Sea lions played in the waves below. A pack of twenty sunbathed on a rock and cheered on the ones playing in the surf in rough, enthusiastic barks. A group fished in the surf crashing against the cliffs, letting themselves be washed against the rocks and then accelerating as the wave subsided to catch stunned fish. A couple of youths play-fought further out. A mother and a baby dove side by side. It wasn't a bad spot for lunch. As I got up to go, five pelicans in formation flew in a close diagonal line a foot off the water, just missing the crest of each swell.

After lunch, I came across a local attraction called the 'Sea Lion Elevator'. This was an elevator down the cliff into what was advertised as America's largest sea cave. The cave was inhabited by a pack of sea lions. I got there and was told there were no sea lions in residence. There was an extensive gift shop though. This being America, it was doing a roaring trade. Who needs animals? I asked a bored attendant why there were a wealth of sea lions a quarter-mile down the road, while the caves below were empty. They were different types of sea lions, one Californian, one Pacific. She pointed out the difference to me on a chart. I think it was something in the shape of the ears.

The sea lion elevator was at the top of a hill. To the south was the Oregon Dunes State Park. From the top of the hill, this showed great promise as a cycling route. A 200m strip of dunes separated the forest from the sea. The dunes undulated toward the horizon. The road did not go through the dunes. I rode through strip mall towns and across historically narrow bridges to camp.

There was one other wanderer at the campsite. John came to talk to me as I was cooking dinner. He was in his mid-thirties, wild locks of blond hair coagulating into dreadlocks. John was very stoned. From what I could decipher, John had been hitchhiking around the US after losing his house down in Galveston, Texas in Hurricane Harvey the year before. He had been to 35 states, hitchhiking, hiking, and sampling the local greenery. We talked about hitchhiking. John said he was trying to bring it back. "I'm chill man, I give smiles, I chat to people, I keep them awake if they are tired." He grinned, "I mean, everyone I rode with is still alive." That doesn't come across as funny when I write it down, but I was pretty sure he hadn't killed anyone.

## Day 86 – William Tugman State Park to Cape Blanco Lighthouse

The morning ride circled Coos Bay, a developed harbour protected by a peninsula. I rode through endless small towns. There were more weed shops than gas stations. "Coastal Highways", "King Kannabis", "Wayhigh 101". Each one was a shack more run-down than the last. King Kannabis had a huge golden crown logo on its billboard and a broken window in the door. Oregon collected $102m in tax revenue on more than $600m of recreational marijuana sales in 2019. You don't need a fancy shop to sell drugs. I read that twenty percent of that tax money goes back into mental health and addiction treatment, which seemed like a good start.

I stopped for coffee at a cafe in the bay. The owner was a character. Long curly grey hair tied back in a puffy ponytail, whip thin and bouncing around behind the counter. Steve asked every single person that came in at 8am where they were from, where they had come from this morning and where they were headed. He was from Canada. He'd taught in the local school for thirty years. He was excited to name all the towns along my route through Alberta and Idaho. He named all the towns along my bike ride south for the day as well, one after the other, and told me to go to an ice cream shop called 'Face Rock Creamery'. What a name. How could I turn that down?

Pre-Face Rock, I stopped in at the South Slough National Estuarine Research Reserve. My guide book promised green herons. Out front, the reserve had a map with 10km of marked trails. I wasn't in the mood to do a full hike in the middle of the day only 40km into cycling. I tried to ask the Ranger whether she would recommend anything specific. This was like asking Santa if she thought kids liked Christmas. "Oh, I'd do all the trails," Joan said. Any in particular? She looked taken aback, "No, none in particular. Just all of them, they are all excellent." You wouldn't say that one is more excellent than the others?

"Oh, it's such a nice day, you should really do all of them." Ok, fine. Joan let me park my bike in the centre. She told me I'd be gone a while.

The path down the hill was lined with forest. Not shit forest like in the Yukon, all pines and no view, but a dense green forest with more than one type of tree, layers of underbrush and birds in the branches. Blue jays squawked at me. With their bright blue bodies, black chests and heads and pointed mohawks, they were as noisy as they looked. The forest was every shade of green. Sun shone through a patchwork of birch, spruce and pine boughs above, dappling a forest floor covered with ferns.

I got down to the marshes. There were no herons in sight. Not green herons, not blue herons, not white herons. No colour herons. I saw a seagull. I walked around the loop trails for a little while, got lost, regretted not taking a photo of the trail map at the start, and had to retrace my steps up through the forest. It was still green, still peaceful.

Face Rock Creamery was all that Steve had promised. It was Saturday and sunny. Ice cream had drawn a crowd. I joined a long line. I asked the woman in front of me whether this was the line for ice cream. "Oh no honey," she smiled, "this is the line for samples, if you want to actually buy something you go over there." I bought an ice cream the size of my head for $2.50. Three and a half days of cycling without eating enough ice cream to kill a kindergarten class; I knew there was something missing from Oregon. After the ice cream, I joined the line for a course of free samples. By the end, I was double-sticking cheese squares with the best of the plebs. The combination of ice cream and free cheese got my legs to the end of the day.

I camped at Cape Blanco State Park. As I arrived, the evening fog rolled in off the sea. In camp, I met a hiker, Pete. He was doing the Oregon coast trail. It sounded hard. When he wasn't walking on the beach or in the dunes, he was on Highway 101, crossing the same narrow, sidewalk-free bridges I was, but on foot. Pete was originally from Massachusetts but had moved out to Portland in 2012. "Everyone who moved there after me ruined it," he said with a grin. "$7 a beer is the going rate now." Pete was another Portland retiree. He'd saved $100k by the time he was 28 and had started doing serious hikes along the Appalachian trail. He was now thirty-two, had finished the

Pacific Crest Trail, the Continental Divide Trail, and three more 1000-mile+ hikes. He had also finished the $100k. He had the beard to match his achievements. Pete smoked two heavy joints and we solved all of America's problems.

## Day 87 – Cape Blanco to Harris Beach

I got up at dawn and went to explore the Cape Blanco lighthouse. It was listed as historic. This was America though, so it was just historic because it was built in 1867. London has Wetherspoons older than that. The fog had all but lifted. The sun crested the hills, and sunbeams illuminated the last remnants of mist in the inlets along the coast. I could see why there was a lighthouse. Islands of rock rose up from the sea on both sides of the cape. The sun, the fog and the rocks made for great photos, but I wouldn't have wanted to be trying to sail around the point in a dense fog and an onshore wind.

After a morning coffee, I passed two cyclists. James was English and Mary was from New York state. They were the beer-money providers of the group in my campsite three days earlier. Mary had finished four years as an Army medic in Alaska and had been travelling ever since. She quizzed me about the female solo cyclists I'd met along the way. I thought for a while, "Well, there was one." James had no clue what he was doing with his life, so I tried to talk him into cycling to Argentina. Why not? Neither of them had adjusted to Alaska pace cycling yet, so I pushed on.

Today's ride was through the most famous section of Oregon coast, the Samuel Boardman Scenic Corridor. It looked pretty much like the rest of the coast, but there were more rocks in the sea. Small islands dotted the coastline. Some were covered in trees, others in bird shit. They all made for photo opportunities, with the associated crowds of RV people. There were rocks that looked like other things. 'Whale Rock' which looked like a whale, 'House Rock' which looked like a house. There were rocks with gaps in the middle. 'Arch Rock' was an arch over a gap, 'Natural Bridges' was a bridge over a gap, and 'Rainbow Rock', which was either a rainbow over a gap, or a rock that looked like a rainbow. Choose your own adventure. After the eighth something-shaped rock I started Googling them to see whether the picture was worth the tourists. Then I stopped Googling and started skipping them.

Adventures in the hiker-biker campsite were unremarkable except for a skunk. The little bastard had no fear, no shame. He strutted through the campsite like he owned it, stopped for a snack under my table and continued towards my tent. Washing skunk out of my gear in a campsite toilet did not sound like it would be fun even once. I shone my phone light at him to check whether he was trying to get into my tent. I'm not sure what I meant to do if he was. Beady eyes glittered back at me in the night. He paused his scratching for snacks to give me a withering stare. I didn't merit long of his attention. He turned back to his search for granola crumbs. My neighbour's tent presented more fertile hunting ground. I retired to sounds of panic.

## Day 88 – Harris Beach, OR to Clam Beach, CA

The best thing about summer ending was being awake at dawn. Further north in July, dawn had been at 3am. As I rode out of the campground, the lowest clouds had the remnants of pink from the sunrise. The islands that dotted the coastline were lit up with a yellow glow. Today, California!

Redwoods! I got my first introduction to redwoods riding up a hill into Del Norte Coast Redwood State Park. The highway went straight through it. There was not much room to stop and appreciate the trees as the cars flew by. They demanded to be appreciated. I looked over the side of a cliff and saw a trunk as thick as I was tall. The trunk was perfectly bare of branches, with thick maroon bark. I looked down. It disappeared below the road. I looked up. I couldn't see the top. The bare trunk disappeared into the canopy. I realised I was looking at only half the tree. My excitement was not shared by people on the highway, my constant stops to take photos audibly not appreciated.

Prairie Creek State Park was quieter and more conducive to honk-free photography. The cycle route diverged from the 101 through the park. At the first opportunity to get off and walk among the trees, I ditched my bike behind a sign and set off down a path. No lessons had been learnt in Utah. The half-mile loop through a redwood forest was deserted except for a group of middle-aged motorcycle tourists in full leathers. They asked me to take a photo of them arm in arm. After they left, I was alone with the trees. It was silent. I walked down the path with my head tilted back, staring at the tops of the trees far above. They were so far away that when I looked from the bottom of a trunk all the way to the top of the tree I felt a hint of vertigo. The smallest of the redwoods were bigger than the largest white pines in Idaho. The atmosphere was eerie. The silence, the coolness, the darkness, and the presence of these huge living things was overwhelming. I reached out to touch a tree. I expected something profound to happen. I had the feeling that when my hand touched the bark something would change. I'm not sure what. Nothing did. It was, after all, just a tree.

After the walk through the trees, the route continued through the State Park. The road narrowed. The trees towered over it on either side. Other paths led into the forest. Cars clustered round each trailhead with people taking photos, setting off up the path and just staring upward, mesmerised. I'd had my spiritual moment for the day and appreciated the trees at speed. It is dangerous to ride through that sort of scenery. Often I caught myself daydreaming, staring off into the forest instead of looking at the road. I was glad to get back out to the coast and the more manageable scenery of rocky islands along the shoreline and the afternoon sun setting into the Pacific.

It wasn't all sunshine and rainbow rocks. I crossed the state line into California and passed through Crescent City. It struck me that a town must be particularly shit when its only feature to inspire a name is its shape. After this curved strip mall of a town, there was a hill. At the bottom of the hill was a sign saying, "No shoulder for 10 miles, watch out for cyclists". It doesn't work like that. Just because there is no shoulder, people don't give you more room. This is the 101, and the 101 is a highway. If there are cyclists on a highway people just get pissed off. They were indeed pissed off. I was honked at. I turned my back light on and hoped for the best. Halfway up the hill, and all the way in the middle of nowhere, I stopped to give a guy sitting on the side of the road some water. He started ranting at me about talking to the seals, how the police had kicked him out of town and how the seals were distraught. I beat a retreat.

## Day 89 – Clam Beach to Burlington

A dense fog covered the landscape as I emerged from my tent. It had settled on everything, and everything was wet. I rolled up my tent and hoped that I'd have time to put it up to dry out in the evening. The route first followed a horse trail beside a beach. It was covered in horse shit. I've never understood why people are required to clean up after their dogs but not their horses. I know it would be a hassle to get off the horse, but it's also a hassle to ride through a steaming pile of effluent in the morning. I was agile. A fellow traveller was less awake. I rode past fresh tyre tracks through a green pile. As some wag put it: "Why do horses get to shit in the street? I'm the one who pays council tax."

After navigating the horse sewer, I joined a road that zig-zagged through cattle farms and over marsh land. The fog fit the marsh. The grey of the mist muted the browns of the grass, mud and murky water. Herons startled by my approach beat broad wings twice to lift off, then floated, silent, low over the water. Through the farmland exotic cows with shaggy coats and short horns enhanced the moor atmosphere. They looked on, indifferent as I battled through morning stiffness and dodged potholes on the rural Californian road. Swallows sitting on power lines took off in hordes, then gravitated back to their perch en masse. A few hawks looked down from solitary positions on telephone poles or glided on open wing over the fields, seeking unwary rodents.

I stopped in a town called Eureka for a mid-morning coffee. No prizes for guessing where that name came from. The town was founded during the California gold rush for export shipping. Unfortunately, the town on the north side of the same bay, Arcata was closer to the gold supply. A snappy name only gets you so far. On the way out of town, I passed a farmers' market. This was a real farmers' market with actual farmers selling actual produce. The middle class in me can't resist a farmers' market. I bought a kilo of apples. Every store sold apples. I picked the guy with the most faded check shirt and the strongest beard.

Distracted, eating apples, I got lost. I joined the freeway and dodged logging trucks. You really knock off the miles quickly when everyone else is going 130km/h. I stopped to recover my nerves with pie in Ferndale. It was turning into a decadent day.

In the afternoon, I left the highway to cycle down the aptly named 'Avenue of the Giants'. The road was quiet and lined with impressive trees. I kept stopping in the middle of the road to get yet another, marginally more perfect, picture of the road stretching into the distance, framed by the giant trunks. Passing drivers honked their appreciation of my camera work.

I stopped at the first opportunity to take another stroll through the park and commune with the trees. I wandered through, trying to stare at the treetops and not fall over. It was windy. The trees swayed in the breeze. One creaked like a rusty hinge. I left that area quickly. It would make quite a different noise if it fell, I was sure. I didn't want to find out what that sounded like. In amongst the peace and mysticism, I noticed that there wasn't a lot of animal life in the groves. Redwoods required steroid squirrels.

The campground was the best of the coast so far, nestled in a grove of redwoods. I pitched my tent on a soft bed of fallen pine needles. In the campground I met a Spanish guy called Raul. Raul had worked in Oxford for four years and still put "si" and "pero no" into any sentence where it seemed appropriate. This was most of them. We cooked dinner together. Living up to the best Spanish stereotype, Raul was the most relaxed cycle tourist I had met yet. He had started in Seattle and was headed to LA. He had meant to cut inland and head through the Sierra Nevada mountains. He'd given up this plan after hitting the first hills out of Seattle. "Si, si, you know, the mountains, they are for other people, not for me," Raul laughed. "For me, I like the flat." This had cut the distance he was planning to do in half. So as not to run out of miles before he ran out of holiday, Raul was going from campground to campground along the coast, 30km at a time. If he liked the area he would stay a day and chill out. He smiled a lot and laughed whenever he got the chance.

## Day 90 – Burlington to Fort Bragg

I had breakfast with Raul in the dark. The redwoods cut out all the light of the dawn. It had been a great night's sleep. The magical trees muffled all sound and their needles made the ground into a soft bed. As we ate, we talked gear. Raul had all his stuff spread out, arrayed around his bike. Four panniers and a duffel bag on top of the back rack. He surveyed the mess, hands on hips. "Si, you know, I do not think I can do without any of the things I have," he said. "I have thought about it, and I cannot. Maybe you can do with less, but for me, I need everything here." Raul laughed. I liked his approach to touring. When I left, he was still eating breakfast, drinking his third coffee and proudly contemplating his mountain of gear.

I left the giant redwoods behind in the morning ride. They were still present all the way down the coast, but the concentration of old trees and large groves thinned out. They were an unforgettable experience.

After leaving the forest, the route bounced on and off the freeway through inland Northern Californian towns of little account. I was in one of these small towns trying to decide whether to get a coffee when I hit a curb and popped my tyre. I was being indecisive about where to stop and tried to jump the bike up on a sidewalk. I didn't lift the front tyre enough, pushed it straight into the curb and was rewarded with a 'woosh' as the air rushed out of the inner tube. Trying to make decisions pre-caffeine is difficult. Three middle-aged, middle-white, middle-American guys were chatting beside one of their trucks. They heard the noise, looked at me and smiled: "That sucks, boy," one said. "It could be worse, it could be raining," I replied. They loved that. As I changed the tyre beside them, they chatted away about how global warming was a hoax, the Paris climate accord was a conspiracy to steal American cash, and how the homeless just needed to get jobs. There was a lot of back slapping: "It's good to know you get it man, you're one of the one percent."

They reminded me of myself talking to Pete the hiker in Cape Blanco a few days before, loudly agreeing. They asked me where I had come from. "Alaska? God bless you, son, God bless you." I never know how to respond to that. They were very impressed that I had the right tools to change my tyre. I thought I was going to get invited to lunch. One of the guys said he would pray for me. That got an even more awkward "thank you" in response. I wanted to ask him to be specific, to pray for no more flat tyres. I only had one more spare and I hadn't seen a bike shop in a few hundred kilometres. I didn't have the nerve.

Either he didn't pray, or Jesus wasn't listening. As I rode up a hill, ten kilometres on, I heard a familiar 'pshhh' noise every rotation of the back tyre. I tried to ignore it, my time-honoured first response to all problems. It ignored my ignorance and continued. Indeed, another flat. And, oh good, no cell service. I flipped the bike over and laid the panniers on the side of the highway. Cars rushed by. The sun baked. A vulture approached. He circled twice, gliding in slow circles. His black eyes stared out of his fleshy red skull, too small for the large black feathered body behind. He checked my water bottles. They were full. He cruised off in search of more immediate pickings. There are lots of vultures in Northern California. Riding warm thermals off sun-baked land, picking at the carcass of the American dream. That image reflected my level of positivity at this moment. As I got the tyre on and stuffed the punctured tube back into my pannier, a middle-aged cyclist approached. Jan was Dutch. With classic Dutch situational tact, Jan told me a story about getting thirty punctures in the first ten days on a trip from Portland, Oregon to Portland, Maine. "Jaa it was ok though," he said, "I was touring with the Trek organisation. They had a van following to change the tyres for you." Thanks Jan, that must have been great. Are they here now? No? Well why don't you have a nice day then, mate? He checked his guide book and told me to cycle back north 100km to the nearest cycle shop, then left me for dead. I resolved to pass him very quickly while looking like I wasn't trying on the next hill. I did this and felt a little better, and a lot petty.

I cycled until I got reception. I discovered that the next bike shop was in Fort Bragg, just past the campsite at the end of the day's ride. Only another 80km. Fuck you, Jan. I just had to trust in the prayers of my climatologist friend. I did have a patch kit, so I would probably not die if I got a puncture. The only issue was that my last experience with patching a tyre was also my first experience. It was also an unsuccessful experience. I ended up hitching a ride to a bike shop with a friendly van driver.

The road to Fort Bragg led over the biggest hill of the Northern Californian section of the route. At the start of the hill, I caught up to a guy about my age. We started chatting as we started climbing. As the climb got tougher, we agreed to shut up and cycle to the top together. After cruising down the back of the 400m hill, we cycled along the flat for a while. Lennart was also Dutch, but showed more sympathy for my tyre situation. He had bought a second-hand bike in Seattle and was cycling down the coast, visiting friends he had made on other trips along the way. He had had his own technical problems with the old bike, with a broken spoke and a broken back pannier rack. We came upon another hill. The unspoken natural competition between two guys on bikes set in. We charged up the hill. According to my memory of the route guide, we had already cracked the biggest hill and we were just in for a short sprint. After 200m of climbing my legs started to burn. Neither of us let up. After 300m we started to encourage each other, "Almost there ... next corner ... must be ... we'll stop at a viewpoint at the top, agreed? Agreed." We made it to the top and started to laugh. "It's good to ride with someone competitive, even if it's not a competition," I said. Lennart grinned, "It's always a competition." We reached the bottom of the hill, and the coast, and stopped for a snack.

The rest of the afternoon was unpunctuated by punctures. When we reached camp, Lennart headed in to find a spot, and I continued into town to find the bike shop and get groceries. Congratulating myself on a day's hard riding, I found the bike shop. It was closed for a two-week holiday. Couldn't wait until the end of the season guys? I found dinner and headed back to camp.

In camp, we met a couple of old Australian characters. Sam and Jenny were from Perth and had retired five years before. Since then, they had done some serious trips. "If I sit at home I just look down at me guts getting bigger," Sam slapped his beer belly. He was right, it was a good belly. They were the least fit-looking cycle tourists I'd met. This made their adventures that much more impressive. They had cycled across the Alps in Europe, the Nullarbor desert in Australia and now the west coast of the US. They had motorbike toured on Royal Enfields around India for two months. When they arrived in India and went to buy the bikes they asked their first taxi driver for advice. He thought for a while, and said, "You need a good horn, good brakes, and good luck." They shared their beers and we chatted into the evening.

## Day 91 – Fort Bragg to Stillwater Cove

It was freezing when I woke up. My tent was wet with dew. I packed it away with stiff fingers. Lennart and I had agreed to do a punchy day along the coast today. In the cold, we started slowly. Eventually we got moving along a coastal path around Fort Bragg. The way was shaded by trees and my hands froze to the handlebars. I tried to put them up my shirt to warm them. I never actually crashed into anyone coming the other way, but some of them definitely thought I was going to.

We stopped into Mendocino, the first town after Fort Bragg, to get a coffee and warm up. I'd meant to catch up on writing I hadn't done yesterday, but predictably we chatted about bullshit and people-watched instead. Mendocino was no Crescent City. It was the uniquely Californian cross of yuppy and hippy. I wondered how some of these towns along the California and Oregon coasts grew into little oases, while others with the same sunshine, same views and same beaches turned into sad strip malls.

We headed out of town to find the bike shop. We took a wrong turn and ended up in a hobby farm. A man was grooming his llamas. Why not? It's a free country. When we found it, the bike shop perched on the side of a hill over a river. It was run by a tanned guy in his fifties. He had a collection of outrigger canoes down in the river below the shop. I said they reminded me of Pacific Island canoes. Jason had built his own canoe based on plans from a guy from New Zealand. He told me it had taken eighteen months of nights and weekends, in between running the shop and parenting. He pulled me behind the counter to look at photos of the canoe and the website of the guy that designed them. They were awesome. A canoe with a single outrigger pontoon and a sail. Jason was starting the process of building the sail. I said he would love New Zealand. Jason got Google Earth up on the computer and we toured the Bay of Islands and Great Barrier. He committed to come to New

Zealand. I committed to build a canoe.

The rest of the day's riding passed quickly. There was a strong tailwind. Lennart and I zipped along, stopping only briefly for lunch. It was easy to forget how much help we had. You never have a tailwind: you either have a headwind or you are having a good day. Every so often we passed a bush or small tree that was blowing in the wind. They looked like they were being mixed in a blender. I thought of the sail on the outrigger canoe. Maybe one would work on a bike? It wouldn't improve my margin of error. We raced up every climb and flew down every descent. The road hugged the coast and cove after cove flew by. In a way, it was an odd landscape, repetitively beautiful. The pictures I took all looked the same. Each cove was a 100m cut into the coast. Bare cliffs enclosed a sandy beach, clear blue water and a collection of rocky islands. The location of the islands changed, but little else.

We arrived in a campground called 'Stillwater Cove' at 5pm. To congratulate ourselves on a ride well done, we'd stopped and bought beers and ice cream on the way. That doesn't sound like a great combination, but after a day of cycling it was the height of decadence. We set up our tents, drank the beers and headed down to check out the cove. On the way down, we walked through a forest. Five minutes out of the campground and we were surrounded by nature. A deer froze as we walked past, wiggling its ears and gazing at us with wet eyes. A little green frog hopped down the path in front of us. As we got to the beach a peacock stalked away. No seagulls in California, only peacocks. The beach was guarded by a sign warning of "the most dangerous beach in California" and "sleeper waves", with a picture of a stick figure being tossed in a swirl below a wave. We looked towards the beach. The sun had just met the Pacific, and ripples lapped the fine sand beach. It didn't look so bad. A Japanese couple were fishing with surf rods and a six pack of beers. We chatted for a while and tempted fate, laughing about sleeper waves in 'Stillwater Cove'.

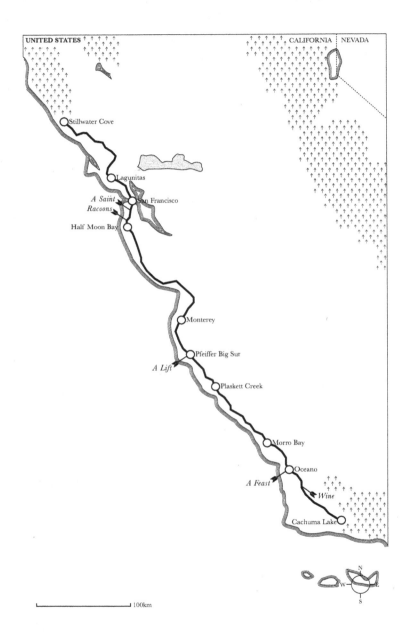

CALIFORNIA : NEVADA

Stillwater Cove

Lagunitas

*A Saint*
*Racoons*
San Francisco

Half Moon Bay

Monterey

Pfeiffer Big Sur

*A Lift*

Plaskett Creek

Morro Bay

Oceano

*A Feast*

*Wine*

Cachuma Lake

100km

N
W · E
S

# Day 92 – Stillwater Cove to Lagunitas

Lennart and I parted ways in the morning. He had 160km of cycling to a friend's place in Marin County and planned to stretch the miles out the full day. I left to catch the early sun over the California hills. The route climbed along coastal cliffs. Cattle farms surrounded the road. Those better be some damn happy cows, because I've never seen a farm with a better view. The cliffs were higher than in Oregon, and the waves crashing against them seemed more dramatic. The cows looked impressed.

I passed into a fog. My route guide mentioned that this part of the coast was sometimes enveloped by huge fog banks. I contemplated the prospect of a day's riding with ten metres' visibility. A car with its fog lights on passed close on the shoulder-less road. Shoulder-less and guardrail-less. The farms were gone. There was now a 100m drop to the sea. I broke through the top of the fog bank. A thick layer of grey hugged the coast and hid the ocean from view. The fog swirled. I felt like I was back in the mountains.

I stopped in another idyllic Californian seaside town, Jenner, for a coffee. I sat out the back of the cafe with a green tea scone and watched pelicans fly low over a glass lagoon. They flapped just enough to gain a foot of height over the water, then glided to within inches of the surface. I was through my second coffee and my second scone, putting on my helmet to go when a middle-aged guy walked through the door. He took one look at me, pointed at my chest, flashed a broad grin and said, "Are you cycling? My nephew will talk to you." With this, he went to the counter to order. I stood, helmet in hand. It seemed odd to walk out, but equally odd to obey the summons. A younger guy walked in. He had a great beard. He took one look at me and said, "Are you cycling?"

Ali and his uncle Sid were from Iran. The family had been in California since the 70s. I told them that I had been to Iran and tried out my best Farsi: "Mar bar Amrika, mar bar Israel", translated: "Death to America, death to Israel." I'd learned the chant at a football match in Tehran. The match was a friendly between Iran and China. The cheerleader was having trouble getting the crowd involved in the game, clash of football titans that it was. He tried the chant out. The crowd loved it. Surreal, it was more like a club anthem than a political slogan. Ali and Sid laughed nervously and looked at the waitresses. Her Farsi was lacking. We took a seat.

Ali had just come back from a tour up the coast from San Diego through Oregon, up to Alberta, then cross country to Maine. He showed me the route with waypoints marked on a map on his phone. I zoomed out. Ali had waypoints over half the world. He had toured through Iran, Turkey, Asia and Europe, with a line of markers running from north-eastern China through Tibet, and down the west coast of India. We swapped stories from the road and about characters we had met. His favourite was a seventy-five-year-old woman with terminal cancer who had toured 70,000km on her bike. She was two years past her doctor-scheduled expiry date, and was in the process of planning a tour into the interior of Alaska, off-road, with a pack raft to float her out further into the wilderness. We laughed about the inadequacy of our trips.

Sid was also a character. He'd worked in tech in San Francisco and was now a semi-professional photographer. When the girls in the cafe had asked his name for his order he had told them to call him "Sidlicious". They'd shouted it out the window. Ali described Sid's style of photography as "harassment" and demonstrated by poking a camera in my face. I told him I found it hard to take good photos of people. He said it was about feeling the vibe, becoming part of the moment and feeling whether the people were okay with having you there recording it. His philosophy of photography was, "notice, appreciate, interact." "Appreciate why something is happening without judgement," he said, "even if it is some crazy racist KKK motherfucker, reflect on the history and why they are the way they are." He'd exhibited at a show in a booth with Bill Clinton. We talked about personal charisma. I laughed at Sid for talking about charisma after he'd stopped me in my tracks while leaving and got the cafe girls to shout "Sidlicious" to a packed cafe.

We sat talking for an hour, Sid and Ali force-feeding me in the traditional Persian style. I reflected again that I was going to miss having random people approach me all the time. These were some of the best experiences of the trip.

I continued, caffeine-fuelled, down the coast. The houses were starting to get more numerous and ostentatious as I got further south. Some specimens of construction had definitely been designed by the owners. As the saying goes: "A man who represents himself in court has an idiot for a client." One in particular looked like it had been built by a plumbing magnate who thought architects were ponytailed wastes of oxygen. "I built my company from the ground up, how hard can designing a bloody house be?" Well, I'm no guru, but I can tell you that circular windows are not a great start.

The route joined the banks of Tomales Bay. The road was dotted with oyster farms and restaurants. I contemplated stopping for a decadent afternoon snack, but decided oysters would be a risky move cycling in the California sun. Besides, some of the oyster bars had valet parking and looked like they wouldn't appreciate a sweat-encrusted cyclist eleven days past laundry day. I pushed on to camp.

## Day 93 – Lagunitas to San Francisco

The final day into San Francisco was a short 50km. I kicked off early for no real reason and stopped in at the first cafe I saw. It was tough to tell whether this was a member of the jet-set California or the hobo California. The cafe was in a second-hand store, and everyone had tattoos, but they were all old. The only other customer was a big guy, about sixty, with a grey moustache hanging over his upper lip in the style of an Old West county sheriff. The barista asked me where I was cycling from and we struck up a conversation. The sheriff said, "I knew you weren't one of the standard Lycra boys. You've got a look about you." I asked if it was because I was particularly dirty. He gave me a serious look, "No. You look like you've been places." This was a great start to the morning. We chatted for a little while. As I left, he gave me a fat green bud. "For your travels," he said. I don't think he was the sheriff.

I cycled through Marin County north of San Francisco. It was a sunny Saturday and the local Lycra brigade was out in force. Forests of skinny spandex legs pumped carbon frames. Whole pelotons passed me by. No one waved back. Cycling fast was serious business. I climbed a mansion-encrusted hill to the edge of San Francisco Bay. I got my first view of the skyline and the Golden Gate Bridge. It was hard to imagine a more impressive entrance to a city. The sun shone down on the Marin Headlands, but as I approached the bridge, I felt the wind coming off the bay. It had a biting chill. Over the bay, the city was covered in the traditional fog. I rode up the headlands around the bridge to take the obligatory tourist photos. Wind whipped at my singlet. I regretted the lack of a jacket, once again. The cycle route across the bridge was hectic. Bikes were confined to one side and crashed past each other, six-lane motorway to the left and 100m drop to the sea on the right. Gusts of wind pushed tourists on city bikes, racers on speed machines and tourers together at random. Taking photos was not encouraged. I got some great ones of Lycra boys giving me disapproving stares as they shot past.

Once in San Francisco, I found a hostel, dropped my bags, walked over to Chinatown, ate as many dumplings as humanly possible, and went for a nap. Great day, well spent. In the evening, I went for a beer with a high school friend, Jerome. It was good to be off the bike.

# Day 94 – San Francisco to Half Moon Bay

After a couple of days break in the city, I started my exit from San Francisco at 6am. I'd agreed to go for a trail ride with Jerome and his friends around Golden Gate Park. I rolled out of bed, already late, and raced through morning traffic in the dark. Nothing wakes you up faster than dodging between cars, trams and homeless people on Market Street. I negotiated the obstacle course, and San Francisco's Escher-esque hills. Vertical rises emerged from nowhere. I never went downhill in two days. I met Jerome's friends at the muster point before he arrived. They looked serious. One of them complimented my bike in terms I didn't understand. I tried to sound grateful and not too clueless. The crew swapped unintelligible stories about building bikes. Everyone arrived, and we were off. Five minutes on the road, then we were racing along single track dirt trails through forest. The trails weren't endless, but it was easy to forget that we were in the middle of a city. After the first track, I'd fallen behind, and raced to catch up. This dynamic continued. These guys were as serious as they looked. Once again, I was reminded that going straight for a long time on a road doesn't make you an expert cyclist. I walked the fine line between trying to go fast enough not to fall behind, and not going so fast that I ended up eating dirt. We ended the outing with cinnamon toast and coffees at a cafe. The boys went off to work. I raced back to the hostel to take full advantage of the free breakfast and have a final shower before setting off for Half Moon Bay.

The ride to the campground Half Moon Bay was relatively short, so I took a scenic route out of town. That is to say, I got lost. I toured along the coast, through the suburbs. I passed a gold domed Orthodox Church. I stopped to take a photo. A lady walked past. She told me, "You should go in, it's dark and wild." That sounded excellent. I locked the bike and went in to find out what she meant. A large bald man stood at a booth beside the inner entranceway. In the dark of a church, I felt suddenly out of place in my singlet, helmet and spandex. The guard gave me an appraising look. In a thick Russian accent and deep voice he said, "I'm sorry, I don't have any spare pants, you can't go in." Oh, no worries, I'll just take a photo. "Next time, wear pants." Ok man, pants, I get it. I joked it was hard to cycle in pants and got no smile. I took my photo and walked out. As I opened the door, a priest in a black cassock with a wild beard was coming in. He leaned towards me. "Did you see the Saint?" He asked me in a fast, low voice. No, I'm not wearing pants, I couldn't go in. He looked me up and down. "Follow me," he said. He didn't wait for a response and rushed in past the bald guy and through the inner door. He said nothing to the guard, so I just pointed to him as I walked past, shrugging. The guard stared, nonplussed. The priest led me over to the side of the church. In a case was a dead body. "These are the relics of Saint John," the priest said in the same low voice, "they were buried under the church here. People come to pray with them. Anything you want, any problem you have. The Saint will answer you." I thanked him. He gave me a grave look. "Next time wear pants," he said, and walked back to his rooms.

The rest of the road out of San Francisco was uneventful. The coast was populated, the riding busy and trafficked. The day was classic Bay Area, a sea fog rolled in off the bay. Tendrils of mist flickered and evaporated as they got to shore. The one escape from the highway was a bike trail around a headland. It was called 'The Devil's Slide'. The road traversed near vertical cliffs. Low clouds covered the ocean. The blue of the ocean in the foreground faded evenly to the grey of the sky in the distance, blending to a constant horizon. I met another touring cyclist. Linda was a middle-aged lady. She didn't look like the typical dirtbag cycle tourist. She looked like my aunt. Looks can be deceiving. She had come down from Seattle and was headed to San Diego. Linda had started her trip through the Cascades and Sierras, but was defeated by wildfires. I had felt lazy for skipping the Californian mountains. Linda reassured me it would have been terrible. We chatted trips. I pitched Alberta and Linda encouraged me to go to Colombia. The year before, she had cycled from Bolivia to Patagonia, solo, through 6,000km and the Andes. Linda was legit.

Half Moon Bay campground was on the coast. At first, I

appreciated the evening breeze from the sea. Then I missed having a jacket. Then I froze. I hadn't been this cold since Alaska. I got into my tent. It was 6pm. More cyclists arrived in the camp. I wanted to go out and say hello, but I also wanted to stay warm. I remained in my tent. Then the raccoons arrived. I must have dozed off. I started dreaming of giant dogs fighting tigers. Slowly, I woke up and realised that those noises were coming from outside the tent. A man's voice narrated, "They're all over your bike," he said in a laconic voice. I tried to figure out whether he was talking to me, and whether I would get out of my sleeping bag if he was. He was talking to his friend, who was already in his tent and was having a similar debate. "What do you mean?" his friend asked, worried. The voice continued, "They're climbing everywhere, do you have any food in there? You must have food in there." "No, I don't." The narrator ignored this interruption, "Yep, these guys are hungry. They've gotten whatever was in your bag." "Great," his friend replied. He sounded thrilled. The raccoons sounded big. They could have been mountain lions. "They look like they are living in that tree," the voice said. There was only one tree. I was camping under it. I decided I wouldn't help the situation by coming out of my tent. I put my earplugs in and hoped for the best.

# Day 95 – Half Moon Bay to Monterey

I got up at the same time as an older guy sleeping in a bivvy bag. The bivvy bag didn't look like it would encourage snoozing. The raccoons had gotten into his panniers. He was more impressed that they could open zips than annoyed that they ate his Snickers. We chatted as I prepared breakfast and he surveyed the damage. Jeremy had come from Maine. He was in his fifties, and looked like a cyclist. I asked him how long it had taken from Maine. "Well, down to Florida was ten days," he said, "across to San Diego was another two weeks and now I'm a week out of Seattle." Not quite as impressive as Linda crossing the Andes, but I had taken that long to get down from Portland. We talked about gear. Jeremy compared the differences between our bike setups. I tried not to let on that I had no idea what he was talking about. I headed off and told him I looked forward to him passing me, only a little bitterly. He got a kick out of that.

The first 50km of the ride hugged the coast. Low cliffs looked out over a clear sky and a calm sea. I almost wished for a storm to add character to the landscape. It reminded me of the ALCAN: impressive overall, but nowhere overly impressive. I rode up repetitive hills, down the other side and looked for tidal waves. The only interest was provided by pelicans. I cemented my love of pelicans. Big ungainly bastards. They floated a foot above the waves. I tried to decide whether this was to save energy in some way, or because they were just too lazy to climb higher than twelve inches into the sky. They flew in formation to minimise drag. Landing was also done on a least-effort basis. They didn't slow, just bombed into the water, belly first. A splash, a spin, a total loss of control, but the water had done all the work of stopping. A group cleaned its wings in a lagoon. They bashed them up and down, churning water. They looked like a swim class of feathery, big-billed toddlers having a tantrum.

The afternoon was split between freeways and farms. The route was well signposted until a freeway turn-off. When the route joined the freeway, there were no signs. There was no indication of the way forward except the gaping maw of the on-ramp. It was like the planners were embarrassed. Off of the freeway: farms. These were no northern Idaho hobby farms. These were feed-the-country farms, with the itinerant workers to prove it. It was harvest time, and whole fields of strawberries, lettuces and artichokes were being denuded. Groups of workers plied rows. Each group came with a set of portaloos on a trailer behind a pickup where they hung their gear. Taco trucks migrated between groups. Two-metre-tall 'No Trespassing' signs in Spanish and English hung outside the farms. I stopped to take photos of the endless fields and half expected to be shown the business end of a truncheon, *Grapes of Wrath* style.

I camped in Monterey, of Steinbeck fame. In true American fashion, Cannery Row had first been named in honour of Steinbeck, then turned into a shopping mall. The campground was in the middle of town. The local homeless and alcoholics had made it a more or less permanent base. I was greeted by another cycle tourist in the hiker-biker site. He said hello, then told me to lock my bike. The only other person there was a lady in her fifties, dead drunk. I don't think she was hiking. Together with the other cyclist, Alan, we had a circular conversation where she told us she was going to be quiet at night, that she didn't do meth, but that she did like a drink. We told her that was great. Then we did the dance over again. Alan's friend Chris arrived. They had met three days before, and were cycling together to LA. Not the best timing, but Alan, Chris and I had discovered the Trader Joe's in town and were competing as to who could produce the most elaborate decadence from their panniers. I came in strong with blueberries, was beaten with kale (who carries a huge bunch of loose green leaves in a cycling bag?). I produced an $8 sack of cookies and a litre of milk. Alan had chocolate-covered ginger and artisanal cider. I claimed a tie but felt defeated. The issue was put to rest with the arrival of other cyclists. Will and Alisha from Vancouver arrived. They'd invested in a full charcuterie board. Prosciutto, salami, Brie, Comte, smoked salmon, fresh figs. All served on a Frisbee. I was amongst masters of the craft. We discussed debauched food choices and where we were going to lock our bikes.

## Day 96 – Monterey to Big Sur

I got up and had breakfast with Alan and the other cyclists. My lack of a jacket made it unappealing to sit around and shoot the breeze while they cooked three-course meals.

I cycled down from Monterey through Pebble Beach. The route followed a road called '17 Mile Drive' around the Monterey peninsula. This was advertised as a worthwhile diversion from the highway. The road followed the coast through Pebble Beach golf resort. This was a serious golf course. Teams of uniformed workers mowed lawns with industrial-scale equipment. Running a golf course really is just an advanced lawn-mowing operation. As scenic rides go, a golf course wouldn't be my first choice. Apart from well-manicured greens, the attraction of the ride was more small dunes and calm seas, and a collection of McMansions. Why someone would want to live in a multimillion-dollar house overlooking a golf course was beyond me. Maybe they just liked watching people mow lawns. Or valued the excitement of wayward balls crashing through their kitchen windows. I zipped through and stopped in the more normal town of Carmel for coffee. One kind of California coast normal, that is: a Ferrari double-parked a Tesla in front of the cafe. Not to be confused with the other California coast normal: tent encampments of homeless people and itinerant workers.

I had pictured the Big Sur coast as a road painted on the side of forbidding precipices. It was less impressive. The most interesting thing about the road around the low cliffs were the isolated mansions. With high walls and security gates, they looked like the Bond villain lairs. I rode along miles of endless rolling coast searching for inspiration. I decided I was being affected by the finish line disease. I wasn't having fun cycling, I was just planning how I could get to the end as quickly as possible. This was self-perpetuating. The longer each day I spent cycling the fastest route down the coast, the less chance interesting things would happen. The fewer interesting things that happened, the more time I was tempted to spend in the saddle. I resolved to get off the bike and do some hiking in Big Sur.

I was the only one in the campground when I got in, so I went for a hike. On my way out, I met a girl riding into camp. Joanna had bright blue hair and matching blue panniers. It turned out she knew Alan, Alisha and some of the other cyclists from the last campground. They were meeting up to ride down to a bike conference in LA. She left to set up her tent and I set off up a hill. The hike was hot. That's the best thing I could say about it. I hiked up a ridge to get a view of the valley below. There was a view, it was of the valley. I became less sure that hiking around Big Sur was going to fix my impatience to finish the trip.

I'd planned to try to convince some of the cyclists from yesterday to do another hike when they arrived in camp. When I got back to the tents, they had arrived and had already raided the camp store for beers. Hiking seemed far-fetched. Alan suggested we go for a swim. This was a better plan. We set off towards the end of the campground. There was a heated debate about whether to bring the bikes. It's hard to detach cyclists from their cycles. After a twenty-minute walk through an endless string of RVs, the decision to leave the bikes in camp seemed less well advised. Eventually, we reached the trailhead for the swimming hole and hiked up the river. Clambering over boulders and up the riverbanks felt like a better use of time than struggling up a hill with the sun beating down. The sun here didn't beat, it shone. It glittered on the stream and warmed the boulders. It hadn't warmed the swimming hole, unless the hole was frozen this morning. The peer pressure of a group and the fact I hadn't showered in a week got me in. Each person had their own method of trying not to look like they were cleaning themselves. We caught the last rays of sun in the valley to dry off and set off back downstream to camp.

Via the camp store for beer and ice cream, of course. I started to appreciate this group camping lark. Back at camp, the full contingent had arrived. Alan and Chris had met on the road. Will and Alisha, of the Frisbee charcuterie, worked at the same bike shop in Vancouver. Joanna had arranged to meet Alisha and Will on the way down the coast. Most of the crew were cycling to 'Bike!Bike!', a conference for community cooperative bike shops. Alan and Chris had picked up another stray, Tucker, that morning. We drank the beers, talked shit about the golf course and the other campers. There was a group of older cycle tourists that Alan and Chris had run into a few days before. One was a former teacher obsessed with Trump. Will had caught a full sermon. Will was English and had moved to Vancouver a year ago. He laughed, "Yeah great man, I agree, he's a dick. You're not wrong. I'm fully on board. So, let's talk action. Let's get practical. I'm English. I'm living in Canada. I work at a bike shop. What do you want me to do? I'm open for suggestions. Happy to work with you on this one. I'm all ears." It seemed like a good crew. They planned to do a 50km ride the next day. This seemed like an opportunity to slow down and enjoy the last days of the trip in good company.

Loath to pass over hiking in Big Sur completely, I tried to convince them all to come hiking the next day. Tucker was keen, Alan seemed like he could be convinced, and the rest showed zero interest. We finished dinner and the bike mechanic enthusiasts discussed gear ratios. I went to bed.

## Day 97 – Big Sur to Plaskett

I was up and ready to hike at 7am. Alan and Tucker had different
ideas. By the time we set off it was 9am. The chill had gone from
the air and the sky was clear. The sun had made its way above
the brown hills for another day of cooking them, and us. As we
walked out of camp, Will was just rolling out of his hammock. It
looked like we would get up and back the 15km before the crew
had finished breakfast.

The hike up was dry and hot. The path was steep. We chatted
about other hikes we'd done. Tucker had grown up in Eastern
Washington and told stories about hiking dry riverbeds with his
dog, killing rattlesnakes. It was Alan's first hike. I tried to slow
down. I hadn't gotten to know Tucker well the night before. Alan
was similar in conversational approach to me. We talked until
we happened to say something interesting. A lawyer by training,
Alan had moved to Montreal a decade ago and gotten involved
with the community bike shop scene as a way to make friends in
his new city. This seemed like a common theme with the crew.
Will had moved from London to Vancouver and described his
social scene as revolving around cycling. He got into bike polo
through the bike shop. He described this as, "like normal polo,
but without the horses, or the dickheads." I got to know Tucker
better on the hike up. Alan and I discussed downhill mountain
biking. We had each done it once. We agreed it was crazy. After
fifteen minutes of airing our opinions, loudly and at length,
we asked Tucker to chip in. He'd built his own trails. After our
ignorance had been revealed on this topic, Alan and I discussed
long-distance trail running. We both agreed it was crazy, loudly
and at length. Neither of us had ever done it. Alan wondered
at the name of very long trail races: "It's like super running or
something." Tucker chimed in, "I think it's called ultrarunning."
"No, not that, I'm sure it's not ultrarunning," Alan said. "Well,
it might depend on the race, but usually anything longer than
a marathon is called ultrarunning." Tucker had just finished

a 50km race around Mt Hood in Oregon: "If you can run a marathon, ultrarunning is easy," he said. Thanks, Tucker.

Alan and I learnt to ask Tucker whether he was an expert at something before we waxed lyrical. We achieved the summit with no further embarrassments. From the top, we could see back across the valley, the dry California hills rolling away towards the horizon. Over the ridge, we gazed out to the ocean. A sea fog still clung close to shore. We would be down on that road cycling in a couple of hours, out of the sun and into the fog.

On the way back, the local reptiles came out to enjoy the sun. We passed lizards basking on the trail and on warm rocks. A snake stopped us in our tracks. Lizards had some appeal. Snakes as a hiking companion I could do without. This guy was stretched over the trail. He was light brown, speckled with darker brown patterns and as thick as a roll of quarters. A roll of quarters dripping with venom. We retreated up the trail and conferenced. First, we threw pebbles to move him along. Next, larger rocks. It seemed needlessly cruel to kill him in the middle of his morning nap. The rocks had no effect. He was enjoying the nap. We decided water might wake him. We threw the rest of Alan's water on him. A full half-litre, a direct hit. No movement. Now Alan was out of water. The water throwing seemed less inspired. As we started to lose hope, he started to inch off the path. As the closest, it fell to me to run by him first. I made a sound which could uncharitably be described as a squeal. The snake paid no mind. We survived. Nothing brings men together like prancing by a napping reptile. At the bottom of the hill, we washed the hike off in the river.

The 50km of cycling to the next campground was the Big Sur I had imagined, the road draped across dramatic cliff sides. The mist we had seen from the top of the hill sat out to sea. We rode in the sun. Wisps of fog tickled the shoreline. Rocky islands out to sea barely crested the top of the ocean cloud bank. The climbs up the cliffs were tough after the hike, and our legs complained. In compensation, the cliffs were picturesque enough to warrant frequent photo stops. We passed Esalen, the famous hippie retreat ($605 for a weekend in a bunk bed, if you're interested). The "Reservations Required, No Visitors" sign and brand new Lexus with a "Peace on Earth" bumper sticker screamed California. The rest of the ride was uneventful except for a stop at a store with the dubious honour of being the most overpriced on the coast. A can of spam was $7. I considered buying it to throw through the window. When I bought my $6 can of beans for dinner the guy told me to "Have a rad day." Thanks, buddy. Still, it provided another opportunity to talk shit. By the time we got in to camp the fog had settled in and crushed our dreams of a late evening swim. No matter. After the hills, the views, the hike and the company I felt much more positive.

# Day 98 – Plaskett to Morro Bay

Today I experienced the trials of riding with a big group. The crew waded through a soup of fog, packing gear and fixing breakfast. By now, I was hyper efficient in breaking down my tent and making breakfast. No fold wasted, no tent peg left behind, a thousand calories of peanut butter, bananas and granola delivered in a hypodermic tortilla needle. Efficiency bought me nothing this morning. I stood around as my new cycling buddies chatted, packed and repacked panniers, fiddled with camp stoves and discussed their methods of coffee preparation. I wore all my clothes, and again, regretted my lack of a jacket. California was supposed to be hot. It was not hot this morning. I ached to get on the bike and warm up. I hopped around the table and tried not to appear impatient. This failed, to general amusement: "You're not ready to go, Otto, are you? I mean, you look pretty ready to go. Where's your jacket? Who goes cycling without a jacket? Didn't you come from Alaska?"

When we finally did roll out of camp, we looked great. Seven fully laden touring bikes had a definite presence on the road. We weren't so much a peloton, as an avalanche of steel frames and PVC pannier bags. This coherent effect didn't last long. At the first hill, the group stretched. Now we just became difficult for cars to pass.

The group separated further as snack stops, hills and photo opportunities competed for individual attention. Most of the crew had started touring alone and marched to the beat of their own drum. With less than half the gear and more than twice the miles, I shot up hills. At the top, Will and Alan "released the gravity bombs" of their comprehensive kit; the potential energy of full packs shooting them down in screaming descents. Alisha, Chris and Tucker kept a steady pace in the middle of the pack, seldom breaking a sweat. Joanna, on her colour coordinated retro bike and four full bright blue panniers, trudged up any incline. Joanna was the best bike mechanic of the lot, the only one that could weld and build frames, but her bike was built for something other than speed.

We passed a group of elephant seals lounging on a beach. They were a tourist attraction. People lined a railing overlooking the beach, taking photos until the smell forced them to move on. There is a reason seals have to bathe for most of the year.

Will, Alan and I reached escape velocity after a particularly pointy hill. We agreed to meet up with the others later. We rode through a cycle race. Lycra-clad racers on bikes so light the wind could have blown them away did loops of the highway. I told Will and Alan about my road game of waving as flamboyantly as possible to serious looking people. We waved in full arm strokes, with open-mouthed grins. Some Lycra boys grinned, some waved, some tried to pretend we didn't exist. One gave us 'the guns', thumb and forefinger extended. Will was excited, "Did you see that? Classic 'cool dad' manoeuvre: I see you there, champ."

We planned to meet the rest of the crew at Hearst Castle, the former summer home of the publishing magnate Randolph Hearst. I had heard about the 'Castle' in Whitehorse. Sarah, the hostel manager, enthused about the tours. One of them involved dressing up in period costume while you explored the house. With our collective mobile phones in various states of no battery, no reception or not having the contacts of the rest of the group, we struggled to organise. Alisha and Joanna went to the visitor centre, Chris and Tucker went to the beach, Alan went to explore the town. Will and I had a beer. By the time we regrouped, by accident, no one else still wanted to go to the castle. I understood the expression "herding cats" at a deeper level. I left everyone lying in the sun by the beach and headed to the castle.

The castle visitor centre had the busy, grimy, tiled look of a bus station. I told the girl selling me the ticket for the tour that my friend in Whitehorse drove down every year in her RV to do a new tour. She was not impressed. Apparently, that was common. RV people love a good tour. The tour I bought was with fifty people and went every twenty minutes, ten hours a day, all summer long. The visitor centre was indeed a bus station. I packed myself into the bus. There were no empty seats and no AC. We rode up the 450 metres of climbing up to the castle at the top of the hill. After the fifth switchback I didn't have to cycle, I viewed the bus and the station in a more grateful light.

The castle was a trip. The architect started out with a brief that described a simple Swiss-Japanese bungalow in the California hills. That's not architecture, that's just a collection of words. I asked the tour guide what "Swiss-Japanese bungalow" meant. She laughed, "I have absolutely no idea." Maybe that initial brief should have been a red flag. The house ended up a 165-room monstrosity in a "Mediterranean village" style. The architect said that her client suffered from "changeability of mind." I found it interesting that someone could be so effective in business – Hearst was the first media mogul – and so ineffective at building a house. To stock the village, Hearst was something of an art collector. He bought around 200,000 pieces of art. This included 100 antique ceilings, mostly from European churches. Each room had its own unique wooden ceiling that had been pulled out of an Italian or German church. Some of the rooms had choir stalls lining the walls. In some ranking of individual collectors, he only made it to 88th place. There were 87 people who felt like they needed more than 100 church ceilings. Whatever floats your boat.

The castle was built on the site where Hearst went camping with his family as a boy. He didn't want to lose that vibe. He insisted on having condiments rather than centrepieces on the tables. The museum staff had kept this, so there were bottles of ketchup and mustard on a 10th-century wooden dining table. He also kept a zoo. I mean, why not? What's money for? There were videos of kangaroos hopping up to investigate cars driving to the castle, and polar bears hanging out in a pool enclosure. At some point he got into financial difficulty and had to sell the animals. When someone came to pick up the zebras, his son and daughter-in-law decided to let them out. There were still 130 zebras running around in the California hills. Freedom!

I headed back down the hill and cycled hard to catch up with the rest of the crew. We reunited at Morro Bay campground, cooked dinner and had a camp fire. After putting the unwashed in the unwashed masses with a tour group, it felt good to be back with the cycling crew, none of whom had showered.

## Day 99 – Morro Bay to Oceano

The now familiar pattern of group touring repeated itself in the morning. I finished my packing and tried not to let on I was freezing and ready to roll. I debated heading off on my own again, but the general confusion and banter of riding with seven people was too much fun to leave. We got going and cycled slowly through farmland. Another fog had set in overnight and we rode through a grey soup with faint views of fields stretching away on either side.

The first goal of the day was San Luis Obispo for a bike shop visit to fix broken spokes, and a Trader Joe's visit to restore depleted supplies. It was a Sunday, and the only bike shop open was next to a donut shop. Fortune favours the brave. While we waited for repairs to be done, Chris and I went off to buy the crew donuts. Chris was the youngest member of our posse at twenty-two. He'd grown up in a Christian family and had until recently attended a religious university. He'd dropped out of university a year ago and had moved to Vancouver Island where he was working in a coffee shop. He'd started cycling alone from San Francisco and described the first few days as foggy and challenging. Then he met Alan, the sun came out and, as Alisha joked, his sun came out. We bought fifteen donuts and headed back to the group. This was well received.

I learned that seven touring cyclists can really take over a car park. When we got back from the donut shop, bags, bikes and spandex-clad legs were strewn across the curb side. The Lycra locusts descended on the box of donuts without regard for the judgemental eyes of passing shoppers or strip mall security guards.

On the way to the campground in Oceano we passed a yard sale. One person stopped, and in the way of the group, the whole group cascaded to a halt. The lady running the yard sale seemed excited to have so many customers in her garden, even if they were us. She came out and gave us fashion advice and lemons from a tree in her backyard. Everything was $1. After surviving without a jumper or jacket for the last three weeks on the road, I was forced by the group to buy something. The consumerism caught on. Helmets and bikes were dumped on the sidewalk and we had an impromptu roadside fashion show. Most of the group ended up with new threads. Chris got a blue and gold silk jacket with a nautical print. Joanna bought him a blue sequinned fanny pack to accessorise. Alan acquired a grey, blue and purple woollen sweater two sizes too small. Alisha found a tropical polyester curtain masquerading as a bomber jacket. It had a picture of a parrot on it. I got a button down fleece with an oversized collar. We departed laden with lemons and colour. I looked forward to warm mornings and increased alarm from strangers encountering the crew.

We rode on to Oceano. The fog set in. The town was full of RV parks and liquor stores. We took advantage of the liquor stores and tried to find a campground. There were none. We ended up in an RV park sandwiched between the highway and a railroad. With one person, it would have been depressing. With seven, we set up a bustling tent city. Five stoves were needed to put the meal together. Anyone not cooking offered instructions. Trains rattled by and the campground was alternatively lit by headlights from the road, then covered in darkness by the fog. We worked our way through the beers and the meal came together. From a pile of shopping bags, to general chaos, to a sudden calm, everything seemed to finish at once. The group was surprised. "We're done? Everything is done? Ok ... let's eat!" Pots which had been cook-pots turned to bowls, mixing sporks became eating sporks. We feasted and retired, serenaded by passing trains.

## Day 100 – Oceano to Cachuma Lake

Our motley peloton cycled out of the campground, newly colourful. Now that we were into Southern California, I started to see where the state had been hiding its forty million inhabitants. I'd thought that once I got out of Oregon, or at least out of Northern California, the ride would become a suburban hell. That wasn't the case, until now. We rode past white picket fences and manicured lawns the 30km from Pismo Beach to Santa Maria. Santa Maria had the last Trader Joe's before Santa Barbara. The prospect of going a day without dried mango and candied almonds proved too much for the group to resist another stop. We piled the bikes against a wall of the store, decimated the snack aisle and spread ourselves out to feast under a tree in the middle of the car park.

We attracted admirers. A middle-aged man came and asked us where we got the money to travel. Once he had satisfied himself we weren't deadbeats, he wondered whether cycling would help him lose weight. A bubbly middle-aged Mexican woman came over and quizzed us about where we had all started and how we had all met. In return, she told us all about her children ("one of them likes white boys like you") and where to get the best tacos in Santa Barbara. Finally, a guy in his mid-twenties cruised over on a BMX. He had a blue bandana over his face, tattoos on his arms, shaved lines on his eyebrows, and a knife on his belt. "Hi, I'm Alex," he introduced himself. Alex was the friendliest of the lot. He asked us where we had come from, and told us he had done the San Francisco route before "with the boys". He told us he wanted to do more cycle touring. We quizzed him about our planned route and he told us to take a road off the highway, into the hills. "There are a couple great vineyards you should definitely check out along that way," he said. When he rode up, I didn't think Alex would be recommending vineyards. As he cycled off, Alex told us, "If you're back this way, come ride with me and the boys, we'll show you how we roll." We all agreed this would be awesome.

After he left, a debate over the best route to take for the rest of the day through wine country broke out. Alan had been doing the route planning for the group. Seven people have a lot of constraints and even more ideas. Route planning is a struggle at the best of times. Route planning with a peanut gallery is unbearable. Open debate on the agreed upon route while sitting in a supermarket car park based on a fifteen-minute conversation with a bandana-wearing BMX rider was one bridge too far for Alan. He decided to split from the group and meet us at the campground in the evening. I was surprised he had lasted so long. I was frustrated by the feeling of herding cats and I wasn't even doing the herding. Alan set off ahead of us to enjoy some solitude, while the rest of us took our time to get our collective shit together and escape the car park.

I was determined to do some wine tasting. Visiting vineyards is not a fun activity alone, but now that I was part of a crew it seemed like a great idea. Vineyard tours provided a great opportunity to stop and see the countryside, get a bit of a buzz on in the sun riding quiet back roads, and to impose six sweat-covered cyclists on a gentile environment. The group was less keen. At the first vineyard that came along I ushered everyone off the road and into the bar. I bought two tasting flights before we could open debate. With wine in hand, people started to see the appeal. We were out of place. The only other people in the tasting room were a couple on their honeymoon. I'm not sure we were part of their plan. The hostess was a cyclist herself, so tolerated us with good humour. She brought us some snacks and vouchers for two more vineyards along our route. The momentum was on for three tastings. This felt like the right number to get a good feeling for Santa Ynez Valley wine country without risking death on the road.

Drinking wine in the sun puts people in a good mood. We cycled slowly along the empty roads in the valley, tackling the small hills with anaesthetised legs. Each vineyard was a green oasis in the otherwise parched valley. The proprietors were suitably impressed that we were cycling through and suitably unimpressed by our attire. Six cyclists crammed into a tasting room passing glasses around and commenting in happy ignorance on the wine was an arresting prospect. In the last vineyard Will confided to the group, "We aren't the best of guests. I can smell myself." The second vineyard we visited was founded by one of the first Englishmen in California. He was famous secondly for his vineyard, and firstly for betraying Mexico to the US. In the Mexican-American war he provided information to the invading Americans about the location of Mexican troops. The Chardonnay had faint notes of treachery.

The final stretch into camp was a busy highway. As cars brushed past us on the narrow shoulder I was grateful that we hadn't got carried away with the wine. A 'ghost bike' commemorating a dead cyclist welcomed us at the bottom of the hill leading into the campground at Cachuma Lake. We were halfway into the campground when we realised we had lost Tucker. I rode back up the hill to see if I could find him. With no response on his phone and the sun setting, I headed back. We were about to organise a more extensive search when he rolled into camp, having gotten a puncture. More relaxed, we found Alan and settled in to cook dinner. The last of the sunset filtered through the trees around the lake, and we realised that it was our last night as a full crew. Tucker and I were headed into Santa Barbara the next day, while the others were splitting off to take the train into LA for the bike conference. After five days of full campgrounds, noisy dinners and chatty cycles, there was a quiet realisation that our time together was over. We laughed, thinking back to our chaotic team dinner packed into our impromptu tent city in the fog-covered RV park the night before: "We will always have Oceano."

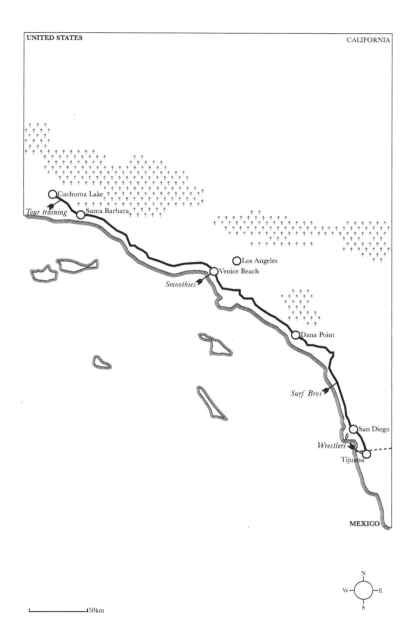

# Day 101 – Cachuma Lake to Santa Barbara

In the morning, Alan said his goodbyes to the group first. He was off to meet some other friends also bound for the conference. After swapping contact details and hugs, he mounted his bike to ride off into the dawn. His foot caught in his pedal straps and he toppled over into the grass. The tension of goodbyes broke. Everyone laughed. He picked himself out of the dirt smiling. I was glad someone else had trouble with poise and fixed pedals. The rest of us had breakfast and continued the morning tradition of taking as long as possible to get on the road. Cachuma Lake was a large campground with a few shops. We cruised around looking for coffee. Tucker and I had a short ride into Santa Barbara ahead of us. We were keen to get off the main road. We spent the morning consulting Google Maps to find a more interesting route across the Santa Barbara hills. By now I had a deep scepticism of small unnamed roads on Google Maps. At one of the shops we had a conversation with the shopkeeper that didn't sound promising. "That there road is right in the hills, it's off the highway," she said. Yes, that's the idea, can we ride it? "The way into Santa Barbara is right down there along the highway." But what about this smaller road? "Oh, that road is off the highway." Yes, it is, but does it go to Santa Barbara? "Oh, yes, the highway goes straight into Union Street in Santa Barbara." We didn't get very far. As we were about to give up and commit to a few hours of tension on a narrow shoulder, we found a Park Ranger. He told us that the USPS Tour de France team used to train on the road. If it was good enough for Lance, it was good enough for us. The road was called 'Camino del Cielo', aka 'The Road of the Sky'. It was hard to resist a great name.

The rest of the crew had a longer day ahead of them and were less excited about the prospect of adding more hills. Tucker and I set off towards the sky road. The highway led to the San Marcos pass through the hills to the north of Santa Barbara. When we got to the pass, the Camino del Cielo split off the main road and continued upwards. After the first 300m of climbing in the sun, we reflected on the group wisdom in taking the fast road. After the next 300m we were confirmed in our assessment. We were also sweaty. Local cyclists enjoying the quiet roads and serious hills flew by. None of them looked casual. One man in full Lycra steamed past us. He must have been about sixty. His calf muscles looked like two clenched fists in leather boxing gloves, punching down on the pedals. His greeting faded into the wind. Tucker and I exchanged glances and re-doubled our efforts. This lasted for a few minutes. The reality of our lack of urgency reasserted itself and we paused again to enjoy the view.

The road followed a ridge along the hilltops. Long driveways led back from high gates to castles nested in the hills. We debated whether the risk of wildfire was worth the view. It was quite a view. On one side of the ridge, empty California hillsides rolled to the horizon. The sky was clear, and five sets of ridges and valleys faded into the distance. The hillsides were every shade of brown. Stretches of rock formations drew a contrasting palate of colour on hills devoid of vegetation. On the other side of the ridge, a fog hung over the sea and the town below. The hillsides were green with the moisture from the clouds and the sea. Not very green, but green for California. We passed the occasional agave cactus, flower spikes growing three metres upwards in a burst of life. We discussed Tucker's trip. Tucker was at the start of a tour from Seattle to Panama, an equal distance to my own, almost completed trip. I felt the pull of continuing the journey. Only another 2,000km to the bottom of Baja...

The route culminated in a screaming downhill into Santa Barbara. After putting up with me cruising ahead of him through the climbs, carrying half the gear, Tucker shot off down the hill. We rode through the hillside suburbs of Santa Barbara and were in town and back at sea level. From empty hills to busy streets in twenty minutes. We felt like we had been catapulted back into civilisation. We had a burrito, bought some beers and sat by the hostel swimming pool to readjust.

# Day 102 – Santa Barbara to Venice Beach

Tucker and I hung around Santa Barbara the next day and explored the standard touring checkpoints of the bike shop, REI and the local taco stands. In the afternoon, we set off to Carpinteria, 15km outside of town, to camp. We passed through the suburbs of Santa Barbara. The road passed by the Santa Barbara Polo Club, which was indicative of the character of the suburbs. Oprah had a house here. We went in for a look. Bone dry hills overlooked football fields of bright green grass. The groundskeepers watched on as horse hooves chewed their manicured turf.

We set up camp at the state beach and headed off to a bar. Carpinteria had two breweries on Main Street. Good. We settled in and chatted to the locals. We were introduced to a couple of guys who had done some cycle touring. One of the guys, Steve, had gone down to Central America. In Guatemala he'd been stung by a scorpion while making coffee by the side of the road. When he screamed, an old man came out from his house. The man told Steve to drink a gallon of warm milk and eat a whole raw onion, which he supplied. After Steve had choked this down, the old man laughed, "Stupid Gringo! That scorpion is harmless. You will be fine in an hour." Steve's friend was also planning to travel to Mexico. He was a cowboy. He had a belt knife with a bone handle and two thick braids of hair snaking out from beneath a felt hat. The cowboy was planning to take a motorboat down to Mexico. He was planning to camp in coves and wherever he could beach the boat. It seemed like a crazy plan, but who were we to judge. Steve offered us a place to stay but we already had all our stuff set up in the campground.

When we returned to camp, Tucker's tent was filled with ants. I felt a bit sorry for him, but a lot relieved they weren't in my tent. Sorry, Tucker.

In the morning, we got up and went for a coffee in town before I set off to LA and Tucker headed back in to Santa Barbara for a cousin's wedding. It felt strange to face the prospect of riding alone after a week with a group. The crew created its own momentum in the morning. It was slow to get going, but once it did there was a communal spirit and drive to ride. Tucker and I reflected on our time together, the crew and our trips. I again felt the nostalgia of my trip coming to an end when his had just begun. We finished our coffees, said our goodbyes and I got back on the road, struggling without the energy of the crew.

Once the blood started pumping and the endorphins kicked in, the prospect of cycling seemed more attractive. It was a flat ride beside the freeway into LA. A few Lycra boys were out for their morning jaunt. One passed me. I tailed him. It didn't take much to get the competitive fire going. He kicked up his speed and tried to shake me. I hadn't taken off my jumper and the sun was coming out. After half an hour of belting along at top speed, I was covered in sweat but had stayed with him. We passed beaches with surfers struggling in and out of wetsuits. I got a kick out of imagining them looking on at this Lycra-clad athlete on a carbon fibre bike being chased by a guy on a loaded touring bike tailing a flapping jumper. They definitely didn't notice. My nemesis stopped on a bridge and I shot past. I waited an appropriate time before stopping to take off the jumper. He zipped passed me laughing and gave me a thumbs up. I thought I saw him say, "This fucking guy." but it could have been my imagination. I tried to catch him again but lost him in a town. Self motivation would have to suffice from now on.

The rest of the cycle flew by. I was caught in the gravity of LA and the flow of the traffic. I shot through Malibu, surfers picking their way through beachfront mansions. No owner-designed monstrosities with portholes for windows here; this was real money. On to Santa Monica, where it was garbage day. Large green bins filled the shoulder. I weaved between the bins, garbage trucks, parked cars and into the traffic. I reflected that it would be poor timing to be crushed by an SUV so close to the end of the trip. The hiker I met on the way out of Yellowstone described cycle touring as Russian roulette. In LA it felt like there were more bullets in the gun.

I got into LA and met the friend I was staying with. She sent me off to walk her dog while she finished work. The dog and I went for tacos. Without my bike or cycling clothes, the taco truck guys were surprised when I put away two burritos in five minutes. I regret nothing. The dog looked impressed.

## Day 103 – Venice Beach to Dana Point

After a week hanging out in Venice Beach, eating edibles and rolling on the carpet with the dog, I set out on the final leg of the trip: LA to Tijuana through the most densely populated part of California. Venice was an oasis of new age decadence in the chaos of LA. I'd spent the week relaxing, trying to avoid buying yet another $15 smoothie, doing yoga, and talking to people about their uniquely LA careers (life coach, breathwork instructor, monkey owner, CBD mogul). This had not prepared me for the grind of cycling through the city. I passed 1st street. Hours later, I passed 236th street. I wasn't sure I was even in LA anymore. At this point the surrounding towns had coalesced to a single sprawl, but that is one hell of a grid system. I passed through classic hip-hop suburbs: Inglewood, Compton, Long Beach. I cycled along Rosecrans and listened to Kendrick. I admired endless strip malls and their stacked signs for the shops inside. Fatburger, Donuts, Colonics. What more could you need? I passed through the industrial district along the LA River. It was lined with homeless camps, these more permanent than the ones in town. I felt like I was intruding. After that, what else is there to say about riding through LA? Very little. At least it wasn't garbage day.

Urban sprawl gave way to affluent beachside communities: Huntington Beach, Newport Beach, Laguna Beach. In between, surfers worked the waves. It was Wednesday but the sun was shining, and the surf was up. I stopped for coffee by the beach and watched the action. Now deep in civilisation, no one wanted to chat. After a long day of stop-start cycling, first through the city and then through coastal suburbia, I reached Dana Point. I was greeted by an RV-only campground. I could camp there, but I had to pay $40 for an RV site. I briefly considered riding out of town and finding an urban campsite but was discouraged by memories of Utah. I decided one bike lost on my trip was enough. I set up my tent on a cement pad and made peace with the ignominy. I couldn't face cooking dinner on a camp stove surrounded by families in RVs and screaming children. I found the local BBQ spot. If I was going to sleep on cement, I was going to do it numbed by pork and beer. I walked in to an empty restaurant but a full bar. Ten people sat around chatting. The bartender came out from behind the bar and introduced himself to me, "Hi, I'm Ritchie, take a seat here man." He pulled out a chair in the middle of the bar. "What's your name? You want some ribs?" I introduced myself and said I was cycling through. Ritchie announced to the bar: "Everyone, this is Otto, where are you cycling from Otto?" Alaska. "Holy shit everyone, Otto's cycled down from Alaska!" Everyone smiled, a lady deep in her Chardonnay let out a small cheer. I felt at home. A guy called Tom pulled up a seat and bought me a beer. He told me about his bikes. We talked about the hills around Santa Barbara. I demolished a kilo of ribs. It was a great evening. I retired to the camp, sedated.

## Day 104 – Dana Point to San Diego

The ride out of Dana Point continued in the same vein as the day before. More endless suburbs by the beach. No hills, no views, but also no chance of death on the highway. My favourite line from Ron Turnbull's *Book of Bivvy* on camping and hiking in Scotland was: "A walk needs hills like a cake needs flour." There was no flour in this cake, it was a sugary mix of flat asphalt, suburbia and the sea. I resigned myself to a placid roll into San Diego. Then I found the interstate.

I'd try to blame Google Maps again, but there didn't look to be an alternative. The coastal road I followed joined an on-ramp. I stopped in front of a large 'No Pedestrians' sign and consulted the internet gods. The blue dot led me to the freeway on-ramp. I dug into my panniers for the route guide. The guide looked like it had an inland road. I backtracked to take it. I arrived at a military base. I was stopped for an ID check. Behind the guard was a green bike route sign. This looked hopeful. The guard gave my New Zealand passport a sceptical glance. I have a great moustache in the photo. I think he appreciated it. "Do you have base access?" he asked. "No, can you give it to me?" He shook his head, "You need to apply for it two towns back." I guess I would have known that if I'd read the route guide. He smiled, I'm sure it was the moustache. "Well, legally, I wouldn't advise you to take the interstate. The only other way is to go back north and take the train down," he said. I laughed, "I'm definitely not doing that." He grinned, "Legally, I can't say that's a good idea. Ride safe." Interstate it was. As trucks flew past, I reflected that no trip to America would be complete without experiencing a ten-lane divided freeway. It wasn't terrible. The shoulder was wide, the rumble strip deep, and wind of thousands of cars headed the same direction propelled me forward. The wind, or the fear; one or the other. After some speedy miles, the interstate cut back inland and popped me back out into coastal suburbia.

I stopped into a cafe by a marina to calm my nerves. On

the way in, an ageing surfer-bro zipped past me on an electric bike. As I got my coffee, he came out and complimented my bike: "Nice wheels man." Bart was out for a rip on his new toy, a $10,000 electric full suspension mountain bike. "I got a deal man, it's $12,000 now The Donald's tariffs have come in. That giant dickhead." Needless to say, the bike was a serious bit of kit. It looked like he could ride it to the moon. He'd just come back from joining a 100km ride with the local Lycra club. He was uninvited. "They were pissed man. Look at me! No helmet, ripped shirt, fat tyres, e-bike," he said. "The only way I could have been more out of place is if I had a fucking rear view mirror." Bart chuckled, enjoying their distain. We chatted about cycle touring. Bart reminisced over tours in his youth: "I always thought jobs were for people who didn't have bikes, or surfboards, or climbing gear, or anything man." He talked me through every spec on the bike, from suspension to handlebar length and wheel diameter. He invited me back to check out his house and to have lunch, but after the specs download I was getting a weird vibe off him. In hindsight it was probably the finish line sucking me on, but at the time I decided it was too late in the trip to end up tortured in a basement.

Along the beach I went. The surf was good. All down the coast, the waves were filled with wetsuit-clad surfers getting amongst it. This was the Southern California from the movies. Blonde pony tails abounded. I headed up into the hills of La Jolla. The whole morning wishing for hills, and when they arrive you actually have to climb them.

San Diego crept up on me. I'd been riding through the suburbs since I left LA, then Bam! Skyscrapers! I checked into a hostel and went to explore. I walked up to Balboa Park, a collection of hills in the middle of the city which houses the zoo and several museums. Nothing interesting happened. I went for ramen. Back at the hostel I met two guys from Manchester who had just "done" Vegas. They tried to drag me out for pints. I resisted. I met two French guys having a dinner of four cheeses, two baguettes and two bottles of wine. It's important to fly the flag when you travel. I laughed at them. They didn't think it was at all funny. Fifteen miles to the border and my finish line.

## Day 105 – San Diego to Tijuana

The trip out of San Diego was full of concrete. The route ran through the city, then along the waterfront through a wasteland of the military industrial complex. Rail yards, warehouses, a naval base, and BAE Systems and General Dynamics office parks. There were 'No Photo' signs on every fence. There were no photos worth taking. America faded into Mexico as I approached the border.

I'd been apprehensive about the time it would take to cross the busiest border in the world. The line of cars on the Mexican side of the border was five lanes wide, stretched back further than I could see, and was immobile. The US side wasn't much better. Vendors wound through the traffic selling snacks. The North American love of the car played in my favour. I dragged my bike through a revolving door of steel bars of the pedestrian section along with the other four people walking over the border that morning and was through immigration in a minute.

In keeping with tradition, I arrived in Tijuana and got immediately lost. I ended up going the wrong way up a motorway shoulder headed back to the border. I passed a parked cop car. The driver was reading a newspaper. He gave me a casual glance. A lost gringo wasn't worth putting down the paper.

I found my way to a bike shop to pack my bike for the flight. My Spanish was in for a test. "Tienes ... una ... caja ... para viajar...?" I ventured. "Oh, sure you want a bike box to go on the plane? No problem. Do you want us to pack it up for you or do you have the tools with you? Where are you flying to?" Classic gringo. I chatted to Mario, the owner. He was disappointed I was stopping my trip in Tijuana and not exploring Baja. He sent me out for tacos while they packed up the bike. I sat on a sidewalk and ate dripping tortillas stuffed with unidentified meat and raw onions. They were delicious. I ordered two more. This got a thumbs up from my neighbour, who had taco grease down most of his wrist. I considered that if I'd started the trip in Mexico I could have eaten more tacos and fewer lentils. Too late now.

Back at the bike shop, I stuffed the box in the back of a taxi and headed to a hostel. The driver was from Tijuana. David asked how long I was spending in Tijuana. I told him I was flying out tomorrow. David was pissed. "What's the point in coming to a place if you don't stay long enough to experience it?" he said. I told him my flight was at midnight the next day and I planned to spend the time drinking Modelos, listening to Mexican music and watching the sun go down into the Pacific. This calmed David down a little. He offered to give me a tour of the area around my hostel. There was an old bullfighting area. We bonded over an appreciation of bullfighting. David told me now that the bullfights were banned, he liked chicken fighting. I asked where I could find a chicken fight in Tijuana. He got cagey. Chicken fighting was also illegal. David had connections. He recommended I check out the Tijuana donkey-zebra, a donkey painted to look like a zebra. I said that sounded fucking stupid. David agreed. Full schedule of bars in hand, David dropped me at the hostel.

My hostel doubled as a Brazilian jiu-jitsu gym. The owner was also called David but had more neck tattoos than my taxi driver. Training was free for hostel guests. Instead of spending an evening relaxing, sipping a cold beer and reflecting on a journey complete, I found myself struggling for breath trapped underneath a sweaty Mexican. It wasn't the ending the trip needed, but the ending it deserved.

*Some days you ride the bike*

*Some days the bike rides you*

*But if you just stick with it*

*You'll see the whole thing through*

*It doesn't happen quickly*

*In fact, it's rather slow*

*But then before you know it*

*You're down in Mexico*

# Afterword

And that was that, the trip was over. I got back on a plane and returned to real life in London. I went back to my desk job. To quote one of my trail buddies in Yoho: "If I go on any more holidays, society won't let me back in." I'm still part of society. I'm still living in London. I spend more time in the pub than on the bike, and no time at all in a tent. Then, was it worth it? Did anything change in my life? The answer is yes, of course.

Lindsay Crouse wrote an article in the *New York Times* about running a 2:53 marathon at 35. Her goal was to qualify for the US Olympic trials. Lindsay isn't a professional athlete, she's a senior staffer at the NYT. That's a serious desk job. She missed the 2:45 cut-off, but the process of training for something she didn't think possible reframed her attitude to what was possible. If the Olympic team looked achievable, what else had she discounted? That reframing is what my adventure gave me. It doesn't matter who you are, what your goal is, or even if you make it. What matters is the work. I had two adventures. The first started in one bike store in London and finished in another in Tijuana. The second started by typing my first notes in my tent in Alaska and finished with publishing this book.

The parallel journeys of writing and cycling shaped each other. I am not a naturally outgoing person. I would very happily not talk to anyone (apart from myself, there was a lot of that in the Yukon) all day. I do love a good story though. Being forced through the process of writing to think about how I would tell the story of each day forced me to experience that day. Whether it was going into a butcher shop in Alaska just to have a chat, observing the details of a mountain or a river more closely, or standing in the way of the bar in Missoula not walking away from Audrey, the writing pushed me out of my comfort zone in more subtle, additional ways than cycle touring did on its own.

I didn't set out to write a book. This book started as a diary of random facts and fragments of thoughts that I hoped in the future would spark memories. One original entry from Anchorage reads: "Met two Poles on shit bikes going to Calgary in 23 days. Felt ridiculous in Lycra." An even less coherent one from Denali reads: "Doesn't take long to start talking to yourself. Accents feature heavily. Pirate Irish. Pirish." Every day I would sit in diners, beside trails or in my tent and tap away on my phone. With practice, I improved. By the time I got to Fairbanks, I was writing in complete sentences. This seems like a low bar, but I started from a low base. The more I wrote, the more I improved and the more my goals expanded. By Whitehorse I had a diary for me, by Idaho I had a present for my parents, by Portland I had something I thought might be worth sharing with friends. By the end of the trip in October 2018 I had written close to 100,000 words. Some of it was even funny.

Back in London, I took three weeks to edit the phone diary into a single text and remove the most caffeine-addled jokes. I printed eighty copies as Christmas presents for friends, family and people I had met during the trip. The reception was positive. A girl I was dating at the time asked me, "What do you have to lose?" This is always a great question. I decided to look for a publisher.

I had no idea what I was doing. I had no connection to publishing. All of the advice I found online was conflicting and confusing. After Christmas, I wrote a cover letter explaining who I was and what I had done, and sent that together with the full text to thirty agents and publishers. This is not typically how things are done, but for a first-time author, there is no typical. In March 2019, one agent decided to take a chance on me. Over the next six months, Nick coached me through the process of writing a formal book pitch to submit to a publisher. In October, a publisher offered me an advance. As I write this in February 2020, I'm about to submit the final edit for publication in June. This has been an adventure quite apart from cycling, with its own unique set of challenges and rewards. It has reframed my possible again.

I'm not a professional adventurer or writer. I did a medium-length, low-stress cycle tour through culturally familiar terrain, on what can only charitably be described as a flexible budget. I've written a book about my day-to-day experience told in the same way I would tell a story to a friend. It is a story for a friend. It's not literature. The objective difficulty of both of these achievements is low. Yet for me, they were improbable goals. Chasing them transformed my conception of my possible. Could I run a 2:53 marathon? Not likely. Would it be valuable for me to try? Certainly. Am I going to do it? Absolutely not. That sounds horrible, I'll pick my own goals, thanks.

My goals were at the limit of what I thought possible for me given my situation. Everyone's situation is different. Maybe my goals seem small to you. Maybe they seem outlandish. If you are supporting a family, it's difficult to take four months to go cycling alone. It is true that I was, and am, in a relatively privileged and free position of being healthy, with limited responsibilities and with an employer that liked me enough to let me leave, but not enough to make me stay. But that isn't the point. What matters is setting the goals at the limit of your own possible, whatever that is for you. Whether it is getting your 10,000 steps in every day for a month, selling a short story to a magazine, or rowing across the Atlantic. What matters is that the goal means something. What matters is the work. My experience was that recording that work enriched it and opened a new door to a new adventure.

As usual Alastair Humphreys has said it already, and said it more eloquently than I would: "It comes down, in the end, to little more than summoning the guts to begin. Concentrate on getting started, then afterwards you can think about everything else. It is a simple solution. Simple but not easy."

# Acknowledgements

Thank you to all the people who read the first draft of this book and were polite enough not to tell me it was total shit. Thank you to the girl who got me into cycle touring with stories of pasta and no flat tyres. Thank you to the girl who encouraged me to try and get this book published. Thank you to Nick and Turku, John and Kassie, Brad, Tony and Ciara, Connor and Nick, Tucker and the Oceano crew, and all the other people I met along the way for making the trip an experience worth writing about. Thank you to Rob, Trevor and Varun who gave me a GPS watch and who are pissed at being left out of the book. You're in it now. Thank you to Jess for giving me your house in LA and letting me play with your dog. Thank you to my agent, Nick Walters of David Luxton for taking a chance on me and for toning down the most excessive of my jokes for the benefit of the British publishing community. Thank you to Peter Crangle and David Burrill at Great Northern Books for rolling the dice on this, and to Ross Jamieson for the editorial comments. Thank you to Claudia for the maps. Last of all, thank you for reading this. I hope you enjoyed it.